The Internet:
The Basics

Here is a comprehensive and jargon-free introduction to the Internet. This easy-to-use companion not only offers practical guidance on everything from email to web design, it also explores the ways in which the Internet has changed our cultures, societies and identities. It looks at:

- How the Internet works
- How to use it for research and communication
- Designing for the Web
- Regulation and ethics
- Hacking
- Cyberculture
- How the Internet is transforming our world

This non-technical, accessible and concise guide is essential reading for anyone interested in knowing more about this fascinating and fast-changing area. It is ideal for all users of the Internet whether beginners or seasoned surfers.

Jason Whittaker is a lecturer on digital media and online journalism at Falmouth College of Arts. He is the author of *Web Production for Writers and Journalists* (now in its second edition and also from Routledge) and is a computer journalist.

Also available from Routledge in this series:

The Internet:

The Basics

ROUTLEDGE

■ Jason Whittaker

First published 2002 by Routledge
11 New Fetter Lane, London EC4P 4EE

Simultaneously published in the
USA and Canada
by Routledge
29 West 35th Street, New York,
NY 10001

*Routledge is an imprint of the Taylor &
Francis Group*

© 2002 Jason Whittaker

Typeset in Times and Frutiger by
Florence Production, Stoodleigh, Devon
Printed and bound in Great Britain by
TJ International, Padstow, Cornwall

*British Library Cataloguing in
Publication Data*
A catalogue record for this book is
available from the British Library

*Library of Congress Cataloging-in-
Publication Data*
has been requested

ISBN 0–415–25745–X (hbk)
ISBN 0–415–25746–8 (pbk)

Contents

Illustrations

Figures

Table

Preface

There is something in the experience of writing a book on the Internet that is not dissimilar to joining a fairground ride. When the idea for this book was first mooted at the end of 1999, dotcom-mania filled broadcasts, magazine pages and the ether of the Internet; by the end of 2001, some doom-mongers were predicting that the very medium itself would not survive the crash of financial markets that had taken place throughout that year.

The Internet, particularly elements such as the Web, is a very immature medium. This is not the same as being very young: at the time of writing, it has existed in some shape or format for over thirty years. Nonetheless, as a medium of communication, particularly as a medium of *mass* communication, those thirty years count for very little compared to print, film, radio and even television. Many people who read this book will probably have had less than five years' experience of using the Internet: prior to the end of the 1990s it was simply too difficult and expensive for most people. It is this novelty, this *newness*, that makes predicting the shape and form of the Net such a difficult task, especially as it embraces rapid change like no other medium.

There have been a huge number of claims made for the Internet: it is (after mobile phones) the most rapidly expanding medium that has been taken up more quickly than anything before; it is revolutionising the way we communicate with each other; business will, in the words of one William Henry Gates, be conducted at the speed of thought with its aid; more than this, our entire consciousness will be transformed as we participate in the first global mind.

As with many claims, there is more than a little hype in the above. The Internet may be expanding rapidly, but in most parts of the world it is still an irrelevance and likely to remain that way for some time: when commentators speak of a *global* system, their frame of reference is often somewhat restricted. If there has been a medium of the twentieth century, it is probably television (with cinema the closest contender), and the fact that the Internet grew exponentially in the final years of that century does not detract from this. It is, of course, in the interests of business to make us believe that we will buy and sell on the terms of major players who make big investments in new technologies, but, while the Net will almost certainly have a much more important role to play in the future of commerce, it has not yet supplanted older ways of doing business.

The book in your hands is not a guide to using the Internet, like countless others that have sprung up in bookshops and newsagents at the turn of the millennium. There is guidance on the concepts and technologies that constitute the Internet, and there is even a chapter titled 'Using the Internet', but it is generally assumed that you have some experience of using computers and online communications, so that this chapter explains in more detail the concepts behind those technologies with the aim of encouraging you to explore beyond the Web and email. The main aim of this book is to combine practical information, for example on how the Internet works and its constituent elements, with theoretical approaches to the study of computer-mediated communication.

This book, then, is divided into two distinct, but overlapping parts: in the first, you will encounter some of the major pointers to thinking about the Internet in practical terms, while the second deals with theoretical considerations from a cultural studies or media studies perspective. It is not intended as a technical work, but, unfortunately, anyone wishing to study the Internet must learn some of its jargon and technical terminology, including perhaps its worst curse, the TLA (three letter acronym). Wherever possible, I have tried to use plain and simple English, or at the very least to explain what is meant when employing technical terms.

Ultimately, the main aim of this book is to try and encourage people to think creatively and critically about what is an important and exciting medium. The Internet may have been over-hyped, claims that it is the most important invention since the Gutenberg press must be approached cautiously, and most people will be sceptical about any easy assertion that we are all cyborgs now. The truth remains, however, that, even with all its faults and foibles, for those who use the Internet the world is a different place, and just because the changes that have taken place are generally smaller and subtler than the claims made by Net-evangelists, for that reason they may finally be more profound.

A companion web site is available for this book at www.routledge.com/internetbasics. Here you will find updated links to relevant sites as well as news stories on new developments online.

Jason Whittaker
Falmouth, 2001

Acknowledgements

I am grateful to Roger Thorp at Routledge for asking me to write this book and to Elisa Tack for her advice and support. As ever, I would like to thank my wife, Sam, for putting up with my irritations and enthusiasms as this book progressed, and colleagues at *PC Advisor* who helped with ideas and contacts, particularly Emma Northam, Rosie Haworth and Andrew Charlesworth. Finally, I would like to acknowledge the assistance provided by the Falmouth College of Arts Research Fund and to thank staff and students at Falmouth College of Arts for feedback on some of the ideas discussed in this book.

Chapter 1

Understanding
the Internet

Introduction

Anyone under thirty has never known a world where the Internet did not exist in some form, although most will not have been aware of this fact until much later. The prototype of what became known as the Internet, ARPANET, was implemented in 1969, the same year that I was born. Unlike that other significant event from the final year of the 1960s, the moon landings, I was blissfully unaware of the Internet's existence throughout the 1970s and nearly the entire 1980s, as indeed were most people. Although I cannot say, unlike many schoolchildren today, that I imbibed this medium with my mother's milk (that was a role played by television), in a sense I would still claim that I belong to the first generation that grew up alongside the Internet.

As with many people of my age, my first contact with the Internet came at university, sitting at a UNIX terminal typing in obscure commands. Returning as a postgraduate student, I was provided with an email account, which slowly opened up connections with

other students and academics, and I gradually became aware that a new piece of software installed on university machines – Mosaic – provided an increasing number of students with a novel pastime, surfing the Web. I was one of them, but in 1993 and 1994 it must be admitted that while a GUI (graphical user interface) made using the Internet much more pleasurable than the text-based terminals I had used five years previously, it did not revolutionise the process of researching for a Ph.D.: the Internet was becoming more fun, but that did not make it (the occasional email aside) especially useful.

It was at about this time that I signed up for my first network account at home: in those days, the main choice seemed to be CompuServe or . . . CompuServe. Even the giant of online connectivity, AOL, was not readily available in Europe in the early 1990s and, although the Internet Service Provider (ISP), Demon, had recently started in business, it was not particularly well known. (Demon was my first ISP a couple of years later, involving the rather painful task of having to configure the modem and protocol settings manually before connection could take place.) Indeed, the Web was generally less useful for finding information than proprietary services such as CompuServe, which also had a robust financial model that provided three hours' free access for £10 and then charged users an hourly rate plus phone charges. In the first couple of months I happily chatted, joined forums and even explored a few web sites using my 14.4 kilobits per second modem; then I received my credit card and phone bills and was more circumspect about my home usage for the next six years or so.

By the middle of the decade, it was still easy to dismiss the Internet as a fad, like CB radio in the 1980s. Most people had still not heard of the Net and, when I began work on the magazine *PC Advisor* in 1995, the big story was Windows 95. In the second issue we carried an article on the Microsoft Network (MSN) subtitled 'The Superpower Goes Online' in which George Meng, then product manager for MSN, predicted that the service would provide *the* route of access onto the information superhighway. In the six years since then, my own experience of the Internet has changed dramatically: my last computer purchase was an iMac, and connecting to the Internet literally consisted of plugging the phone socket into the wall and entering the phone number, user name and password for my ISP. Amongst the students I teach, knowledge of the Internet is not quite ubiquitous, but each year more and more new undergraduates demonstrate complete familiarity with the Web, email and chat rooms.

Some commentators still like to compare today's Internet to CB, but this is simply nonsense: the Internet is often over-hyped and frequently underpowered and has not delivered, nor can, deliver on all the promises that have been made in its name. At the same time, the number of users grows every year and the amount of data transferred across the Net at least doubles. In one of my favourite stories, Bob Metcalfe, the inventor of Ethernet, predicted that the Internet would hit gridlock by the end of the 1990s, and that as users and data transfer exploded so the infrastructure would not be able to cope. A couple of years later he ate his words – literally, after mulching a copy of his article in a liquidiser the better to consume it – when the Net had failed to stop. On a more sombre note, following the destruction of the World Trade Center on 11 September 2001, many commentators remarked on the role played by the Net: the Internet could not compete with television in terms of conveying the horror of that disaster, and yet, as many web editors and managers remarked, traffic increased by as much as 2,500 per cent as users went online in search of information (Gibson 2001). We now see that the Internet is not going to replace every other medium, and the changes that have taken place in the past decade indicate how difficult it is to predict the future shape of telecommunications. This book, however, will demonstrate and explore some of the most significant features of the global information system that is the Internet.

More like Germany, less like a hammer

A typical starting point for any book on the Internet is to provide some sort of definition. The easiest way to think of the Internet is as a 'network of networks', the collective noun for the thousands of networks found in businesses, universities, governments, ISPs and other organisations. This is what you will find in just about any user manual that deals with using the Internet, for example *The Complete Reference Internet, Millennium Edition*, which concisely defines the Internet as 'a network of networks that connects computers all over the world' (Young 1999: 4). As Young goes on to point out, such networks consist not only of the physical hardware (computers, cables, satellites, etc.), but also the rules, or software *protocols*, that govern the exchange of data between machines.

Yet more than hardware and software, the Internet has established a series of particular – even peculiar – relationships with its users. Print has long developed a series of special fetishes (as in the bibliophile who collects books he or she never reads), and various media theorists since Marshall McLuhan have examined the symbiotic dependence we formed with television in the twentieth century, but the potential for interactivity across the Internet has often focused special attention on the people who use the Internet, its audiences and even communities. For Katie Hafner, Matthew Lyon and John Naughton, the Internet is particularly valuable as an arena of technological innovation, one that coincidentally transformed geeks into the epitome of nerd chic (Hafner and Lyon 1996; Naughton 1999). Howard Rheingold (1995) extended this notion of community to a much wider and more diverse range of users, while Esther Dyson distinguishes the Net from the Internet: the latter is the technical medium, the 'house', while the Net is a 'home' that 'includes all the people, cultures, and communities that live in it' (1998: 14). Unsurprisingly, perhaps, the inventor of the World Wide Web, Tim Berners-Lee, found the Internet a chaos of conflicting standards upon which he imposed order (1999), while Charles Jonschler points to the *medium* of the Web, its use as a communication tool that is profoundly affected by the format of its messages that, in turn, affect us (1999).

Very quickly, then, we see how a simple definition of a 'network of networks' fails to explain clearly what the Internet is: as well as hardware and software, it is a series of communication rules in the widest sense, as well as a space of social interactions, between groups of users who form audiences and communities in addition to operating as individuals; it is the different media of email, newsgroups and the Web; it is itself a culture and a meeting place for cultures; and it is a remarkable experiment in technology. As Mark Poster explains:

> The only way to define the technological effects of the Internet is to build the Internet, to set in place a series of relations which

constitute an electronic geography. Put differently, the Internet is more like a social space than a thing; its effects are more like those of Germany than those of hammers. The effect of Germany upon the people within it is to make them Germans (at least for the most part); the effect of hammers is not to make people hammers, though Heideggerians and some others might disagree, but to force metal spikes into wood.

(2000: 205)

The Internet is very much a material entity, but its effects cannot be traced from its causes as simply as hitting a nail with a hammer will drive it into wood. In perhaps the largest survey of the effects of information technology on society, *The Information Age* (1996–7), sociologist Manuel Castells argues that a network society results from the convergence of three independent strands: the IT revolution of the 1970s, the restructuring of capitalism that took place in the 1980s, and the cultural and social movements of the 1960s and 1970s. An 'informational economy' is one where companies and countries depend on information, technology and management, these feeding into other sectors (such as agriculture and industry). It is also very much involved with the process of globalisation which, Castells states, is not the same as a world economy that has been in existence since the sixteenth century. A 'Network Society' is structured around (capitalist) networks and, although not produced by information technology, it could not be such a pervasive social form without the Internet.

The global Internet

Who, then, uses the Internet? As the chart in Figure 1.1 shows, Internet growth, fuelled mainly by the Web and email, exploded in the mid-1990s as the number of hosts grew at a geometric rate, more or less doubling each year. It should also be noted that the rate of growth has also begun to slow in recent years and will probably hit a plateau by 2010. Converting fairly reliable statistics on Internet hosts into actual users is always problematic, but a common assumption that there are, on average, ten users per Internet host means that, by 2001, there were approximately 420 million people worldwide with access to the

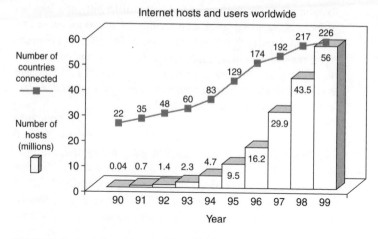

FIGURE 1.1 Internet growth to 2000.

Source: International Telecommunications Union

Internet, though this figure may be as low as 250 million users out of an estimated 8 billion global population. Statistics on Internet usage were relatively accurate until 1996, when the US government deregulated provision of Net infrastructure; since then, it has been widely assumed that the Net is expanding sixteen-fold every year, although the most accurate recent estimates suggest a two-fold to four-fold growth every year.

While the majority of countries, then, had connected to the Internet by the end of the twentieth century, there remains a long way to go before its usage extends much beyond 5 per cent of the inhabitants of the world. Likewise, the Internet also has far to go before its content becomes truly global. As Figure 1.2 shows, the vast majority of Internet hosts (nearly two-thirds) are located in the US – hardly surprising considering its development – with Europe far behind in second position, accounting for fewer than one quarter of hosts. Yet it is less than a decade since nearly all hosts were located within the US and, as rapid expansion will occur outside a North America that is reaching saturation point, so the West will account for fewer and fewer Internet users while remaining the dominant force for some years to come.

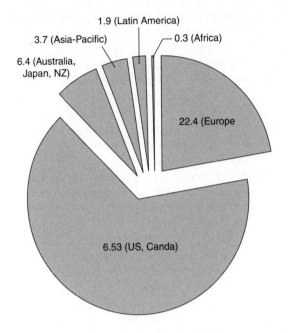

FIGURE 1.2 Internet hosts by continent, 1999.
Source: International Telecommunications Union

The development of the Internet is often seen as integral to the notion of globalisation, indeed, as one of its defining features. While parts of the Internet have had global aspirations from their moment of inception (most notably the *World Wide* Web), the gap between aspiration and reality with regard to online communications has been huge. While America, western Europe and parts of eastern Asia lead the way in terms of Internet usage, the spread of computer media communications is extremely patchy, with less than 0.1 per cent of the population having access to the Net in many countries. Nonetheless, the number of countries that have no Internet provision has declined rapidly so that, for example, North Korea became one of the last countries to prepare for Internet access in 2001 (amidst claims that officials in Pyongyang already had limited access).

While communication networks capable of spanning the globe have been available since the invention of the telegraph (and, arguably, since the first sailing ships circumnavigated the world), modern globalisation has its roots in the process of trade liberalisation that began after the Second World War, which brought with it increasing inter-penetration of worldwide media markets, and which was consolidated by the General Agreement on Tariffs and Trade (GATT) and the World Trade Organisation, based in Geneva, as well as by the collapse of the Eastern bloc in 1989. Although globalisation and reactions to it are complex, ranging from the managerial role of the World Bank to protests in Seattle and Prague, there have been three general phases of response to globalisation. In its initial phase, western countries saw the process as almost entirely beneficial, as one contributing necessary investment to the 'developing' world. As this developing world grew in confidence, particularly as the OPEC countries realised their signifi-cance in global markets and previously colonial nations found their voices, so a backlash within the UN referred increasingly to cultural and media 'imperialism', extending colonialism by new means (Sreberny-Mohammadi 1996); more recently, thinking on globalisation has tended to emphasise a new 'pluralism', both in trade and the media so that, for example, the Portuguese-language media of Brazil are much more significant globally than those of Portugal itself, while John Tomlinson points out that, although the West currently dominates glob-alised media and commerce, the 'triumph' of globalisation signals the end of the West as a distinct entity and 'may be actively problematic for the continuation of Western cultural dominance' (1996: 29).

Nevertheless, currently the West's cultural power remains supreme and throughout the 1990s there was an extension of US media and economic power across international markets. Globalisation remains complex, however: media companies in the US, for example, have found that their best chances of success lie not in pouring Western paradigms down the throats of other cultures, but by adapting to local conditions – in the words of Disney, to 'think global, act local'. In devel-oped global markets such as book publishing, film and music, major players maintain oligopolistic conditions: for example, 90 per cent of the global music market by the end of the 1990s was controlled by just six companies – PolyGram, Time Warner, Sony, EMI, Bertelsmann and

Universal, formerly MCA (Herman and McChesney 1997). While commercialisation and deregulation of media had begun in the 1970s and 1980s, it was during the 1990s that these processes reached full speed and the growth of the Internet as a deregulated medium owes much to this fact. While the Internet raises special considerations compared to other media, had it developed alongside, say, television, then we could have expected to see greater governmental involvement.

Globalisation, then, depends on the interdependence of worldwide financial markets and the ability to move capital from one market to another, though controls on movement of capital remained in countries and regions such as the EU until the 1990s. In certain markets, such as music or Hollywood film, this can lead to oligopolies, so that films made in Mexico for a Hollywood studio squeeze out local media in countries such as France or India. The Internet is an increasingly important force in globalisation on several levels: as a means of moving capital more efficiently and cheaply; as a potential global marketplace; and as a product of media, or cultural, dominance.

Yet as Figure 1.3 shows, globalisation is far from a homogeneous process. While North America dominates Internet usage, there are small, highly concentrated countries such as Monaco or Singapore where a higher percentage of the population is online. Yet Asia and Europe are very mixed regions, both including some of the digitally poorest countries of the world as well as the richest. Even statistics for 2000 cover some surprising changes that may occur in the early years of the twenty-first century. China, for example, is expected to transform its economy as it enters global trade: there were already seventy million mobile phone users by the end of 2000, a figure set to double within a year. If the wireless Internet becomes a reality, some experts have argued that China could bypass much of the transitional development undergone elsewhere. Likewise in eastern Europe, while certain countries such as Russia will remain largely dormant over the coming years, Internet usage is expected to triple in the space of three years in places such as the Czech Republic and Hungary.

Furthermore, variations and heterogeneity can occur within national boundaries. In the UK, for example, the government's own research from the Office for National Statistics for October 1999 to September 2000 raised concerns over a perceived 'digital divide'

Internet penetration by percentage of population over 14

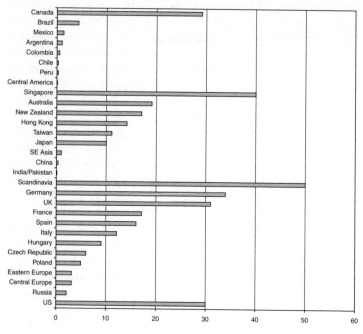

FIGURE 1.3 Internet usage by continent, 2000.
Source: eMarketers

between haves and have-nots, which largely (although not completely) reinforced stereotypes of a north–south divide between the richest and poorest parts of the country. The biggest discrepancy was between London (where 34 per cent of households had Internet access by the end of 2000) and Northern Ireland (with only 16 per cent).

Despite commitments by the government to provide total Internet access across Britain by 2005, it is increasingly evident that socio-economic factors affecting wealth in the country, where manufacturing centres in the north have declined as service and financial sectors in the south have been relatively prosperous, are repeated in terms of Internet access and usage. Nonetheless, on a national level Internet access across the entire country has been growing at an increasing rate: whereas 27 per cent of households had Internet access between April and June 2000, that figure had increased to 32 per cent between July and September of the same year. Other surprises occur when Eire is taken into account: this small country with a population of just over 3.5 million had, by the end of the 1990s, transformed its traditionally poor economy into a high-tech industry as large as the UK's, achieving this by combining low corporation taxes with government incentives to foreign businesses and a forward-looking ecommerce act.

Yet the issue of Internet access and growth should not be confused with Internet usage. The Virtual Society, a project comprising some twenty-two projects amongst seventy-six researchers in twenty-five universities across Europe and the US and sponsored by the Economic and Research Council, includes amongst its aims the task of mapping out a demographic of the development of the Net. Since the end of 1999, researchers have noted that the overall trend of growth in Internet usage is also accompanied by slump periods, when people who were previously connected stop going online. While teenagers seem more likely to drop out very quickly, this is less apparent for those over twenty.

More significantly, the Virtual Society suggests that the Internet is not replacing other forms of communication, particularly mobile phones, but simply adding to the volume of traffic, although only for those privileged enough to have access already. Widespread take-up of the Internet amongst the poorer sections of society is simply not taking place, something that does not look likely to change in the near future. For this and other work from the Virtual Society, see its web site at virtualsociety.sbs.ox.ac.uk.

History of the Internet

Origins

When discussing the history of any medium, whether print, broad-casting or the Internet, there are several problems of methodology. Probably the most obvious red herring for any form of technological historicism is what used to be known as the 'great man' theory of history: while this dominated older forms of historiography, which proceeded by listing kings and generals, it has generally been dismissed, or at least displaced from general historical accounts by social and economic analyses, and would appear to be less relevant to media history. Nonetheless, the temptation still exists to mark out the pioneers of any technology, their Gutenbergs, Bells and Marconis; while biographical details have their importance as a nexus of historical and material conditions, to isolate an individual 'genius' from technological, economic and social relations distorts any account of origins more than it illuminates. If the Net as we know it would not have taken its current form without figures such as Paul Baran or Tim Berners-Lee, it could not even have been conceived without the cold war and economic imperatives of the computer industry.

The next problem facing media history, particularly when dealing with the Internet, is more subtle, but much more problematic. Technological determinism, at least in its strong form, assumes that the historical development of a medium is a process of necessary 'laws', whereby the development of a new medium creates the conditions for social and psychological interactions. Computing seems especially vulnerable to this form of determinism, particularly since the enunciation of 'Moore's Law', usually interpreted to mean that computer power will double every eighteen months or so – although, as we shall see, taking this individual law out of context generates its own problems. While theories of technological determinism can be very useful for escaping the humanistic tendency to place men and women at the centre of history, one exceptional example being Manuel de Landa's *War in the Age of Intelligent Machines* (1991), such a view does not remove the fallacious tendency to see the history of technology as one of intrinsic progress. A readable account of technological history that demonstrates some of the virtues and vices of such determinism is Paul Levinson's *Soft Edge* (1997).

As Gary Chapman remarks, transactional or deterministic models of technological history are much poorer than those that take into account social and material conditions, particularly the willingness of governments, businesses and markets to invest in new media: 'Computers, like other machines, are material representations of a long process of innovation, error, improvement, more error, more improvement, consolidation of features, the extinction of superseded practices, intellectual breakthroughs and dead ends, and so on, all embodied in the physical object and the way we use it' (1994: 304). Patrice Flichy has made a similar observation with reference to radio and other communications media, that 'what appears today as a series of naturally articulated steps is, in reality, the history of a difficult passage from one domain to another' (1995: 100). With regard to another culturally important innovation, television, Raymond Williams has argued against the paucity of technological determinism, or 'symptomatic technologies' removed from social and cultural forms: such inventions are comprised not from a 'single event or series of events', but depend for their realisation 'on inventions made with other ends primarily in view' (1989: 13). In particular, notes Williams, technologies such as telegraphy or electricity required a change in social perceptions before they were considered useful.

As with the computer, in the past few years the Internet has been granted a prehistory, the so-called 'Victorian Internet' of the telegraph, which was inaugurated with Samuel Morse's transmission of the first electric telegraph message, 'What hath God wrought?' in 1844. Over the following decades, telegraph lines were installed across North America and Europe and, in 1866, the first transatlantic cable was laid. As telegraph links spread across the world, augmented by telephone lines following Alexander Graham Bell's invention in 1876, the foundations were laid for a global telecommunications system (Moschovitis et al. 1999; Standage 1998).

The development of such a system was boosted by the invention of the electronic computer. Although Charles Babbage, perplexed by the problems of calculation in what Doron Swade has called 'an age of quantification' (2000), had designed and partly built his Difference Engine in the early nineteenth century, it was not until the early twentieth century that the principle of an all-purpose computer – able to read, write, store and process data – was established. Alan Turing, who had attended King's College, Cambridge, and Princeton University, established the principle of a mechanical computer, the 'Turing Machine', in his paper 'On Computable Numbers'; significantly, Turing also argued that not every mathematical problem was solvable, and that there are some problems for which no algorithm exists that could be fed into a computer. Nonetheless, most problems, when converted into a series of digital sequences of 1s and 0s, could be fed into a machine by tape, recorded and solved for output.

At the same time that Turing was outlining the theoretical principles of the computer in the 1930s, Konrad Zuse constructed the first primitive electronic computers, the Z1 and Z2; the Z1, begun in 1936, used mechanical gates to count binary numbers (Zuse having chosen binaries over decimals because they could be computed more quickly). In the Z2, these gates were replaced by faster electromagnetic relays, of the sort used in telephone exchanges, but it was not until the construction of the Z3 in 1941 that Zuse completed a fully-functioning, programmable computer. Most devices of this time were really no more than calculating machines. The ability to process and perform many different functions did not begin until the invention of the Z3 and other fully-programmable, electronic devices: ENIAC (Electronic Numerical Integrator and Calculator), housed at the University of Pennsylvania at the end of the Second World War, and the Colossus, built at Bletchley Park in 1943 and designed to crack codes produced by the German Enigma machine.

These early devices, which were accompanied in 1944 by Howard Aiken's and IBM's Mark I and the Manchester 'Baby' in 1948, were huge machines. ENIAC, for example, covered 650 square feet, while the Mark I weighed five tons, and such early, gigantic computers were filled with erratic vacuum tubes and relays (the term bug is traced back to a story that one of the first computer programmers, Grace Murray Hopper, found a moth in the Mark II in 1947). For the first time, however, they represented the potential of ever-increasing computer power. The UNIVAC (Universal Automatic Computer), based on the ideas of John Von Neumann, was the first commercially available computer and the first such machine to store data on magnetic tape. The next task was to find something to do with this power, and some commentators have even suggested that the mid-twentieth century mania for centralising information owes more than a little to the growth of these behemoths in government and large corporations. Throughout the 1950s and 1960s, mainframes such as the System/360, along with the much more powerful 'supercomputers', dominated public thinking and comprised huge cabinets in specially cooled rooms attended by trained technocrats.

As the number of mainframes increased and were employed by an increasing number of academic industrial and military institutions, so the need to connect these computers began to arise. Initially, the primitive precursor to networking occurred only on a local scale, and consisted of little more than connecting terminals to mainframes so that more users could make the most efficient use of such immensely expensive machines. By the 1960s, however, the demands of national security in America led to the strategic implementation of a network that could cover a much wider area. The beginning of the Internet proper is conventionally dated to that decade, though one convenient starting point is the launch of Sputnik in 1957, the first artificial satellite that began the space race and increased the importance of the telecommunication system that the Internet would plug into.

Following the launch of Sputnik, the Advanced Research Projects Agency (ARPA) was founded, essentially funded by the US Department of Defense but also oriented towards academic research. In the climate of the cold war, a main concern was that a nuclear assault would reduce the ability of centres to communicate with each other. John Naughton has recently criticised the cliché that the Internet was simply the product of what Eisenhower called the military-industrial complex. John Licklider headed the project to build a communications network that developed into work advancing the contemporary state of computing and, as Naughton (1999) observes, the actual impetus that led to the first computers being connected between institutions was an engineering 'solution' to the problems computer scientists encountered when working on collaborative projects. Nonetheless, as Edwards has pointed out, the development of post-Second World War telecommunications and computing was closely tied to the military requirement to 'defend every place' during the cold war; certainly Paul Baran's designs for a survivable communications network owed much to the work at RAND Corporation, a Californian think tank, to provide an effective counterforce to potential Soviet nuclear attacks (Edwards 1997; Hafner and Lyon 1996).

ARPA itself, then, was part of the military-industrial economic climate that provided the funding and metaphorical delivery forceps for the multi-billion-dollar computer industry, even if the actual events leading to the development of the Internet *per se* had little to do with a particular military initiative. Between 1963 and 1967, ARPA investigated the feasibility of building a computer network and selected nineteen possible participant computer hosts to join ARPANET, as it had become known. The programme plan, entitled 'Resource Sharing Computer Networks', was submitted in 1968 with a several-year, multimillion-dollar schedule, work beginning with a contract with the Stanford Research Institute in 1969.

Much of the essential work at ARPA consisted of providing the protocols that would enable the physical backbone to communicate. Of especial importance was packet-switching (PS) software: a common misconception is that the Internet sends information – such as email text or graphics – as a single, discrete file. In fact, each file is split into small packets, each of which can be sent via different hosts so that significant amounts of the file could still reach their destination even in the event of a host being wiped out during conflict (Moschovitis *et al.* 1999; Hafner and Lyon 1996; Naughton 1999).

Extending the net

During the 1970s, individual networks such as ALOHAnet in Hawaii began to connect to ARPANET, and there were international connections with the University College of London and the Royal Radar Establishment (Norway) in 1973. Work also proceeded on improving the protocols that remain the standard for Internet transmissions such as File Transfer Protocol (FTP) and Transmission Control Protocol (TCP). In 1979, the National Science Foundation (NSF) established a computer science research network, and Usenet, a distributed network of bulletin board systems, was established by Jim Ellis, Steve Bellovin and others at Duke University. At this stage, however, although fundamental work was being done on the communication systems used by the Internet, it remained a niche for academics committed to scientific – particularly computer – research, with users being numbered in the hundreds.

More significant development began in the 1980s, and it is hardly a coincidence that the largest network in the world began to take off as the personal computer (PC) gained ground, introducing more and more people to the notion of computing. Although mainframes formed the basis of machines linked together by the early Internet (and the role of large, UNIX servers as the backbone of the Internet cannot be underestimated), the computing revolution that led to the widespread adoption of personal computers can be dated to the late 1970s and early 1980s. What is significant about the PC in all its different variations (such as Macs and IBM-compatible machines) is that it encouraged a distributed model of computing, with information spread over a wide distance and away from centralised control.

Intel invented the first microprocessor, the 4004, in 1971, and this was followed in 1973 by the 8080 and the 8086 in 1979. Initially, such microprocessors were used in pocket calculators (the first one being constructed by Texas Instruments in 1971), but by the end of the decade they had become the backbone of the PC. As processors have moved from 4 bits (the amount of information they can process simultaneously) to 8, 16, 32 and even 64 bits, they have roughly followed what is known as Moore's Law: named after Gordon Moore, co-founder of Intel, the original Moore's law stated that the power and complexity of integrated circuits would double every year (he wrote this in an article for *Electronics* magazine in 1965, six years before the invention of the microprocessor), but this has since been modified to include computing power in general and extended slightly to about eighteen months (Jackson 1997).

Early personal computers, or microcomputers as they were more commonly known in the 1970s, debuted with the MITS Altair 8800. The Altair was, in many respects, a particularly unimpressive piece of kit: it was sent in pieces to hobbyists and, once constructed, had at its heart the slow Intel 8080 chip with 256 bytes of memory, but no keyboard, monitor or any way to get information in or out of the machine. (It was apparently given its name by the daughter of the editor of *Popular Electronics* after she had seen an episode of *Star Trek*.) Yet MITS had problems keeping up with orders, and the release of the Altair resulted in an early computing boom as enthusiasts for the first time had access to their own computer. Amongst these early adopters were Paul Allen and Bill Gates. Gates (who shortly afterwards was to drop out of Harvard) and Allen converted the programming language BASIC for the Altair and, in the spring of 1975, founded the company Microsoft (Gates 1995; Wallace and Erikson 1994; Cringeley 1996).

More successful in terms of breaking into the lucrative business market at this stage was the Apple II, launched in 1977. Apple, founded by two Steves, Jobs and Wozniak, was the archetypal garage start-up: the two friends had met at a local electronics club and their business rapidly expanded from the company's base in Cupertino (Carlton 1997; Cringeley 1996).

In the meantime, some employees at IBM, the world's largest computer manufacturer and responsible for the mainframes that had dominated post-war computing, believed that personal computers could be profitable. Because IBM worked so slowly, Bill Lowe, operating from the IBM business unit in Boca Raton, Florida, determined to get the PC (codenamed Project Chess) to market in less than a year. To succeed, Lowe and his team had to use readily available parts such as Intel's microprocessor and an operating system provided by Microsoft. In a now famous incident, IBM had originally attempted to lease another operating system, CP/M, from a competitor to Gates, Gary Kildall, but he had preferred flying to meeting the company (more significantly, his wife had refused to sign a draconian non-disclosure agreement), so Lowe turned to Microsoft, which bought an operating system called QDOS (Quick and Dirty Operating System) from a small Seattle company (Cringeley 1996; Gates 1995; Jackson 1997). IBM released its first PC in 1981, but the open architecture of the IBM model resulted in the widespread proliferation of clones, with the result that it was not IBM that made the most profits from the personal computer, but Intel and Microsoft.

At the same time that computing began to move away from the post-war model based on a centralised mainframe and terminals, the Internet (and related networks) began to expand both internationally and in terms of capabilities. In 1981, BITNET (Because It's Time Network) began distributing information out of the City University of New York and Yale, while the Minitel system was deployed across France. The next year saw the formation of EUnet (European UNIX Network) to provide email and Usenet services, with the Joint Academic Network (JANET) being implemented in 1984.

Alongside ARPANET and various other official national and international networks, the spread of computers also encouraged the growth of Usenet, 'the poor man's ARPANET'. Emerging from the collaborative work undertaken on UNIX, the operating system devised at Bell Labs, Usenet was only taken up slowly at the beginning of the 1980s, but grew steadily as the decade progressed. Unlike ARPANET, Usenet was open to all (or at least those with appropriate hardware and software) and encouraged the spread of information in an autonomous and uncensored way that was to have important implications for the emergence of the Web in the 1990s. Usenet articles are distributed from server to server, with users logging on to a local ISP; such articles are arranged into 'hierarchies', with a top-level category providing the most general classification, such as alt for alternative, or sci for science, followed by more specific classification, for example alt.fashion or alt.fashion.crossdressing (the latter, unsurprisingly, somewhat more eclectic than the former).

The 1980s also saw the introduction of the Domain Name System (DNS), to allocate addresses to host computers and a higher-powered NSFNET. Throughout the late 1980s, with DNS in place, all these different networks could access computers anywhere, meaning that the Internet was in place by 1990, the year when ARPANET, its work finished, ceased to exist. And yet, although the number of Internet hosts had broken the 100,000 mark in 1989, it was still the preserve of nerds, geeks and scientists (terms interchangeable in some quarters). It was only in the 1990s that the Net became a wider communication medium, due almost entirely to the World Wide Web and email.

The World Wide Web

While the Web, in many respects, represents the most exciting aspect of the Internet (and certainly the part that most attracts the attention of the media), it is email that is the Net's 'killer app', an application so useful that people will buy a product or subscribe to a service simply to use it. In the late 1970s, the killer app that stimulated the personal computer market was the spreadsheet VisiCalc for the Apple II; for the Internet it is email.

As Naughton remarks, email was something of a surprise to the developers of ARPANET, who had intended the early Internet as a system that enabled research scientists to share scarce resources. By 1973, however, three-quarters of the traffic on the Internet was electronic mail and a large part of this could be constituted as 'chat' (Naughton 1999). Although it is not the first recorded instance of email, the most famous early example concerns Leonard Kleinrock, who had returned to Los Angeles from a conference in Brighton, England, and realised that he had left his razor in a Sussex dormitory bathroom. As he had left the conference early, he hoped that he would be able to contact another member and reached Larry Roberts via a Teletype connection, TALK. The grand plans of ARPANET were already being used to convey the small desires of its users (Hafner and Lyon 1996).

Another small desire, which was to become transformed into a big idea, stemmed from one user's frustration at trying to access information stored on servers around the world. By the end of the 1980s, the number of hosts attached to the Internet was increasing, but, while there were standards governing the communication protocols connecting those machines, there was no certainty that a user seated at one computer would be able to read information stored on another if it was formatted differently. At the European Centre for Nuclear Research (CERN), a consultant, Tim Berners-Lee, had written a short program entitled modestly 'Enquire Within Upon Everything', which allowed links to be made between documents. ENQUIRE, as it came to be known, was Berners-Lee's big idea and it became even bigger in 1989, when he submitted a paper entitled 'Information Management: A Proposal', which mooted the idea of using hypertext for accessing documents. In 1990, the first text web browser was developed at CERN and so the World Wide Web was born (Berners-Lee 1999; Hafner and Lyon 1996; Naughton 1999).

CERN continued to develop the Web as an academic tool, but by the end of 1992 only twenty-six hosts were serving web sites, and even in early 1994 there were only 1,500 registered web servers. The boom in Web – and Internet – growth came with the development of Mosaic, a graphical browser capable of displaying images as well as text, by Marc Andreessen at the National Center for Supercomputing Applications (NCSA). Before Mosaic, users had to master a series of esoteric commands for UNIX, which severely limited its mass appeal. The first versions of Mosaic still ran on UNIX only at first, again restricting their usage, but as versions appeared for PCs and Macs by the end of 1993 it began to seem that the Web could finally be more than a tool for scientific research. As Robert Reid remarks, 'the phenomenon is not about doing things on the Internet, but rather it's about using the Internet to do things differently' (1997: xxvii).

In 1994, Andreessen left to form Mosaic Communications, which then changed its name to Netscape Communications. What was most significant about Andreessen's work was that he actively began to promote the Internet as a platform, like UNIX or Windows, and that this made for a commercial market that could be pursued aggressively. Netscape Navigator was released in October and was much faster and more sophisticated than the competition. The year of the Web was 1995, when it went from being undervalued to overvalued in a matter of months. Nonetheless, as the Web became a more attractive environment, Navigator had an estimated ten million users worldwide and, when the company went public, Netscape Communications was valued at over $2.5 billion on Wall Street. The four stages of Internet evolution, according to Reid, are experimentation, novelty (in which the Internet, and particularly the Web, began to enter mainstream consciousness), utility (whereby it became easier to use and real applications were found for it), and ubiquity (Reid 1997). The latter has not yet arrived, particularly compared to television, but the timeline for the Internet and the Web in particular has been faster than for any technology other than the mobile phone.

Nevertheless, the rapid growth of the Internet and particularly Netscape's belief that the browser was more important than the operating system (OS) of a computer raised the alarm in at least one quarter. By 1995, Microsoft had 80 per cent of the OS market, making founder Bill Gates the richest man in the world. Microsoft initially dismissed the Internet as just another fad, intending to supplant it with its own Microsoft Network. By late 1995, however, it was plain that this strategy was a non-starter and so Microsoft started pouring vast amounts of its resources into Internet-ready products. The growth of Internet Explorer as an alternative to other browsers such as Navigator led to concerns that Microsoft was exploiting monopoly conditions to exclude competition in this new marketplace. In 1997, specific concerns about Microsoft's role in distributing its browser led to an investigation by the US Department of Justice into the company's alleged anti-competitive practices.

The computer industry has become a multi-billion-dollar industry, one that has been particularly significant in reviving the fortunes of the US at the end of the twentieth century, as its manufacturing, automobile and electronics industries suffered in competition with other Pacific-rim countries. The importance of the Internet is easily demonstrated by the fact that the most important software company was brought under greatest scrutiny because it gave away an application that generated no direct revenue, and for which people seem unwilling to pay at any time in the near future. The Microsoft investigation arrived at the time of the dotcom gold rush, when investors, businesses, and individuals made – and lost – fortunes, handing over money in an attempt simply to establish a presence in the new electronic market. If the first rush was a search for fool's gold, however, that does not mean that already the Web and Internet have not transformed global telecommunications forever. As Janet Abbate comments, 'If there is a constant in the history of the Internet, it is surprise' (Abbate 1999).

The next generation Internet

The exponential growth of the Internet, as well as fax, multiple phone lines and other telecommunications strains, has led several commentators (notably Bob Metcalfe) to predict that the Internet would be unable to cope with the huge increases in traffic – that the end result would be data gridlock. Certainly the theoretical limit defined by Claude Shannon for analog communications, 56 kilobits per second (Kbps) looks unlikely to be extended much past current specifications. These speeds create massive bottlenecks compared to advances in computer hardware and software and, thus, one of the major developments affecting the next step of the Internet is the movement to faster, more reliable broadband access.

Copper wire and optic fibre are capable of moving electrons or photons at two thirds the speed of light (124,100 miles per second); copper and fibre cannot increase the *speed* of transfer, but they can move bits of information in increasing multiples, hence broadband technologies such as ISDN (Integrated Services Digital Network), ADSL (Asymmetric Digital Subscriber Line), cable and wireless.

22

ISDN is the poor relation which has also been around longest, offering improved digital connection, but only offering 64 Kbps, although channels can be combined for 128 Kbps. ADSL has the advantage of using ordinary telephone lines: voice information sits in the 0–4 kHz range transmitted by such lines, leaving between 4 kHz and 2 MHz for data transfer at typical rates of 512 Kbps downstream and 256 Kbps upstream (hence *asymmetric*), although theoretical speeds of up to 2 megabits per second (Mbps) are available. Cable, which connects the user to a cable Internet LAN (Local Area Network), offers theoretical transfer rates of 36 Mbps and in the early days radio networks such as LMDSs (Local Multipoint Distribution Services) could transfer data at 1.5 *giga*bits per second. Gigabit networking is fully expected to be a reality within a few years in countries such as Sweden (which already enjoys access at 10 Mbps thanks to the communication company B2). Gigabit networking will also work its way into MANs (Metropolitan Area Networks), with the networking company Cisco having demonstrated 10 Gbit Ethernet and outlined plans for a 100 Gbit version.

If broadband is one aspect of the near future of the Internet, its complement is ubiquity. At present, the vast majority of users connecting to the Net do so via a personal computer, but, while such computers have extended considerably into our lives over the past decade or so, the complexity and expense of this technology still mean that it remains alien to most users. A smaller number of users can access services such as the Web via the great success story of the twentieth century, the television, while an infinitesimal group of users can, at the time of writing, elect to use the Web via a mobile phone.

Drawing upon innovations made by individuals such as Marconi and companies such as AT&T, the movement of wireless to mobile technology was a particularly difficult and drawn out process. Bell Labs began to experiment with cellular-based communication in the 1970s, using a limited selection of radio frequencies shared between low-power transmitters that would not interfere with each other and that culminated in the analog Advanced Mobile Phone System (AMPS) in 1983. At the same time, the European Groupe Spécial Mobile (GSM) was established to outline standards for a digital system that was launched nearly a decade later – by which time GSM had come to mean the Global System for Mobile communications. Using 900 MHz and then 1,800 MHz and 1,900 MHz frequencies, GSM became immensely popular in Europe and parts of Asia, although Japan and the US continue to operate their own standards.

While GSM and other, so-called second generation mobile services are able to carry data, as opposed to analog cellphones that could only carry voice signals, traffic is very limited. Third generation, or 3G, services are currently being implemented to handle increased data traffic, including audio and video, combining broadband with mobility. Predicted data throughputs indicate rates of up to 384 Kbps or even 2 Mbps in certain circumstances, compared to typical rates of 9.6–14.4 Kbps for GSM; in conjunction with developments such as Bluetooth, a technology that offers wireless connections over short distances, the aim is to make networked services ubiquitous, invisible and immersive. Yet broadband connection on mobile phones does not indicate that such services will automatically be accepted and (more to the point) paid for: when the Wireless Application Protocol (WAP) was outlined in the late 1990s, enabling users to browse specially constructed web sites from mobile devices, it became evident very quickly that this was an invention very much in search of an audience. A MORI poll at the beginning of 2001 found that, although fourteen million Britons had mobile phones, only 2 per cent had WAP versions, which was bad news for the companies such as BT, Vodaphone and Orange, who paid £22.4 billion for 3G licences in the UK.

The growth and acceptance of new technologies cannot always be predicted. At the same time that WAP was proving to be such a failure in Europe, a similar technology, i-mode, has become immensely popular in Japan. Similarly, the number of mobile phone users worldwide is expected to reach one billion in 2003, rather than 2005 as originally expected by manufacturers. Despite recent setbacks, then, the Internet continues to extend more and more into different areas of our lives, gradually becoming faster, more reliable and more ubiquitous.

How the Internet works

The basic architecture of the Internet is what is known as a client/server model. A server, a computer running special software capable of sharing files with other systems, hosts a range of services such as email and web pages that are accessed by client software running on a remote computer. In the vast majority of cases, to access these services and files requires an ISP, with only the very largest companies and institutions being able to connect to the Net without an intermediary.

An ISP operates a network using common software rules, or protocols, and this is linked to other networks and agreements to pass traffic between them: this combination of networks comprises the Internet as we know it. Each ISP has a range of Internet Protocol (IP) addresses allocated to it for its own business and users, and uses its servers to match IP addresses to domain names, the basic information that is required to tell others where you are connecting from. Most users will connect using dial-up or leased-line accounts that offer Point-to-Point Protocol (PPP), with a few still using the older Serial Line Internet Protocol (SLIP) to connect.

Typically, a PPP communications program, such as Windows Dial-Up Networking, connects to the network by dialling via a modem, then logs into the ISP's network with a user name and password. Windows application producers created a standard way for Internet clients to communicate called Winsock (short for Windows sockets) and Dial-Up Networking is Winsock-compatible. The equivalent standard for Macs is called Open Transport/PPP in earlier versions of the MacOS, and Apple Remote Access in the latest version.

Internet structure

The Internet consists of two main parts: the hardware/communications network, and the protocols governing data transfer across that network. The actual computer hardware is relatively insignificant, in that it can be upgraded regularly and is changed frequently. More important is the communications infrastructure, the cables and satellite links, which are much more difficult to change and limit the bandwidth, the amount of data, that can be transferred from computer to computer. A common metaphor for bandwidth is a pipe, but this is incredibly misleading: the assumption is that, if you increase the width of the pipe, you can pour more data down it. A better metaphor is of a road network: simply widening roads may not help traffic jams, but smaller and faster cars, as well as improved traffic control systems, may help more drivers get from A to B.

Of the four main ways to connect to the Internet in addition to a leased line – standard modem, ISDN, ADSL, cable modem – by far the most common is via a standard modem. Modem stands for modulator/demodulator, referring to the way in which a modem changes binary instructions into tones (modulation) that can be transmitted across a phone line and decoded (demodulated) at the other end. Speeds for modems are measured in bits, or kilobits per second, with various standards governing how such modems connect at their fastest rates: the current standard is V.90, which covers modems capable of downloading information at a theoretical maximum of 56 Kbps (though access is usually at around 44 Kbps) and uploading information at 33.6 Kbps, with V.92 currently being ratified at an increased upload speed of up to 48 Kbps.

Of the other techniques for connecting to the Internet, ISDN does not offer huge speed increases over a standard modem but, by connecting to a digital network, as the name implies, it can connect more or less immediately rather than having to negotiate with a modem at the other end of the line. In addition, ISDN lines can be combined to double the speed of such modems from 64 Kbps to 128 Kbps. More substantial improvements are promised by cable and ADSL. ADSL connects across ordinary lines, but, as with 56-Kbps modems, the speed for download and upload is asymmetrical, offering 512-Kbps download rates and 256 Kbps for upload. These rates are typically those of cable: although cable can offer much faster access speeds, with networks offering anything up to 36 Mbps, in reality no one can ever use such capacity because the bandwidth has to be shared between everyone on a local cable network. With optimum conditions, ADSL would download a 1.5-Mb file in under five seconds, compared to approximately twenty seconds for ISDN and a minute for a 56-Kbps modem.

In addition to the networks used to connect to the Net, protocols control how data is transferred across that infrastructure, the most important ones being collected together as TCP/IP (Transfer Control Protocol/Internet Protocol). TCP/IP operates on four levels: network access (to facilitate transmission and routing of packets); network protocols (governing the delivery service); transfer protocols (ensuring the machines are capable of receiving and sending packets); and application protocols (either applications themselves, or providing service to applications running across the Internet). TCP/IP is the most important set of protocols and will be dealt with in more detail below, but other, more specialised protocols include: Hypertext Transfer Protocol (HTTP), used to enable web servers and clients to share data regardless of where they are held, HTTP addresses being indicated by a Uniform Resource Locator (URL, signified as http://); FTP, developed before HTTP to enable users to access files held on remote servers; Internet Relay Chat (IRC), one of the forms of real-time communication enabling users to chat to each other; and Telnet, which allows users to log into a remote computer and send commands controlling the operating system, so that the local client operates rather like the terminals that were used for older mainframes.

At its highest level in Britain, a 'tier one' ISP has its own international connections and links to other UK ISPs at the London Internet Exchange (LINX). Smaller ISPs connect to these larger companies, reselling that connectivity. In the Net's early years, ensuring connectivity was largely a question of academic and research institutions (the main backbone of the Internet as run by the National Science Foundation) agreeing to transfer traffic to each other; as the Net has become a larger, commercial environment, however, information routing can sometimes be more difficult. If an ISP does not have an agreement with another network, it cannot pass traffic across that route. Thus routing on the Internet is no longer simply determined by need: companies that invest millions of dollars in infrastructure, including the transatlantic cable connecting Europe to the US, insist on so-called peering and transit agreements, often for a price.

While most of the major UK ISPs connect to LINX, for example, they do not necessarily connect with each other: when a user on one UK ISP requests a web page on another UK provider, but there is no agreement between the two companies, information may be routed via LINX to an international link in Europe or the US that does have an agreement with that party. This is one reason why certain ISPs seem slower than others – as well as having too many users or not enough hardware to support their services, they may also lack suitable transit agreements. Connections are made, employing the Internet's famous resilience, but not all connections are equal.

TCP/IP

While the obvious tendency is to consider the Internet as a collection of hardware – computers, satellites and telecommunications links – it is also a set of software instructions, or protocols, that are arguably more important. While the hardware components of the Internet are regularly replaced, the software enabling communication between those different parts is upgraded much more slowly and carefully as this is the glue binding together the entire network.

As mentioned earlier, the family of protocols that takes care of passing information across the Internet and certain other networks, such as LANs, is known as TCP/IP, or Transmission Control Protocol/ Internet Protocol. When information is transferred across the Internet, computers along the way know where to redirect messages due to the instructions provided using TCP/IP. Increasingly, TCP/IP is used to refer to a wider range of Internet protocols that include the subset for TCP and IP, as well as protocols dealing with other aspects of routing information. To understand TCP/IP requires a basic grasp of four networking fundamentals: addressing, packets, protocols and routers. These can be best explained using the metaphor of sending a hand-written letter by mail.

When you write a letter to a relative or friend and seal it in an envelope, unless you intend to deliver it to them personally the first thing it requires is an address. Likewise, for a file to transfer across the Internet and be received by the right person it must also have an address: for email, this is usually a name followed by an @ symbol and ISP name; for a file transfer to a web site, it usually consists of an Internet domain name. Domain names are matched against IP addresses (see 'IP addressing and domain names' below), and, while such addresses may seem confusing at first, it is best to consider them as akin to a post- or zip code. Zip codes and postcodes correspond to certain areas of the country, but you don't need to understand them to use them; you do, however, need to enter them correctly if you do not want your letter delivered to the wrong address.

When sending our letter it leaves our hands and arrives at its destination in one piece (if not, we want compensation). Across an electronic network, however, this creates problems. First of all, sending large files clogs up the network so that nothing else can be transferred while your file is on its way. In addition, errors can occur as a file is sent and even small errors may prevent the file from opening, requiring the whole lot to be re-sent. This is where packets come into play. Our virtual envelope is snipped into a number of small pieces (packets) that are then reassembled at their destination. Each packet includes information added to it, so that software can check for errors, and so that it knows that the message begins 'Dear John Doe' and ends 'Yours sincerely, Jane Bloggs'. If one packet has become corrupted during transmission, the error-correcting software requests that the packet be re-sent.

To enable the computers that are sending and receiving messages to understand how to handle and reassemble packets, protocols are required. These include the instructions for splitting and assembling the file, as well as instructions for directing it to its intended address and mechanisms for saying that a packet has been received or requesting that faulty or missing packets be re-sent.

Our handwritten letter requires a final component to arrive at its destination. Assuming that we have affixed a stamp, we drop our letter in a postbox and wait for the Post Office or mail company to deliver it to the address on the envelope. On the Internet, the role of the postman and mail company is handled by what is known as a router. When you connect to the mail server of your ISP, that computer works out the details of passing the file across the Internet to its destination. In the vast majority of cases, rather than connect directly to the recipient's ISP across a country or even the world, the router will pass the file to another router that will in turn pass it to another, using Internet protocols to work out which route is most efficient.

IP addressing and domain names

An important function of Internet Protocol (IP), as mentioned already, is addressing, the basic means by which computers are identified on the Internet. An IP address is a 32-bit number that uniquely identifies each host and network as four octets from 0 to 255 (for example, 10.126.58.192). In theory, such a 32-bit number provides over four billion addresses, but when IP addresses were first allocated they were divided into four classes, of which A, B, and C are the most common. Class A networks range from 1.x.x.x to 126.x.x.x, class B from 128.n.x.x to 191.n.x.x, and class C from 192.n.n.x to 223.n.n.x, where x indicates a number that can be allocated by the ISP, and n a number that is determined centrally. Thus a class C network has a possible 256 addresses, for example from 201.15.15.1 to 201.15.15.256, a class B has 65,365 and a class A network 16,777,216. Of the missing numbers above, any address that begins with 127 is known as a 'loopback' address because it points (or loops back) to the network card in the local machine rather than to one elsewhere on the network, while addresses beginning 224–239 are used for multicast addresses, and higher numbers are reserved for administrative use. It is because the smallest unit of allocation is 256 numbers that the Internet is running out of addresses.

Because of this, the Internet Engineering Task Force (IETF) and Internet Architecture Board (IAB) have designed a next generation Internet protocol, IPv6 (or version 6), which increases the number of addresses available under the current standard as well as improving how messages are routed across the Net. It is assumed that IPv6 will eventually replace the current protocol, but it has also been designed to coexist with older networks.

Also important is the Domain Name System (DNS), without which the Internet could not function, although domain names were not a part of the early Internet. Before the implementation of DNS, servers had to have an up-to-date copy of a single text file listing every host on the Internet and its IP address. DNS evolved for a number of reasons, including the difficulty of using IP addresses in numerical form, and also because, as the Internet expanded, it became impossible for networks to keep track of every IP address in circulation across the Net. DNS, then, is a hierarchical database that is distributed across the Internet, with information being distributed to the lowest level possible. What this means is that an ISP holds DNS information for its own systems, so that when an email is sent for another user on that system, such as from user1@example.com to user2@example.com, the message can be transferred by matching the address in the server's own database. When a message is sent to another domain, however, for example to user3@myisp.co.uk, the server must ask a higher-level server for information, such as who holds information for .co.uk. At the highest level are the 'root servers' that hold information about which name servers around the world have information for each of the top-level domains, such as .com, .uk, .org and so on.

It is vitally important, then, for an ISP's servers to maintain up-to-date DNS information, particularly as this system is used to redirect traffic using aliases and because servers cache information to help traffic flow more quickly across the Net. When a user sends an email, then, requests are passed up the Internet chain until eventually they find a DNS table listing that host. Information passed from computers is broken into packets, each one with a heading that identifies that packet; when they reach their destination, the packets are reassembled into the complete message. Some of the protocols governing TCP/IP are error-checking protocols: if the message is incomplete, the destination computer requests the packet to be sent again.

Further reading

There are a number of books outlining the history of the Internet in some detail, of which Naughton (1999) is probably the best, along with Abbate (1999). Hafner and Lyon (1996) approach the same subject with considerable enthusiasm, although some of their material is beginning to date now. Berners-Lee (1999) concentrates (unsurprisingly) on the events that led to the development of the Web, but, as a contributor to the open standards movement that has provided much that is best on the Internet, his opinions are worth reading. Reid (1997) is similarly restricted to the Web and now is frankly out of date: nonetheless, *Architects of the Web* includes a number of interviews with important figures involved in the development of technologies that we take for granted (as well as a few that have deservedly disappeared) and, as a 'historical document', offers some fascinating insights into the utopianism that gripped Internet development in the mid-1990s before this was replaced by simple greed. Although it deals with computers rather than the Internet, a highly recommended read is

Cringeley (1996): the author, who worked on the US magazine *InfoWorld* for a number of years, had very close dealings with some of the major players in the computer industry and writes wittily and incisively about the foibles of the IT revolution.

There are a huge number of manuals and technical books on how the Internet works, but perhaps the best text for beginners, which is both comprehensive and simple to understand, is Young *et al.* (1999). The Internet itself is a good place to start here, for example the World Wide Web Consortium (www.w3c.org) and the Internet Society (www.isoc.org).

Chapter 2

Using the
Internet

Introduction

While this book provides theoretical and contextual
material about the nature and purpose of the Internet,
it is also important to understand applications in order
to develop best practice. This chapter will not necessarily explain how to use specific programs (many of
which could take up an entire book in their own
right), but will cover general principles behind common
technologies; exercises and instructions can also be
found on *The Internet: The Basics* web site at www.
routledge.com/internetbasics/techniques.htm.

The main reason for understanding how applications work, as well as how to use them, is very simple.
I frequently encounter students, readers and friends
who, while perfectly happy with a familiar program
employed for email or chat, cannot get to grips with
one which is unfamiliar, even though it does exactly the
same thing. Much of the blame for this must be laid at
the feet of programmers and designers, particularly
when they employ idiosyncratic interfaces or hide away

important information in obscure menus, but Internet users can also improve their practical skills by understanding the technologies that underlie many commonly used programs. As such, this chapter will outline the main elements of online communication – email, the Web, file transfer, Usenet and chat – and then offer advice and guidance on using the Internet as a research tool.

Email

As we saw in Chapter 1, one of the first possible instances of electronic communication familiar to current users of email came in 1973 when Leonard Kleinrock wished to recover a razor: logging onto ARPANET and using a program called TALK, Kleinrock found a US delegate willing to retrieve his precious razor.

As John Naughton (1999) observes, this incident was really an example of online chat rather than email *per se*: Kleinrock's exchange with another conference delegate took place in 'real time', or was synchronous; email, on the other hand, is *asynchronous*, that is, sender and receiver do not need to be connected at the same time. As Naughton further comments, the emergence of email was something of a surprise to ARPA, particularly when a survey in 1973 revealed that three-quarters of online traffic consisted of email – a considerable amount of it having nothing to do with computers. 'Here was this fantastic infrastructure built at government expense for serious purposes – and these geeks were using it for sending messages to one another!' (1999: 141). As email quickly came to fulfil a social purpose, so it succeeded where other applications had failed.

Email concepts

Technologies do not simply evolve and become successful according to some necessary law of internal determinism – for every VHS or MP3 player there is a Betamax or laser disc. Even technological superiority may not be sufficient to guarantee success, as with the example of Betamax and VHS: while Betamax was held up by experts as providing better quality videos, there were simply more titles available for its competitor. Alongside marketing and careful product placement and distribution, then, there must be a social use for a technology for it to prosper, its so-called 'killer app' (see Chapter 1).

On the Internet, while plenty of books (including this one) will concentrate on the glories and marvels of the Web, virtual reality and streaming audio-video, the simple fact is that email is the real killer app on the Net. Email as a communication medium is non-intrusive and asynchronous: like a letter, but unlike the phone, it does not depend on the recipient being available at the time communication is made, and email messages can be read when he or she has time. Like the phone, but unlike a letter, it is also (when it works well) extremely fast, with reception being almost instantaneous.

Email does have its drawbacks, however. The speed and casual nature of email means that people may fire off messages without thinking through the consequences, and the practice of junk email (or spam) can render accounts more or less unusable. Email can also be easily misunderstood, lacking as it does the nuances of facial or verbal expression. Nonetheless, as a means of communicating around the world, email is probably the most valuable Internet tool that can transform the way we work, study and even play.

Receiving and sending email

Most people access email through a mail client, such as Outlook Express (included with Internet Explorer), Netscape Mail (or Messenger in Communicator 4) or Eudora. Such an application sits on a local PC and uploads or downloads messages to and from a mail server (see 'How the Internet works' in Chapter 1). Alternatively, users may access email via a web-based email server, such as Hotmail or Yahoo!, or through commercial and proprietary applications, such as AOL's mail program or Lotus Notes.

Email is sent to a unique email address. When a mail client connects to the Internet, either through a permanent connection or across a modem, it links to a mailbox that stores incoming email sent to that particular address on a mail server, a computer permanently attached to the Internet and set up to handle email. Mail servers use two main sets of rules, or protocols, to receive and send messages, the most common protocol for receiving and storing email being known as Post Office Protocol (POP, or POP3 after the current version). Sending email requires a similar process, the rules governing the transmission of messages being known as Simple Mail Transfer Protocol (SMTP); SMTP is understood by all email applications that transfer your message to its final destination.

Email addresses are indicated by the use of the 'at' symbol (@), and are divided into two main sections: the username, which precedes the @ symbol, and the host or domain name, which follows it. The username is used to identify someone and may be an actual name or variant of a name, such as 'wblake', or a nickname, 'tyger', while the host or domain name is the Internet location of the mailbox, usually the ISP or company that owns that domain name. Thus, for example, wblake@jerusalem.com could be the address of William Blake on a server owned by the ISP called Jerusalem.

Many domains have special addresses, such as info, sysadmin or postmaster@domainname.com, which are used to provide information or services, such as the reporting of spammers or help with web sites. When using email addresses, capitals are usually unimportant, but some servers insist that you use the correct case (WBlake). In addition, while user names can contain numbers, underscores and periods, such as 'william_blake' or 'blake25', they cannot contain commas, spaces or parentheses. If you are sure that you have the correct address, but your message is not getting through, check your entry for capital letters, spaces or commas instead of full stops. To retrieve email, the client application must also be correctly configured, so that it points to the correct mail server, for example mail.myisp.com.

Spam and security

Most of us have become used to receiving junk mail through the post – colourful or not-so-colourful brochures, letters, competition announcements and other paraphernalia from companies seeking to entice us into buying something. While snail junk mail can be a pain, at least companies sending out such material have to pay for postage and the cost of bulk mailing acts as a brake (however slight) on their activities. For marketing and sales people seeking new

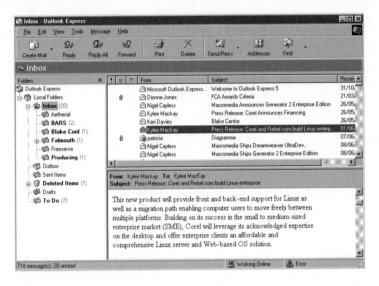

FIGURE 2.1 An email client, Outlook Express.

customers, the ultimate nirvana is a system that allows them to send out mail to anyone at minimum cost: enter one of the curses of modern email – spam.

Spam is the term used to describe unsolicited email, usually from a mailing list, newsgroup, or web site. Sometimes a spammer may simply guess at an email by prefixing a common name to an ISP's domain name, such as john@myisp.com. Spam is a double curse because, as well as filling your email box with inappropriate and unwanted email, many users have to pay telephone charges to download messages. To try and control spamming, be careful who you give your address to, particularly when using newsgroups, and set up filters to move mail to designated folders (such as the delete bin if you receive certain messages frequently). Don't unsubscribe unless you are receiving mail from a company that you subscribed to in the first place – you may simply be confirming to the spammer that your email address is valid. A very simple technique, which is useful if you participate in a lot of newsgroups, is to adjust your email in a simple but obvious way, for example jane@myNOSPAMisp.com. This will still allow other users to email you, but will confuse automated programs used to cull email addresses from newsgroup postings.

Several ISPs have begun to sue spammers who use their systems because of the bad reputation that this causes. If you feel that you are on the receiving end of particularly annoying spam, you can research further by going to the web sites for the Coalition Against Unsolicited Commercial Email (www.cauce.org) or the Network Abuse Clearinghouse (www.abuse.net). Finally, if you want to advertise your wares on the Net, bulk mailing probably seems just what you have been waiting for: resist the temptation – at best you will annoy many potential customers, at worst you could face fines and legal action.

Another major issue affecting Internet users, particularly with regard to email and the Web, is security. We shall consider issues around privacy and the effects of recent European and North American legislation in Chapter 4, and, as email is used increasingly to send sensitive information, security has become more important than ever before. The means of securing your email revolve around various types of cryptography, that is, encoding messages, or substituting letters and numbers with different characters, in order to encrypt the information. The contents of a message appear scrambled to users who do not enter the right password, either a secret key that is transmitted by the sender or a 'public key' system, where two different but related keys are used to encrypt and decrypt messages; a common public cryptography package is PGP, or Pretty Good Privacy. (For more on how cryptography works, see the section on encryption in Chapter 4.)

Email mailing lists

Mailing lists are a popular means of enabling groups of people to keep in touch: whether an academic subject discussion that continues over decades, or a specific project with a clearly defined beginning and end, such lists provide a convenient way for users to contact each other and keep up to date. These lists are organised by a mailing lists manager, typically an application that stores a catalogue of subscriber addresses with input from a human administrator. Lists may be open or closed, that is, anyone may subscribe or subscription may be limited, and there may or may not be restrictions on posting to such groups. To work effectively, mailing lists also require two further email addresses: postings to subscribers are sent to the list address, for example PROJECT-L@listserver.com, which then redirects them to everyone on file; requests for subscription to a list or removal on it are addressed to the administrator address, for example PROJECT-L-request@listserver.com, usually with an instruction to subscribe or unsubscribe in the subject heading.

Because maintaining a mailing list can be labour-intensive, most are managed by programs with only very occasional human intervention. The three main mailing list managers are LISTSERV (www.lsoft.com), ListProc (www.cren.net/listproc) and Majordomo (www.greatcircle.com/majordomo), of which LISTSERV is the most popular. To subscribe to a mailing list, of course, the first step is to find a list that interests you, and the easiest place to start is the large database at www.liszt.com. The company responsible for the LISTSERV program also maintains a useful set of links at www.lsoft.com/lists/LIST-Q.html.

The Web and file transfer

While email is probably the real killer app for the Internet, it is the World Wide Web that attracts most attention from the media and many users. The Web consists of millions of files stored on tens of thousands of servers around the globe, each one capable of transmitting text, images, video, sounds and programs as part of the largest and most diverse collection of information ever seen.

The foundation of the Web comprises HTTP (see Chapter 1), which provides a means of linking files and transferring them from one computer to another, and text formatted in HTML (Hypertext Markup Language). By following such links, the Web can appear as a seamless document, with the potential for crossing from almost any web site or page to any other.

Browser concepts

A browser is a client, similar to an email client such as Outlook Express or Eudora, that enables a computer to communicate with web servers and view the files, or web pages, that are downloaded to the local machine. At the very least, a web browser must be able to display text according to the rules of HTML, but most users will also be able to view images and multimedia including sound, video and 3D. While one of the first publicly available browsers that could display images was Mosaic, the two most commonly used browsers are Netscape (previously known as Navigator) and Microsoft's Internet Explorer. Some users will employ other browsers – one growing in popularity amongst certain web users is Opera, available from (www.opera software.com); users of AOL's older software may employ a proprietary web browser; and there are a number of alternatives such as Lynx (a text-based browser from lynx.browser.org) and Arachne (www.naf. cz/arachne/xch).

A typical browser can be divided into several sections: the menu bar at the top, similar to those employed by WIMP (windows, icons, menu, programs) graphical user interfaces (GUIs) such as Microsoft Windows or Apple's MacOS; toolbars, containing buttons for the most common tasks performed in the program and located beneath the menu bar; an address or location window or bar, usually located near the toolbars; the main viewing window where web pages and content are displayed; and a status bar, at the bottom of the screen, which provides information on such things as the current status of a page download or the web address of a link.

As web pages may be scattered all over the world, so the system of protocols used to access such documents requires a method of addressing that will enable users to transfer files from web servers. As mentioned earlier, every file on the Internet has an address known as a Uniform Resource Locator, or URL for short, which specifies the transfer protocol (usually the hypertext transfer protocol, entered as http://), the host name of the Web (see 'IP addressing and domain names' in Chapter 1), and sometimes information about directories and files on the host computer. Thus, for example, http://www. routledge.com, is the domain name URL for the publisher of this book, while http://www.routledge.com/internetbasics/default.htm will direct you to the page containing information for *The Internet: The Basics*.

It is worth noting that, while a domain name can give you some information about a web site, geographical location is not necessarily part of this. Many web sites use .com, which could be in Alabama or Albania, while other sites end with a top-level domain name (TLD), such as .uk for the United Kingdom, .fr for France or .jp for Japan, which does provide geographical data. This does not mean that the server is necessarily located in that country, but such addresses are often helpful for people looking for nationally specific information (for example support from IBM in the UK rather than in the United States). Other domain names indicate the type of organisation using the server. The most common type, .com, indicates a business, and this is also often found with country-specific domain names such as .co.uk or .co.jp; .org is used by (usually non-profit) organisations; and .gov is reserved for government organisations. Less common but becoming more important are domain names for specific types of business or organisation, such as .tv for television sites and the recently introduced .museum for museums or .pro for professionals. Domain names are maintained and organised by ICANN (Internet Corporation for Assigned Names and Numbers, www.icann.org).

Recently, however, the issue of who controls these domain names has been confused due to an American company, New.net, offering an additional 30 TLDs, such as .family, .inc, .ltd and .xxx. Many of the new codes were turned down by ICANN, but can still be activated without reference to that authority because they are routed via New.net: www.mycompany.inc is really www.mycompany.inc.new.net. While ICANN has made threatening noises against New.net, recognisable domain names are the real estate of the Web, with more and more users willing to pay for easy-to-remember TLDs and this may only be the beginning of commercial operators challenging the established organisations that administer the Internet.

FTP

While files are transferred across the Internet all the time, as email or pages in a browser, the File Transfer Protocol (FTP) deserves a special

FIGURE 2.2   The Netscape 6 browser.

mention. In most cases, files that are transferred across the Net are of a special type, whether text messages for email or graphics and text files encoded as HTML for web pages. FTP, however, enables users to transfer any kind of file across the Net, whether it is a word-processed document, a spreadsheet, an application or a video file. In addition, while such files can also be transferred to remote users as an attachment to an email, FTP is designed for transferring files to a number of users using a client/server system. Files can be sent to a central server and then downloaded by other computer users.

There are thousands of FTP servers across the Net, usually indicated by ftp:// instead of http:// at the beginning of the URL. While such servers can be accessed by web browsers, however, they are independent of the Web and can also be accessed by other clients, such as WS_FTP for Windows or Fetch for the Macintosh. Although many users load private files onto FTP servers, some servers also make available a selection of files to the general public; this is referred to as *anonymous FTP* because no password, or the user's email as password, is required, whereas users of protected servers log on to directories protected by a password known only to them. Although it must be emphasised that FTP servers are separate from the Web, most FTP access occurs via browsers (in most cases to anonymous servers so that files can be downloaded).

Usenet and newsgroups

Usenet is one of the longest-running services on the Internet, and still one of the most valuable. While applications such as Gopher and Veronica have come and gone, Usenet remains immensely popular because it requires very little in terms of computing power and can be very interactive – similar to email, except that postings can be read by a multitude of people and responded to. While this has its drawbacks, particularly in terms of attracting unwanted attention that can lead to 'flame wars', it also means that Usenet can be extremely valuable as a research tool because pertinent responses to a particular question may come from anywhere around the world.

Usenet developed out of the growth of UNIX in the late 1970s: a researcher at Bell Labs developed a program called UUCP (UNIX-to-UNIX Copy) that enabled computers to deliver software updates automatically to other machines. Graduate students at Duke University worked on this program in order to search for changes in specific files and copy these files to their own computers: by 1980, this had become known as Usenet News, the 'poor man's ARPANET'. As postings are made to various newsgroups, so the Usenet protocol ensures that any news server can connect to another server and automatically transfer that material across, usually at set times during the day. Usenet is, strictly speaking, separate from the Internet in that information can be transferred over direct connections between UNIX computers; in the early 1980s, however, researchers at Berkeley created links between Usenet and ARPANET and today the vast majority of newsgroup users read and respond to postings via the Internet.

THE INTERNET: THE BASICS

Usenet concepts

As Usenet distributes messages, also known as postings or articles, like a widely dispersed bulletin board, and because so many postings are made each day, it became obvious very quickly that its collection of articles would become too chaotic to be useful. As such, messages are organised into newsgroups, which in turn are arranged hierarchically; the first part of a newsgroup name indicates the category that the newsgroup falls into, there being eight main categories:

- alt: alternative newsgroups
- comp: computer-related topics
- misc: miscellaneous topics
- news: information relating to Usenet itself
- rec: recreational topics
- soc: social topics
- talk: general discussion

After the category comes a name specifying the main topic of a newsgroup, such as alt.religion, which provides alternative discussions on religion. In turn, more specific newsgroups begin to emerge looking at ever more particular topics, such as alt.religion.catholicism, or alt.religion.scientology.

Subscribing to newsgroups is slightly different to subscribing to mailing lists, requiring you to download a list of newsgroups available from your local ISP; once you have a list of newsgroups you do need to select a newsgroup that you may wish to read. While some newsreaders allow users to search for topics, this is not true of all, although an easy way to access (and search) newsgroups is by using a web-based reader such as Dejanews (now acquired by Google) and is available at www.google.com.

To access a newsgroup, your ISP needs to have a news server configured: this is true of most ISPs, although the particular newsgroups that are available from the server vary greatly; in particular, many servers do not carry postings for alt hierarchies that tend to carry pornographic images or other material that can be considered offensive. Some newsgroups are moderated, meaning that postings can be

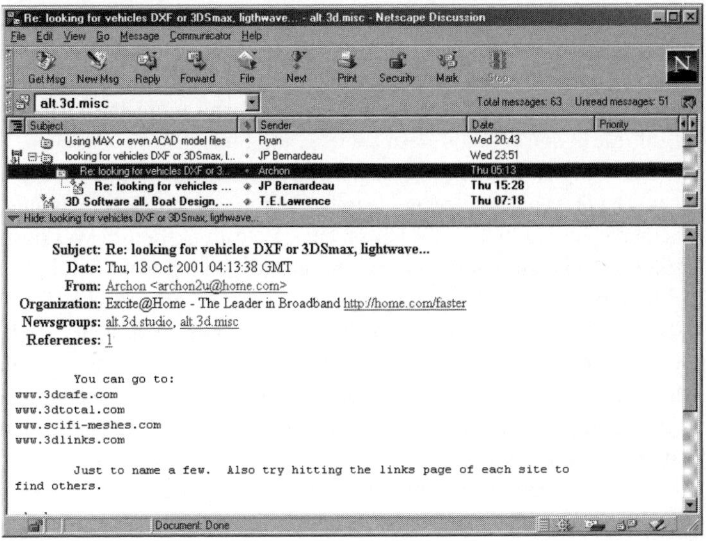

FIGURE 2.3 A typical newsgroup reader.

deleted by the individual or group of individuals in charge of the newsgroup, whereas others are very much a free-for-all.

Netiquette

While etiquette and manners (or the breach thereof) on the Net, or 'netiquette' as it is commonly known, is not the preserve of Usenet, some of the most particularly virulent examples of the breakdown in polite interaction can be found in newsgroups, highlighting the importance of the (often unspoken) rules that enable communication to continue. The ease with which modern applications enable users to quickly fire off an email or a posting in response to a message that they have just read can result in 'flame wars', where words do their best to rival sticks and stones for breaking bones (or egos at least).

In certain rare cases, flaming can be a particular form of almost poetic rant, not particularly directed at any specific user or group of users, but simply intended to let off steam against a cruel and unfair world. It is not the intention of this book to denounce what can be an extremely individualistic and entertaining form of communication; in most cases, however, flame wars demonstrate no more than what is pitiful, mean-spirited and despicable in the human spirit. As such, a few voluntary rules can go a long way.

The first and simplest guide to facilitating communication online, whether it be via email, Usenet or chat, is to think before you post: hitting the send button as soon as you read something that offends you is the surest way to blow up an issue out of all proportion. If you decide, on careful consideration, that you do wish to hurt in return, then fair enough: you are prepared for the consequences as you are talking to real people, not computers. In addition, it is not uncommon to encounter 'trolls', messages intended to provoke a response that demonstrates the respondent's ignorance of Net conventions.

While simple anger, bile or malicious spite are the surest ways to irritate your fellow netizens, there are also certain other practices that can rile experienced Internet users, but are something of a mine-field for new users. Thus, for example, typing COMPLETELY IN CAPITALS is considered to be shouting; the reason why it is probably so irritating is that, while using capitals can help to emphasise a point, it actually makes longer messages harder to read. Alongside this, checking spelling and proofreading text is advisable, although the text message bug ('cul8er') is spreading faster than ever before.

There are some features of netiquette that are specific to Usenet. It is, for example, important to read a newsgroup's FAQs (go to www.faqs.org/faqs for a list) to see the remit of a particular group. Also, before you post a question, read through previous postings to check that the same question has not already appeared – the worst way to announce that you are a newbie is to fail to check what has been posted before and, while many Usenet posters will try to be as accom-modating as possible, it is only human to become annoyed when forced to answer the same question repeatedly.

While cross-posting to different newsgroups can be a useful way of ensuring that your message is seen by a number of readers, overuse of this technique will be seen as spamming by some users and some newsgroups will not accept it. Cross-post only if you believe your message will be genuinely interesting to different groups, and it is good form to begin a cross-posting with a brief apology and list of where else the message appears. If you feel you must cross-post, send the message to a limited number of groups (in most cases two or three).

Finally, if you make a mistake in a posting, remove it as soon as you can. You may be too late to prevent the eternal game of Chinese whispers that takes place on the Internet, but you have a responsibility to limit the misinformation that you may cause.

Chat, conferencing and instant messaging

One of the most popular forms of communication online is via chat, that is real-time conversation via text on screen, voice or even video. Such communication is akin to telephone conversations, with users seeing or hearing messages as they occur and responding quickly. As explained earlier, such chat is often referred to as Internet Relay Chat, or IRC, but most chat really occurs via web-based chat rooms, in proprietary chat rooms such as those found on AOL, or increasingly through instant messaging.

Another form of discussion that lies somewhere between chat and newsgroups is conferencing. This can occur in real time, as through a conferencing program such as Microsoft NetMeeting, but may also be asynchronous, with participants responding to messages left on a bulletin board or forum.

Chat concepts

When using a chat application, the first step is to locate the type of chat area that you wish to participate in. For those using IRC, the user needs to connect to an IRC server and join a channel where conversation is taking place. Because IRC requires the user to learn a variety of commands and is considerably more complex than using a browser, in recent years chat rooms on the Web or proprietary services such as AOL have been booming.

Chat rooms or channels tend to be organised around topics, though it must also be admitted that the relation between a channel and its ostensible topic may be tenuous. Topics can be based around

47

films or other media, hobbies, religion, sex, romance, research interests or simply hanging out. Once the user has located a chat room or channel, the next step is identification. While an email address indicates who you are to a mailing list or newsgroup, chat rooms require a nickname, screen name or 'handle'. Sometimes, such names will need to be registered in advance, while other systems will require a handle each time you log on: if someone else has chosen that name you will need to select another.

Another difference between newsgroup or bulletin board discussions and chat is that, while the former are usually organised into 'threads', chat rooms display messages as and when they are transmitted to the server. Some will use different colours to try and differentiate users, but in general you have to be paying attention to follow a chat discussion, as several conversations may be (and usually are) taking place at the same time. Chat, particularly as it appeals to teenage users or children, has often raised concerns about safety; as the old joke goes, 'On the Net, no one knows you're a dog'. Likewise, no one knows your real age or gender and, as relationships can and frequently do form online, there have been several stories of predatory people using chat rooms to meet younger males and females. Some systems, such as AOL, provide parental controls, but in general chat usage – like so many forms of communication – requires users to develop a healthy scepticism about the material they receive and some caution when providing personal details or meeting others face to face.

One fast growing subset of chat is messaging: applications such as AOL's Instant Messenger or Microsoft's Messenger enable users to send messages to others online. By creating a list of users you may wish to chat to, the message application informs you when one of them comes online, so that you can chat to them directly. So popular have such messaging systems been that AOL and Microsoft have engaged in an ongoing struggle to convert as many users as possible to each of their systems.

Researching via the Internet

The Internet is a remarkable resource for research – a huge international library – although one frequently lacking in quality control.

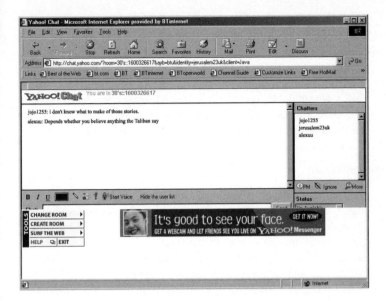

FIGURE 2.4   Using chat applications on the Web.

With that proviso in mind, the Net also provides materials from many of the most respected and important institutions in the world, institutions that most people would not have been able to use previously. What is more, much of the information provided is freely available, in a form accessible to anyone with a computer and Internet connection.

The following pages will concentrate on web-based sources of information; if you are using the Internet to research a project, however, do not neglect other sources: relevant mailing lists or newsgroups, for example, can be particularly rich. As such, you should consider subscribing to such services, especially as the ease with which participants can contribute via emails and postings means that these are often a source of the most up-to-date information. This open participation brings, of course, its own problems: the Internet is a great medium for gossip and speculation, and I frequently read student essays where the most ridiculous claims are made on the basis of spurious information posted to a newsgroup or web site. This is not to say that there is no editorial control on the Internet – as with any medium, you should check the quality of your sources (I have, less frequently, read equally ridiculous claims that have made their way into print). One simple technique to check the quality of information is to triangulate it, to reference it to at least two other sources, one of them ideally not online. This is not infallible, but does have the advantage, when practised, of cultivating a proper attitude of careful scepticism towards a medium that often deals more easily with casual rumour than definite fact.

Finding material

The starting point for researching material on the Internet is a search engine. The principle of searching through web sites began with two US students at Stanford University in 1994: David Filo and Jerry Yang spent a large amount of time cataloguing available pages on the new medium of the Web, hosting this database on Netscape's servers in 1995 as Yahoo! (for Yet Another Hierarchical Officious Oracle). While Yahoo! operates on the principle of quality not quantity, whereby an individual checks pages by hand before they are included in its directory, such an approach obviously neglects the vast majority of pages. In 2000, the US research company Cyveillance (www.cyveillance.com) produced a study called 'Sizing the Web' in which it estimated that the Internet had more than 2 billion web pages at that point, with 7.3 million new ones being added every day and a potential one per cent, or 21 million, being updated. This means that a search engine would need to analyse 6 Mb of data per second to stay up to date, which is why such sites tend to lag behind by a month or two.

As the Web increases at such an astonishing rate, most search engines employ automated programs known as 'spiders', 'crawlers' or 'robots' to read and index the text of a web page before looking for links to other pages, following them and repeating the process all over again. This raises problems of classifying and ranking such pages, which is why many search engines frequently return apparently useless results. The first attempt to resolve this was to use metatags, special HTML instructions not displayed in a page but used to indicate contents more specifically. Unfortunately, metatags require a page designer to enter information honestly and accurately, and a common trick to try

TABLE 2.1 The main search engines

Name	URL	Comments
AltaVista	www.altavista.com	A fast search engine with multiple advanced search options, although it does not always return the most relevant results
Ask Jeeves	www.ask.com	A natural language directory, useful for some searches, but with fewer direct links than other search engines
Dogpile	www.dogpile.com	A metasearch site that searches through other search engines
Excite	www.excite.com	Average directory and search engine
Fast	www.alltheweb.com	Generally lives up to its name: fast with very good results
Google	www.google.com	Probably the best search engine, which uses an innovative page ranking system to improve relevance
HotBot	www.hotbot.com	Metasearch site that is best used for business and technology
LookSmart	www.looksmart.com	Directory that uses a pay-for-placement model
Lycos	www.lycos.com	Directory that uses Fast as its search engine
MetaCrawler	www.metacrawler.com	The first of the metasearch sites, although no longer the best
Northern Light	www.northernlight.com	Excellent for research, particularly as it includes links to reports and articles
Yahoo!	www.yahoo.com	Directory that also uses Google as its search engine and, although not the most comprehensive, often provides more relevant results

and enhance the ratings of pages in search engines is simply to list the most common search terms as metatags. In 1998, Playboy sued adult sites for including the word 'Playmate' in their metatags, receiving $3 million compensation.

A more innovative, and effective, means of ranking pages is offered by Google (www.google.com). Its Page Rank system uses links to define a page's score: the more links to a page, the more important it is considered, particularly if those links come from pages that are themselves weighted more heavily, such as MSN or Yahoo! This combination of automation and more efficient page ranking has made Google a very useful search engine, but it still cannot process the entire Net and so the other search engines listed in Table 2.1 are worth considering.

While there are plenty of search engines around, the vast majority of these are powered by the same databases: for example, Netscape's Open Directory Project (www.dmoz.org) powers Google, Lycos and AltaVista, while Inktomi is used by LookSmart, MSN and HotBot. While search engines augment these services, they also feel the pinch when dotcom advertising dries up; for example, AltaVista laid off 25 per cent of its workforce in early 2001 and Disney closed its Go.com engine. What this means is that you will need to check that your favourite search engine remains available, and some pages may be overlooked as search engines insist that users pay to have sites listed. In any case, it is probably advisable to use a metasearch engine such as Query Server (www.queryserver.com) or Metor (www.metor.com), which do not index the Web themselves but pass queries on to other engines and then remove duplicate results. If you are looking for country-specific databases, Search Engine Colossus (www.search enginecolossus.com) has a comprehensive list.

Despite their difficulties, search engines remain an important source of information on the Web, though if you know you require specialised information it is probably advisable to visit a search engine or database dedicated to a particular topic, such as MedNet (www. mednets.com) for medical information or Euractiv (www.euractiv.com) for events in the EU. There is a list of search engines included in the appendix to this book: in my experience, search engines tend to vary in quality, though Google and Northern Light are ones that I tend to use on a regular basis, the latter also offering a library of pay-per-view full-text articles.

The Internet has become particularly useful for keeping up with ongoing research: publishers continue to produce printed catalogues that list forthcoming and new publications, but information about these as well as relevant tables of contents (TOCS) can also be received online. Zetoc (zetoc.mimas.ac.uk) offers TOCS based on the British Library's electronic data, which has been available since 2000 to all higher and further education institutions in the UK, and subscription to ZetocAlert will ensure that TOCS from chosen journals can be emailed on a regular basis. Likewise, the Bookmark Alerting service (bookmark.iop.org/alerts.htm) and BOOKNews (www.booknews.co.uk) offer similar alerts for new book publications. Finally, you should consult online stores such as Amazon (www.amazon.com) and the Internet Bookshop (www.bookshop.co.uk) as sources of information on new publications. For further information, see *The Internet: The Basics* research resource page at www.routledge.com/internetbasics/pages/resources_searchengines.htm.

Search tips

Typically, when entering a keyword into a search engine, a site will return a huge number of hits that are too general to be useful. Most sites support the use of speech marks, so that "designing for the web" will return pages with that phrase, rather than every page with the words 'designing' and 'web'. Several web sites, such as AltaVista and Google, also offer support for Boolean searching, which uses keywords AND, OR and NOT to make a search more specific. HotBot is an example of a site that employs such options in a very user-friendly manner, asking if you wish to search for an exact phrase, any word in a sequence or to exclude certain terms.

Of these Boolean operators, AND looks for pages combining search terms (William AND Blake), NOT excludes one or more terms (William NOT Wordsworth), while OR looks for either word (Byron OR Coleridge). In addition to these Boolean terms, proximity operators, such as NEAR, can search for pages where one keyword is within ten places of another. Thus a Boolean search on a site such as

Altavista could look something like (William Blake) AND (Byron OR Coleridge) NOT (Wordsworth). Two other options supported by some sites include the terms DOMAIN, whereby you can search a certain domain, such as .uk sites, by using the query DOMAIN:UK, or specific hosts, such as HOST:www.microsoft.com "Internet Explorer".

If a search engine does not specify Boolean or advanced search options, there are still a few things that you can try. As well as using quotation marks to try and restrict searches to a phrase, using the plus sign before a word acts as an implicit AND term, for example +Derek +Jarman. For further help, try out Search Engine Guide (www.searchengineguide.com) and Search Engine Watch (www.searchenginewatch.com). Finally, when using search engines, read the instructions on each site (most will tell you how to get the best results) and be specific but not too concise.

Search engines

Table 2.1 lists the main search engines, but there are a few other sites that you should consult when using the Web for research.

- Names and addresses: In the US, Google provides phone numbers and addresses when you search for a combination of name and zip code or state (www.google.com), while other sites include Lycos's Whowhere (whowhere.lycos.com), 411 Locate (www.411locate.com), Bigfoot (www.bigfoot.com) and Switchboard (www.switchboard.com). In the UK, go to Yell (search.yell.com) and Infobel (www.infobel.com/uk/).
- Images, video and music: Image search engines include Alta Vista (www.altavista.com/sites/search/simage), Excite (www.excite.com/search_forms/photosearch) for Associated Press and Reuters images, while other image bases include the Smithsonian and NASA at the University of California's ImageFinder (sunsite.berkeley.edu/imagefinder), and a library of fine art, design and architecture images at ADAM (adam.ac.uk). For video, check the Lycos VideoCenter page (video.lycos.com), AltaVista's Video Search page (www.altavista.com/sites/search/svideo) and StreamSearch (www.stream

search.com/radiohome.asp). StreamSearch also returns finds for audio, which, post-Napster, can also be found on the Alta Vista Audio Search page (www.altavista.com/sites/search/svideo), Lycos Music (music.lycos.com/downloads) and AudioGalaxy (www.audiogalaxy.com).

- News: Most of the world's news producers have devoted a considerable amount of time and energy since the mid-1990s to building up substantial web sites: many of these are listed in the resource section in the appendix to this book, as well as on *The Internet: The Basics* web site at www.routledge.com/internetbasics/pages/resources.htm. More general search engines include Lycos News, which serves recent AP and Reuters stories (www.lycos.com/news), TotalNews for the BBC and Washington Post (www.totalnews.com), Moreover for a broad range of (not always immediately up-to-date) news sources (www.moreover.com) and, for a less mainstream version, News Is Free (www.newsisfree.com).

Further reading

There are plenty of books and guides devoted to using the Internet: if you are a novice, then the Idiot guides or Dummy books are extremely simple to use (as the pejorative titles suggest). If you need something more detailed, Young *et al.* (1999) provides an extremely comprehensive guide to just about every technology you will encounter. Books that cover using the Internet for research (particularly for students) include Holland (1999) and Stewart and Mann (2000).

Chapter 3

New media and
web production

Introduction

New media is a catch-all term applied to the various
components that constitute digital production, whether
for the Web or other formats such as digital video.
Most so-called 'new' media have a very strong relation
to their precursors, whether digital imaging, audio or
video; hypertext may offer a genuine innovation, something that could not be done before the advent of
computers (although cross-referenced textbooks may be
one form of proto-hypertext), but other media can
generally be viewed as developments of other techniques, however radical those developments may be.
There are, however, two main differences between new
and old media: first of all, the movement away from
analog towards digital formats is accelerating a process known as *convergence*, whereby processes that
previously required very different technologies (such as
for editing video or processing still photographs) can
be performed on the same computer; second, digitised

57

media offer greater scope for interactivity, whether at the production level or when used by consumers.

The distinction between analog and digital formats is crucial to new media. Analog information, such as a sound wave, is a continuous stream of data: digital information, on the other hand, is *discrete*, with distinct breaks between one piece of data and the next. A common analogy is to compare analog processes to rolling down a hill and digital ones to walking down steps. In practice, digitisation represents most information as bits, or binary digits: on/off, 1/0. There is no intrinsic value to a bit other than the fact that it represents a state of an electronic circuit: nearly all information travelling around a typical computer consists of bits, ones and zeros, but these different streams of binary numbers are then output as words, images, audio files or videos depending on how they are interpreted by software.

Digitisation offers a great many advantages to media production: editing a digitised image is much simpler than using an airbrush or chemical processing, and video editing can be enhanced with clips captured to a hard drive. Digitisation is not, however, automatically better, despite the claims often made for new media. Many experts, for example, claim that analog media such as vinyl or tape offer a 'warmer' sound than audio CDs or crisper digital tape. Likewise, the vast majority of digital cameras offer poorer image quality than the average SLR 35mm film camera, despite costing between five and ten times as much. Digitisation, then, offers many changes to practice, but not all of them are improvements.

Text and hypertext

A fundamental component of the World Wide Web is hypertext: without a standard protocol for transmitting documents using the HTTP, the Web would not exist, and without a standard format for creating pages, including the ability to link between them (hyperlinks), web pages would lose a great deal of their usability. Tim Berners-Lee was obviously the inventor of hypertext as the series of protocols and file formats for transferring information across the Web, but important innovators include Vannevar Bush and Theodor Nelson. More contentiously, British Telecom launched lawsuits against Internet companies at the beginning of 2001, claiming that a patent application made in 1976 and granted in 1989 for a system known as Hidden Page was the source for hyperlinks.

What, then, is hypertext? The term was coined by Nelson in the 1960s, and later explained in *Literary Machines* as 'non-sequential writing – text that branches and allows choices to the reader, best read at an interactive screen (1993: 2)'. George Landow, an influential theorist on the relation between hypertext and postmodern theory, describes hypertext as 'text composed of blocks of text – what Barthes terms a lexia – and the electronic links that join them' (1997: 3). Like many influential ideas, the simplicity of hypertext belies its impact, which is the ability to cross-reference, quickly and easily, a multitude of documents, texts and files on the Internet. In addition to connecting text, hyperlinks may work with other components such as images or videos, creating hypermedia that link from page to page, image to image, video to video, or any combination of these.

Perhaps the fundamental idea of hypertext came from a paper entitled 'As We May Think', published by Vannevar Bush in a 1945 issue of *Atlantic Monthly*, in which he described a mechanically-linked information retrieval machine, the 'memex', which would store books, records and communications on a microform reader that could be searched mechanically, using similar word associations and links as utilised by human brains rather than the rigid classification systems then employed (Bush 1945; Landow 1997). Bush's ideas were immensely influential on pioneers of hypertext and the Internet, including Douglas Engelbart and Ted Nelson. Nelson, who has been hugely critical of the Internet of today as an inefficient means of connecting information, planned a universal, democratic hypertext library, or 'docuverse', known as Xanadu, that would provide the sum of human knowledge rather than mere data. Despite funding from Autodesk in the 1980s, Xanadu was, like Coleridge's poem celebrating the pleasure gardens of Kubla Khan, never finished (Wolf 1995).

As computers became more widely used and information had to be linked, so hyperlinks were a useful means of connecting information contained in different files or even different machines. It was with Tim Berners-Lee, however, and the invention of the World Wide Web that hypertext and hyperlinks became more widely used and recognised. As we have seen in Chapter 1, HTML and HTTP, the formatting language and communication protocols that form the basis of the Web, were devised by Berners-Lee as part of a proposal to connect multifarious documents together while he was at the European Centre for Nuclear Research. The original remit of 'Enquire Within Upon Everything' was relatively simple (the ability to access scientific documents and research papers held on computers in Europe, the US and elsewhere), and thus it was a success as opposed to Xanadu, 'the longest running vaporware project in the history of computing' in the words of Gary Wolf (1995: 137). Berners-Lee has since compared the Web to a global human brain which will enable 'creativity [to] arise across larger and more diverse groups' (1999: 210).

Hypertext and intertextuality

The way that hypertext may reconfigure textuality has been of increasing interest to literary theorists who are concerned with the way that we read texts. A variety of texts, such as the difficult, modernist poetry of Stéphane Mallarmé or Ezra Pound, or allusive literature that calls upon the reader to make associations with canonical or popular texts, have been invoked as prototypes of hypertext.

Richard Lanham, in *The Electronic Word*, has argued that, in our daily use of computers (for word processing and reading documents such as emails or web pages), we treat computers as rhetorical machines:

> We have always, from Pascal to the present, thought of computers, especially digital computers, as logic machines. Whether they helped us with our weaving, our business tabulations, our artillery trajectories, or our atomic bombs, we have always located them where we locate logic; at the familiar Platonic, mathematical center of human reason ... I would like, as a supplement and complement to this view from philosophy and theory, to suggest that in practice, the computer often turns out to be a rhetorical device as well as a logical one, that it derives its aesthetic from philosophy's great opposite in Western thought and education, the world of rhetoric.
>
> (1993: 30)

While Lanham had little to say about the Internet, George Landow and other theorists have argued that hypertext in general, and the Net in particular, provides a rich testing ground for postmodernist and post-structuralist theories (Landow 1997; Plant 1997; Baudrillard 1993). This is hardly surprising, considering that one of the most famous essays on postmodernism, Jean-François Lyotard's *The Postmodern Condition* (1984), was commissioned as a report on the sociological effects of information technology.

For postmodern and post-structuralist theorists, hypertext fulfils many of the conditions of textuality argued for by thinkers such as Roland Barthes, Jacques Derrida and Jean Baudrillard. Thus, for example, hyperlinks shift the boundary between consumption and production of 'a text': if no two readers ever begin and end in the same place, how logical is it to speak of an author or even a text, ideas that have grown up and developed alongside the book? If such logic is no longer applicable, then the Internet becomes the clearest example of Barthes's argument that the Author is dead as an ideological point of closure for the text. Likewise, as Barthes and Derrida attempted to demonstrate with more conventional and literary texts, hypertext is open and intertextual from its very inception: the ability to click on links and surf or browse from page to page (the metaphors of reading very different to the incisive, concentrated application one would expect with a book) tends less towards a unified experience of our universe and more towards a 'docuverse' – what Derrida refers to as *assemblage*, a cognitive montage.

In addition to this transformation of our perceptions, the growth of hypertext and the Internet has *decentred* the book and made us aware of print as technology – a critical process going back to Marshall McLuhan (1962), who was one of the first to argue that the Gutenberg printing revolution transformed our epistemological relation with the world via the saturation of media. While humanism tends to assume that the arts are non-technological, hypertext provides a mirror that attenuates such assumptions until they are difficult to maintain. At its crudest, arguments around how our processes of reading and perception are transformed by hypertext tend towards a simplistic technological determinism, for example Paul Levinson's suggestion in *Soft Edge* (1997) that monotheistic notions depend upon the invention of the alphabet. More useful is the argument made by historians of technology, such as Alvin Kernan (1987), that we must understand the material conditions under which textuality is produced, that is, understand the logic of technology, without submitting to technological determinism. As Landow (1997) remarks, hypertext historicises our assumptions about reading, literature and experience.

Digital imaging

As far as the Web is concerned, in the beginning was the word, and the word was good, but the image quickly proved itself better. It is over a hundred and fifty years since the invention of photography, the chemical – indeed alchemical – process of capturing images that has not only transformed the arts but also changed the way we view societies and the world. Through the magazine photo, the cinema and the instant snap, we are so used to these windows on our lives and the lives of others that this realm of images now seems entirely natural. How different that world would be if we had not been able to see those events that cross all sorts of cultural boundaries: bodies of soldiers in trenches during the First World War, the collapse of the Berlin Wall, and men walking on the Moon.

Yet the selection of these events is significant. There was a time, until very recently, when the photograph was the touchstone for the truth of an event: if seeing is believing, a photo is the closest thing to being there because, as Barthes (1977) noted, such an image *denotes* events. The selection of images, however, their framing and the associations we bring to them will affect their meaning, their *connotation*, from viewer to viewer. Since the end of the twentieth century, moreover, the floating world of the image has become much more suspect even at its most basic level. While photo retouching has always taken place, for example to serve propaganda (as in the removal of Trotsky from images depicting Lenin), it was always a laborious and time-consuming task, almost as intensive as the art of painting from which it evolved.

The power of the computer has changed all that. We are now beginning to treat the image with the same suspicion once reserved for the printed word: just as we do not believe the words we read in the papers, so we no longer trust everything we see.

Image basics

There are two basic steps involved in capturing a digital image: sampling and quantisation. Differing intensities of light are sampled along a grid and then quantised as pixel values on the screen, that is, the intensity is calculated in terms of brightness, of red, green and blue, and the result approximated to an integer, or a digital value or number that can be measured. This two-stage process is known as *filtering*. Painters do a similar thing manually when they represent a scene, approximating the colour of a leaf or building to a pigment and brush stroke. Whereas this manual process is very subjective, however, digital sampling and filtering is mechanical and much more consistent (though not necessarily more artistic). Another way to think of filtering, especially when used in scanning techniques, is of a finger sensing Braille dots at regular points on the surface before translating these dots into a coherent image (Bovik 2000).

These digital values produced by filtering are then displayed as pixels. Each pixel is a discrete element of a picture, similar to the dots that you see in a newspaper photo if you look at it through a strong magnifying glass. The quality of the image depends largely on the sampling grid: too coarse and valuable detail will be irretrievably lost. On the other hand, a theoretically infinite resolution (where the individual dots can never be perceived no matter what the magnification) will require infinite storage space. A trade-off is required, therefore, to communicate a satisfactory image. A basic rule of thumb is that the human eye sees clear resolutions at one-sixtieth of a degree, or about 600 dots per inch at the distance of one foot. For an eight- by ten-inch monochrome print, then, this requires $4,800 \times 6,000$, or $28,800,800$ pixels to appear completely smooth – or 3.6 Mb. That, however, is just for black and white: to record the same image in 256 colours, what is known as an 8-bit 'colour depth', because there are eight bits of information for each pixel, requires 28.8 Mb of uncompressed storage space. Similarly, 24-bit colour (with eight bits per pixel for red, green and blue, producing up to 16.7 million colours) would require 86.4 Mb for a completely smooth image at 600 dpi.

It's easy to see, then, why a full-page, colour image for a magazine often takes up 20 to 30 Mb. The above figures are for

FIGURE 3.1 A black and white image saved at 1-, 4- and 8-bit colour depths.

uncompressed data, but almost all digital images involve compression and compromise of some sort. Compression of up to a half can be achieved with no loss of image quality, and compression of between one-tenth and one-fiftieth can be achieved with no perceptible loss of quality. The reason for this is that an image will contain many of the same colours that can be described by a more compact algorithm; what's more, although many of the 16.7 million shades are theoretically perceptible to the human eye, in practice most of us find it hard to perceive the most refined distinctions in terms of vividness. Also, because no image can have more shades of colour than the number of pixels (and very few images have as many as 16.7 million pixels), colours can be mapped onto palettes to save space (Mitchell 1992; Bovik 2000).

Computer monitors work by using an additive model – that is, when the three primary colours (red, blue and green) are mixed in equal amounts, white is produced. Printed images, by contrast, use a subtractive model produced by reflecting light from cyan, magenta and yellow (this model is subtractive because the more light is absorbed, the less it is reflected and so the darker the colour). When these colours are mixed in equal amounts, black is produced or, rather, a close and slightly muddy approximation of black. Because it is difficult to generate true black by this process, extra black is usually included as a fourth colour, hence CMYK. As though these two colour systems were not enough, it is also possible to define colours in terms of hue, brightness and saturation. Hue is specified by a colour between 0 and 360 degrees on a colour wheel, with brightness and saturation being set as percentages.

A further distinction is between bitmap and vector images. While bitmap, or raster, images work by recording information about each pixel in an illustration, vector images use equations to describe the position and direction of lines on a screen. Thus, whereas a bitmap may have to describe each pixel that constitutes a line, a vector is defined in terms of two points and the distance between them and, as you may recall from calculus, complex curves can be defined in terms of a relatively short equation expressing their relative velocity (curvature) at any given point.

There are two main advantages of vector images over bitmaps. Firstly, because complex figures can be expressed by short equations, the size of a vector image tends to be considerably smaller. At the same time, while it may not be as 'realistic' as a bitmap photo, such an image does not lose its clarity at different resolutions. Bitmaps store information about individual pixels on a sampled raster grid: increase the size of that grid and you spread the amount of information between each point. Because vector images are defined mathematically, however, increasing the resolution of such an image simply requires it to be recalculated on screen, preserving its sharpness.

FIGURE 3.2 Raster and vector images magnified.

A brief history of digital photography

William Henry Fox Talbot, tracing a view of Lake Como with the help of a camera obscura, pondered how to imprint such images durably. By 1839, he had perfected the art of chemically fixing these images on specially treated paper 'by the agency of light alone, without any aid whatever from the artist's pencil'. At the same time, in France, daguerrotypes – named after Louis Daguerre – made their first appearance. Photography had been born (Mitchell 1992).

Throughout the nineteenth century, there were plenty of writers who pointed to this new art as evidence that painting was dead. (Painters, in the meantime, were having none of it, and there were plenty of artists, such as Edgar Degas, who were more than willing to employ photography as an aid to their compositions.) In addition to those image processes that reproduced single events, Eadweard Muybridge used twenty-four cameras in 1887 to transfer a series of images in rapid succession onto film and the age of the camera moved from still life to the movies.

While the science of film and its development made more than a little contribution to the evolution of the art of photography, the quantum leap in digital imaging came in the mid-1950s. Russell A. Kirsch, working with a team of colleagues at the National Bureau of Standards, constructed a mechanical drum scanner that could trace variations in intensity from a photograph's surface, converting the signals into an array of 176 by 176 bits that was then fed into a primitive SEAC computer and reproduced as a digital image. One of the major factors contributing to the progress of this new process, as with so many technological innovations, was the space race. NASA used digital image-processing in 1964 to remove imperfections from photos of the moon sent back by the Ranger 7 spacecraft, and from 1972 satellites such as Landsat and ERTS have been sending their images through the ether, spying on Earth and its weather systems as Voyager and Magellan spread the eyes of Earth's inhabitants throughout the solar system.

As photography expanded into the macrocosm, so it contracted to provide surveys of the hitherto unexplored microcosm closer to home, when, during the 1970s, scientists at IBM's Zurich Research

Laboratory, headed by Gerd Binning and Heinrich Rohrer, captured the first pictures of atomic particles. Nor did the route of technological progress halt with outer space and microscopic worlds. Wilhelm Röntgen's discovery of X-rays began a process of 3D imaging – computerised tomography (CT), positron emission tomography (PET) and magnetic resonance imaging (MRI) – that is now common in medical science, enabling doctors to capture detailed images of human anatomy that are then processed by computers (Mitchell 1992).

The expensive techniques involved in digitising images remained part of a technological arcanum until the late 1990s, when companies such as Canon, Nikon and Sony began to provide hi-tech cameras for a mass audience and scanners started to flood the market. In addition, the compact disc, devised as a sound-recording medium and as an inexpensive way to store images, was united with the camera in 1990, when Kodak announced a system called Photo CD. As the ability to capture, edit and print images became ever more sophisticated, this was not without its problems: in America, the National Press Photographers Association called for a code of ethics to regulate image editing, just as the Artists' Rights Foundation was set up to deal with electronic tampering. A hundred and fifty years after the birth of photography, reproducing images is more a source of confusion than ever before.

Audio and video

While digital images are apparent on almost every page of the Web, broadcasting in the form of digital music and video is only just beginning to take off across the Internet. Although computers have been a prominent part of audio-video (AV) editing for a considerable time, the speeds with which modems connect to the Internet have only recently made any form of live video possible, combined with improved compression techniques that reduce the amount of information that must be transmitted to the end user.

Despite improvements, however, for the vast majority of users connected to the Net streaming video (see 'AV basics' below) remains impractical in any but the simplest formats. Promises of full-screen video being transferred across the Internet are impossible for anyone without broadband access, and, although videoconferencing is beginning to proliferate alongside webcams, these still operate at very low frame rates and resolutions. Nonetheless, streaming media and different types of webcasting have become more popular, particularly with the music format MP3 and web radio.

One thing that helped the development of streaming media was Mbone, an experiment in Internet webcasting or broadcasting. The introduction of Mbone in the mid-1990s meant that, rather than having to send a packet of information to every computer, it could be multi-cast, or addressed in such a way that multiple computers could access the information at once. As outlined in Chapter 1, certain parts of the IP addressing system are reserved for multicast addresses, and Mbone was originally used in universities for sharing meetings and conferences. This multicast system reached a wider audience in 1994 when the Rolling Stones gave the first rock concert online, while, more recently, Madonna's exclusive London concert was multicast by MSN.

The next step required to bring multicasting to home users was taken by Real Networks, which provided an audio compression and webcast system known as RealAudio. Early RealAudio sound was distorted and prone to fade in and out, but kickstarted the web radio phenomenon and was soon followed by improvements to Real's audio and video formats as well as other media formats such as QuickTime, MPEG, and MP3. MP3 in particular has demonstrated the popularity of multimedia webcasting beyond the combination of text and image that has dominated the Web for the past ten years. With the movement towards digital broadcasting, convergence between the Internet and television becomes a real possibility. At the same time, the emergence of standards such as Synchronized Multimedia Internet Language (SMIL), a schema for XML (Extensible Markup Language; see p. 77) that standardises how streaming media clips behave, for example how they appear in the browser, means that more and more browsers should be able to play streaming media without the need for complex plug-ins.

AV basics

Digital AV media are usually referred to as streaming media, although strictly speaking not all audio-visual material streams, that is, begins to play on a system as soon as data is received. Until fairly recently, digital music and video files had to be downloaded completely before they began to play, but the use of Real Time Streaming Protocol (RTSP) and Real Time Protocol (RTP) by various media players means that a clip can be opened after the initial packets of data are received and can continue to play as the rest is downloaded.

Since the invention of the phonograph and film, AV media have traditionally been used in an analog format, such as vinyl, audio or video tape, and 16 mm film. Such material must be digitised and transferred to disk before it can be processed by a computer, although increasingly a number of video and audio recorders can save sound and images in digital form. The use of Analog to Digital Converters (ADC) is responsible for this process, but must also be matched by corresponding Digital to Analog Converters (DAC) for output to most monitors and speakers. When preparing video, another important distinction is between *offline* and *online* editing. Offline editing consists of using copies of original clips to mark out a sequence, or edit decision list (EDL), and can be as simple as writing down time points for scenes while watching them on a VCR. Online editing is a more complex process, where all editing is done on the same machine that will produce the final cut, and when digital video clips are compiled into a final cut all such editing must be done online.

There are a number of AV formats for digital video, including Microsoft's Audio-Video Interleaved format (AVI) and Audio Waveform (WAV), Apple's QuickTime, and MPEG – Moving Pictures Expert Group – the organisation responsible for international standards for compression of streaming video and data. Another major factor that affects how AV is transmitted is the use of codecs: like digital images, uncompressed video requires a huge amount of storage space and is impossible to transmit across the Internet in this format, so AV codecs (compressors/decompressors) are used to reduce the data rate and file size of streaming media.

Video compression works in two main ways: spatial and temporal. Spatial compression, sometimes referred to as run-length encoding, compacts the description of the visual area of a frame by looking for patterns, for example repeated patches of a particular blue in a scene of a sky, which are then described by a shorter phrase to

69

the effect that 'all pixels in this area are dark blue'. As spatial compression increases, the picture loses sharpness and definition, but even the lowest level of compression can reduce file size by over 50 per cent. Temporal compression compacts the description of scene changes during a sequence of frames so that, for example, there are fewer changes in a sequence of a person standing in front of a static background than of a car chase through town, meaning such scenes can be compressed more. When most pixels in a frame are different, it is best to describe the entire frame again, resulting in what is known as a keyframe. This technique, also called frame differing, is important to MPEG video and can achieve very high compression rates without loss of quality.

The popularity that MP3 has achieved in the past couple of years makes many people think that it has only emerged recently, but the standard was actually formalised in 1987. MP3 is an abbreviation of MPEG1 Audio Layer 3 and is the audio part of the MPEG standard. Layer 3 refers to the fact that MPEG covers a number of compression standards, each one more complex than the last and offering higher standards of compression: Layer 1 can compress audio at the rate of about 4 : 1, or about 384 Kbps for CD-quality audio; Layer 2 compresses audio by between 6 : 1 and 8 : 1, or 256–192 Kbps; and Layer 3 (MP3) can achieve compression rates of between 10 : 1 and 12 : 1, or 128–112 Kbps.

Thus, a song stored in the MP3 file format can be downloaded from the Web ten times more quickly than one stored in the normal CD format. How MP3 achieves such compression without apparent loss of quality is due to 'perceptual coding', drawing on the fact that the human ear is limited in the range of sounds that it can hear. Doubling the amplitude of sound, for example, does not double the loudness, while very high and very low frequencies are outside the range of human aural perception. So, MP3 uses what is called a 'psychoacoustic model', a set of rules that determines what parts of a wavelength can be removed without sound degrading in quality: that this is not merely an acoustic model is due to a psychological process known as masking, whereby we tend to prioritise sounds at the expense of others (usually quieter noises) which can then be removed. A similar process occurs visually, so that our eyes tend to respond to movement

FIGURE 3.3 Online digital editing.

while background visual detail can be removed without perceptible loss of quality.

MP3 is a popular medium, but far from the most effective audio compression technique available on the Internet. MPEG2 Advanced Audio Coding (AAC) and two proprietary formats based on this, MP4 and Microsoft's Windows Media Audio (WMA) can offer similar quality audio as MP3 but at half the size, but the fact that AAC is not backwards compatible, and that MP4 and WMA are proprietary, means that these have not been adopted so quickly as audio standards for the Web.

Web radio, webcasting and DVD

The first video played when the cable channel MTV was launched on 1 August 1981 was the deliciously ironic *Video Killed the Radio Star* by the Buggles. As a number of commentators have observed, video

71

was the making of many a radio star in the closing decades of the twentieth century, and announcements of the death of radio have been somewhat premature. What is perhaps most surprising, however, is how, a hundred years after Marconi first transmitted a radio signal from Cornwall across the Atlantic to Newfoundland, the Internet has come not to bury radio but to praise it.

Traditionally, anyone who wishes to run a radio station would have to purchase a slice of the airwaves for a commercial channel or provide public services (hence the proliferation of pirate stations during the 1970s and 1980s), but the Internet has provided an opportunity for 24-hour radio coverage with a potentially worldwide audience. Although the common protocols used across the Web, TCP/IP and HTTP, are not really suitable for audio streaming (with their emphasis on reliability rather than speed, these protocols request information to be re-sent, resulting in pauses during audio downloads), a standard alternative to TCP, UDP (User Datagram Protocol), does allow for streaming by sending out datagrams, or packets of data sent out without checking for errors: if a datagram is missed, there is a brief break in the transmission before it continues as normal. Even if UDP is not used (firewalls, for example, break such transmissions), TCP and HTTP can be used for pseudo-streaming, whereby programs such as RealPlayer buffer information on a local hard drive before playing the audio file.

A common misconception is that most web radio consists of authentic broadcasting to multiple users, but various forms of webcasting are actually cleverly disguised unicasts, that is, each file is sent out to individual listeners. Even if recipients listen to the same file simultaneously, the server sends out multiple files so that each listener gets individual files. The problem with this is that networks can quickly clog up with data, but, although UDP does allow true multicasting, all parts of the network must be set up to pass on the data, meaning it is rarely used across the Internet. Despite these difficulties, sites such as www.real.com offer a broad spectrum of radio stations from around the world and across a wide range of formats and genres. While bandwidth is generally unsuitable for video for most users, the Internet has proved an exceptionally versatile medium for audio.

While web radio has grown immensely over the past few years, the road to digital video for general consumers outside the Internet has been a surprisingly difficult one for film and media producers. When DVD (Digital Video Disc, or Digital Versatile Disc) finally began to emerge in the late 1990s, following a similar path to audio CDs a decade earlier, there were huge concerns about video piracy as well as the cost of the medium and players. Perhaps an even greater hindrance to DVD production than copyright, however, was the issue of playing back movies from around the world. When the DVD was first touted as a medium for distributing film, studios were concerned not only that digital formats could be copied easily, but that viewers in different parts of the globe (such as Europe or the Middle East) would be able to buy films released on DVD in the US that were not even showing in cinemas elsewhere. This was less of an issue for video, in that different speci-fications such as PAL and NTSC meant that videos produced in North America simply would not play on European VCRs, but this was not the case for digitised DVDs. With the rise of the Internet as a possible conduit for international commerce, customers around the world could purchase American DVDs before a film was released in local cinemas and cut into the studios' profits; thus, Hollywood insisted that discs be coded as belonging to one of six regions so that they would only play on specified machines.

The fragility of this status quo was revealed when two European programmers were able to use software DVD players such as WinDVD to crack DVD encryption, their intention being to enable playback on the Linux operating system. The resulting code, DeCSS (CSS being the technique used to encrypt DVDs), enables movies to be copied to disk and played back without the need for encryption. US federal judge Lewis Kaplan made the first decision to interpret the 1998 Digital Millennium Copyright Act to rule that code is not free speech, and since then attempts to publish the code have been blocked. With ever more efficient AV codecs such as DivX, a hacked version of the MPEG4 codec that is capable of reducing video files to one-tenth of the MPEG2 standard used by DVD, and with the increase in broad-band Internet access, producers are worried that video could be spread as easily across the Net as pirated MP3 music files.

Web production

One of the most exciting aspects of the Internet is the ease with which users can publish content in contrast to other media, such as print and broadcasting. The simplicity of web publishing can be overstated: for countries and social groups without access to the Net, and where computer equipment is not readily available, the obstacles facing users are enormous. Even where these are not an issue, learning the skills required to move from using the Internet to web production can be a major hurdle.

Nonetheless, such production is a possibility for many people who use the Internet for work or play. Students on new media courses in particular will often be involved in web production at some level and, therefore, the rest of this chapter is intended as an introduction to the theory and practice of web production as well as to the different media formats encountered on the Web. However, it is not a complete reference or manual on the theory of web design, and students wishing to follow this through in more detail are recommended to read *Web Production for Writers and Journalists* (Whittaker 2002), also published by Routledge.

HTML

As stated in Chapter 2, the core of a web page is HTML (Hypertext Markup Language), the basic set of commands used to format pages for display across the World Wide Web. While it is possible to create a web page without any experience of HTML whatsoever, for serious web designers a knowledge of the fundamentals is essential for both troubleshooting and speeding up web design. It is also noticeable that, in the past few years, many employers have begun to specify a knowledge of 'hand coding' (the ability to use a text editor to write code) as an essential requirement. This is for a variety of reasons: a web designer who does not understand the principles of HTML will probably also not understand many other factors of web design; only the best web editors can keep up with innovations in HTML, so advanced features have to be hand coded; in addition, many web editors include spurious lines of code that involve designers in a search and destroy operation. For more information, see Whittaker (2002) or one of the very detailed manuals on HTML available, such as Thomas Powell's *HTML: The Complete Reference* (2001).

Rather than being a full (and very complex) programming language, HTML employs tags, indicated by angular brackets, such as <p> for paragraph, to surround commands. These tags are interpreted by a browser, such as Netscape or Internet Explorer, to control how the page is displayed and, in most cases, must enclose content, the final tag being marked with a slash, for example <p>Paragraph one</p>. In addition, HTML enables developers to create documents that link to other documents on the Web – hence hypertext. HTML is defined by the World Wide Web Consortium (W3C), which sets certain standards governing how HTML can be viewed by any browser on any computer in the world. HTML 2.0 covers the basics for formatting text, displaying images and linking to other documents, and is much less sophisticated than versions 3.2 and 4, which extend the facilities of HTML in terms of presentation, dynamic features and their ability to work with more complex scripting languages.

Formatting a page for the Web is very different to designing for print, as a print designer has to work within certain material and technical constraints: the type of paper, ability to use colour, whether this is spot or four-colour, the type of press and other factors affect the overall appearance of a page. Once these constraints are taken into account, however, the designer has considerable control over the final layout of a page limited only by his or her competence and skill. While certain technical constraints are much less important on the Web (it is, for example, much easier to use colour on screen than on paper), a web producer will have much less control over the final appearance of his or her site. The most common problem is that different browsers do not interpret HTML tags in the same way.

While the content of web pages varies greatly from instance to instance, most will include four main tags, grouped in pairs, which begin to structure the page:

- <html> and the final tag </html> These are the fundamental marks surrounding every word on your page and indicate to the browser the language used to mark up the page.

<head> </head>   These contain information about your page, including meta-descriptions.

<title></title>   Look in the blue bar at the top of your browser. This is where you'll find the title of your page, usually a short description that is used by search engines to find information on the World Wide Web.

- <body></body>   The body tags contain the main bulk of your content, that which appears in the window of your browser.

Thus, for example, a very simple web page would appear in HTML as follows:

```
<html>

  <head>
     <title>My first web page</title>
  </head>

  <body>
     <center>
     <h1>Hello World</h1>
        <p>Hello World! programs are very simple
        programming exercises designed to give users their
        first taste of coding. Creating such a page marks your
        successful entry into the world of HTML design that
        can be hosted and read anywhere on the World Wide
        Web.</p>
  </body>

</html>
```

If you open a text editor such as Notepad or SimpleText, enter the code above and save it with the filename hello.htm and you will have created your first web page that can be viewed in a browser.

XML, style sheets and the future of web design

HTML will be around in one form or another for some time to come, but there are several problems that arise from using hypertext markup language in its current incarnation. In the ten years since its inception, HTML has been pushed to fulfil a number of functions that its original inventor, Tim Berners-Lee, could not have foreseen. Particularly problematic is the fact that web pages jumble together very different types of code, including structural markup, presentation and design tags and the content that is displayed. While the ability to combine content and design creates the conditions for some truly innovative pages on the Web, it is also responsible for many that are simply execrable. One way to overcome this is to enforce HTML rules in order to prevent lazy coding, this being the task of the new XHTML specification.

Rigorous coding, however, will not overcome all the problems associated with poor web design. It is, indeed, very rare to find an individual who combines all the abilities needed to create a compelling web site, from the visual and written content displayed on pages to the combination of these in a visually appealing and navigable format, and who also possesses the knowledge of back-end systems required to make sites dynamic. When web pages were simple text documents created by research scientists, this was not a problem, but today we expect much more: we want Pulitzer-winning material presented by award-winning designers on systems that work seamlessly.

Thus, one of the biggest tasks facing the future of web production is the separation of design from content. One of the main ways of achieving this is through the use of style sheets, also known as the cascading style sheet (CSS) system, because style sheets can be nested, or cascaded, within each other. At their simplest, style sheets provide information governing the position and styling of text, using the <style> tag to determine its appearance. For example, a simple style tag would read <style="font-size: 10pt; font-color: red">. Style sheets can also be created separately to HTML files and linked to them, enabling designers to make site-wide changes by adjusting the contents of one or two files. Because CSS allows designers to exercise greater control over pages and enables writers to concentrate on

77

writing, CSS is making great inroads and will remove the burden of presentation design from HTML, which will increasingly be used for formatting the fundamental structure of pages. When combined with scripting languages such as JavaScript, CSS can be used to make pages more dynamic, responding to user interaction as visitors navigate around a site.

In addition to issues surrounding design and presentation, another problem with web pages is that they mix up the logic of content with presentation and other coding: unlike a database, where it is easy to tell a name from an address or telephone number (providing they have been entered correctly), HTML files do not separate such material logically. While an increasing number of professional web sites link front end HTML pages to a database, one proposed solution consists of XML (Extensible Markup Language). XML provides a means of distinguishing different types of content and is also extensible, that is, users can define their own tags. For example, a customer invoice could look something like:

```
<name>John Doe</name>
<address>
    <street>1, Broad Lane</street>
    <town>Hometown</town>
    <country>UK</country>
</address>
```

XML cannot replace a well-defined database – it will not, for example, speed up searches across an unindexed site, but it will probably make it easier to exchange information between different documents and applications in the future.

Finally, the two biggest changes facing the Internet are the arrival of broadband access and the use of devices other than PCs to access content. As discussed in Chapter 1, while the roll-out of faster Internet access has faced many obstacles, it is gradually arriving and will be responsible for a greater movement away from static HTML pages to broadcast-style content. In addition, while technologies such as WAP have been overstated as a means of viewing the Web, producers will have to take ever greater account of the fact that future visitors may be viewing their sites on a television, mobile phone or small computerised device, and so tailor content accordingly.

Elements of a web page

Good design covers more than how a site looks and includes navigation, content and usability, but appearance is still very important: how text and image are presented will have an impact on how visitors react to a site, from the most basic instinctive reaction to more subtle ways of manipulating the meaning of images by framing and selection. As such, when designing your own web pages or analysing those you encounter of the Web, you should be aware of the individual components that make up a web page.

Text

Text still remains central to web design and, despite the importance of the convergence of the Internet and audio-visual material, this remains one of the main ways in which the Web is defined, as opposed to broadcast media that rely on sound and the moving image. The way that text is used, therefore, has an impact on a visitor's experience.

Compared to print, text is relatively crude on the Web and techniques that are simple on paper may be difficult, or even impossible, to achieve using HTML and CSS. Thus, for example, the Web does not support particular page widths; browsers may render text in unexpected ways, particularly if a typeface is unavailable on the computer; typographic facilities to control such things as the space between lines or characters (leading and kerning) may not be available; and a user may change the size of font in such a way that it completely ruins the flow of a page. While there are ways to wrest back control – for example, by converting text to graphics – text remains invaluable: it creates smaller file sizes than graphics, is more accessible to users with visual impairments (in that they can use text readers to spell out words), and can be searched and organised more dynamically than graphics.

When using text, it is worth bearing in mind some of the basics of typography, beginning with the concept of fonts. Strictly speaking, different styles of text are typefaces, while a font is the particular size of a typeface, usually measured in points; however, the term font is commonly used to cover both these features of text, for example 10-point Arial or 24-point Helvetica. Fonts are also distinguished as serif or sans serif, as well as proportional or monospaced. A serif font has a short start or finish stroke, while sans serif ones do not; proportional fonts use characters that take up only as much space as they require, while monospaced fonts use the same fixed width for all characters, for example:

- Times: proportional serif font

- Arial: proportional sans serif font

- Courier: monospaced serif font

Typically, serif fonts, by providing a little extra information, are easier to read for larger chunks of text, while sans serif fonts make bolder headlines. Monospaced text is not usually encountered – its principle uses seems to be when designers wish to emulate typewritten pages or distinguish instructions within a web page. A good text that deals with conventions of typography (not necessarily just for the Web) is Robert Bringhurst's *The Elements of Typographic Style* (1996).

HTML uses the <font></font> tag to determine the size and type of text, as well as other features such as colour, for example <font face="Arial, Helvetica, sans-serif" size="3" color="red">. Just because you can use any style of font on your computer does not mean that you should do so: if users do not have such a font installed, then the latter will revert to a default, such as Times or Courier, and will cause a page to reflow. Netscape and Internet Explorer can use down-loadable fonts, known as Dynamic Fonts and OpenType respectively, but these are still not widely employed.

Basic formatting to indicate such things as bold, italicised or underlined text is done using simple tags such as <i>*italics*</i> or **Bold**. For more sophisticated results in terms of text for-matting and positioning, CSS is a valuable tool: as well as enabling designers to stipulate an overall look and feel very quickly, CSS provides greater control than HTML over such features as font sizing, text alignment, kerning and line spacing. Unfortunately, not all variants of supposedly CSS-compliant browsers support all of these features, but this is gradually changing and CSS provides one of the main means of extending the functionality of typography on the Web.

Finally, when using text on the Web, it should be repeated that conventions of print typography should not necessarily be applied. Copy fitting (fitting text to a given space), for example, is important in the production of magazines, newspapers and books, but while pages on the Web could be limited to a certain size, this does not always make sense and, in any case, is rendered unworkable when a visitor resizes text using the browser defaults. Although this can be restricted, insisting that text is viewed only at a certain size could prejudice the site towards users who have good eyesight. Therefore, remember a very simple rule: be flexible.

Colour and images

While text is an extremely important factor in conveying information, colour and images obviously have an important part to play and are obviously significant to the way that web pages are read. The Web is, after all, a visual medium and if images or colour are misused pages will be perceived negatively. The principles of digital imaging have already been covered in this chapter: here we are concerned with how images are used on the web page itself.

HTML defines colour by means of hexadecimal code, three double figures that define RGB (red, green and blue) values with 0 as the lowest value and F as the highest (representing the number 15 in hexadecimal notation), preceded by the # sign. Thus, for example, #FF0000 signifies pure red, while #C0C0C0 is the HTML code for silver. Using a visual editor, colours can be chosen from charts, and certain colours such as aqua or purple can simply be written out: most of the 16.4 million colours that can be displayed on a screen, however, must be defined using hexadecimal notation. Document-wide settings are usually defined in the <body> tag, for example <body bgcolor ="#800080" text="ffffff" >. Like fonts, however, just because a designer can use millions of colours does not mean that he or she should. Visitors with older computers may be restricted to using moni-tors that can only display 256 colours, hence the use of so-called

81

'web-safe' colours: because of differences between the standard colours supported by Macs and PCs, these are 216 colours that can be displayed on most computers and represent the lowest common denominator.

Beyond the technical practicalities of using colours, they have 'meanings' related to cultural, emotional and psychological factors, so that brown may be 'warm' or 'dirty' in different circumstances, and red 'lively' or 'aggressive'. Making simple assumptions for a worldwide medium is difficult: in some cultures black is the colour traditionally associated with mourning, for example, but in Japan the colour of mourning is white. Despite these pitfalls, the most successful sites use colour to create themes, provide contrast to pages and even to aid users as pointers to navigation.

Alongside colour, images are often essential to web page design. While many images on the Web may be purely decorative, they are also a communicative medium in their own right, conveying and representing information alongside, or in place of, text. Of the various image formats used on the Web, the two most common are GIF (Graphic Interchange Format) and JPEG (Joint Photographic Experts Group, the committee responsible for this standard). GIF is capable of supporting only 256 colours, but it is a lossless compression format, that is, it does not discard information, so it is good for compressing images where only a few colours are used, such as a logo. In addition, the GIF 89a standard supports transparency and animation. JPEG, by contrast, is a lossy image format, capable of displaying 16.4 million colours while achieving high compression rates, though there is a trade-off between image quality and file size. JPEG is best suited for photographs on a web site, GIF for line drawings or converting text into graphics.

Other formats encountered on the Web include PNG (Portable Network Graphics), which combines GIF 89a features with greater colour depth and will probably replace GIF, though not currently widely supported; and Flash, a vector-based format (where images are defined as lines and blocks of colour, rather than pixel by pixel) designed by Macromedia and capable of displaying very sophisticated – but very small – images. Flash is probably the most widely-supported vector format on the Web, particularly as it can be used for complex animations and scripting.

FIGURE 3.4 A photograph in JPEG (left) and GIF formats.

Images are incorporated into a web page by using the <img> tag, which must include an 'src' attribute to indicate where the image is located, as well as other possible attributes, such as image width, height, alternative text that is shown should the image not be displayed, and space around an image. For example, the instruction <img src="whitehouse.jpg" width="200" height="150" align="left" hspace ="10" vspace="10" alt="The White House"> displays a JPEG photograph of the White House 200 pixels wide by 150 pixels high, with a 10-pixel margin around it and text indicating what the picture is when the mouse moves over it.

When incorporating images into a web page, it is important to take into account their usability and usefulness. Images are the most common hindrance to download times across the Web, with pages taking much longer to display if they are loaded with graphics. In addition, there is a tendency to rely on colour in images for visual clues such as navigation and information, neglecting the fact that many people are colour-blind. When optimising images for use on the Web, there is nearly always a compromise that must be made between file size and image quality, so it is best to restrict the use of images wherever possible, and also to reuse images that have already downloaded to the visitor's computer and are stored in his or her browser cache.

Layout

Text and images must be presented as part of a web page: at its simplest, a page is what appears in a browser window, but a quick glance at any number of web sites will indicate that not all web pages are designed to fit in such a window. Most pages you encounter will, at the very least, need to be scrolled up and down and even (particularly if you browse using a monitor capable of showing no more than 640 pixels at any one time) from side to side.

In theory, a web page can be extremely long or wide; in practice, users get bored after too much scrolling and it is generally better to include links to multiple pages. There is, however, no standard web page, and in some cases, a very long document may be preferable to one that is navigated by a series of links. For example, if your site includes a novel that people usually want to print off, visitors may be best served by one long file, or, at the very least, files of whole chapters, rather than a series of short, irritating sections. Size, therefore, should be appropriate to the content: in some cases big really is best, but in others a small package is favourable. As a rule of thumb, restrict content so that a page can fit vertically within four screens, unless there is a good reason to do otherwise.

This is not the case when dealing with screen width, the reason for this being that there is a standard series of resolutions that monitors use, the most common being VGA (640 × 480), SVGA (800 × 600) and XGA (1024 × 768). While nearly every new monitor supports XGA, even until recent years this was not the case and there are plenty of VGA monitors in use. In terms of design, it is very good practice to provide page sizes that support VGA, but that deal with larger sizes either by expanding (the default for text) or by being centred. The resolution 640 × 480 may be too restrictive, and 800 × 600 seems to be becoming a more acceptable standard; however, if you use this size it is still worthwhile breaking up the page so that it still appears coherent when viewed at the smaller size, for example by moving boxouts or links to the extra 160 pixels on the right-hand side. Insisting that visitors view your site at a certain size is equivalent to telling those who can't to go away.

When adding content to a page, the default for HTML is to begin on the left-hand side and run down the page from top to bottom. Using the align tag, content can be moved to the right or centre of a page, but to place text midway down two-thirds from the left edge can be extremely difficult in simple HTML. There are two ways to overcome this: the first, and older, method is via tables; the newer method (supported only in 4.x browsers and later) is to use layers.

A table is a grid that holds content in rows and columns forming cells into which content can be entered: thus, in a table that is three rows deep and three columns wide, it is indeed possible to enter text that is halfway down the page and occupies a position two-thirds of the way across the page. Tables are defined using the <table> ... </table> tag, with rows defined by <tr> ... </tr> and columns by <td> ... </td>. Thus, for example, a very simple table one row deep and two columns wide would look like this in HTML:

```
<table>
   <tr>
      <td>row 1, column 1</td>
      <td>row 1, column 2</td>
   </tr>
</table>
```

The use of tables for more sophisticated layouts is due to the fact that tables can be nested within each other (for example, column 2 could contain another table divided into four cells). What is more, rows can span multiple columns and columns multiple rows, enabling web designers to create, for example, a single cell across the top of a table that could hold the title to a page.

Tables are compatible with a wider range of browsers and can be used to achieve advanced effects, such as those created by changing background colours or images. While it is possible to regulate the size of tables to some degree (for example, by defining their width or height as a percentage of a window or pixels), it can be difficult to position

85

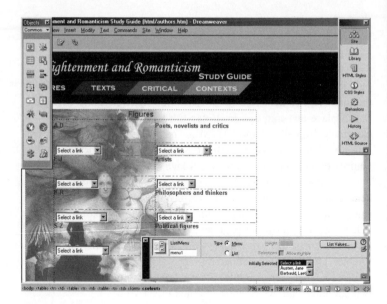

FIGURE 3.5   Using tables to design pages.

pixels in absolute relation to a page and, while tables can be nested, they cannot be laid one over the other. A more recent method allows design elements to be positioned anywhere on a screen and for layers to be overlaid: with dynamic scripting, this can create complex effects by hiding, showing and moving layers in response to certain other actions (such as pressing a button or loading a page). Layers have not been as widely adopted as they should have been, however, because version 4.x of Communicator used a proprietary <layer> tag that would not display in Internet Explorer (which uses the <div> tag).

Hyperlinks

While we have covered most of the fundamentals of web design in terms of graphics, text, layout and navigation, it must be repeated that the feature that separates web design from most other forms of media is the ability to link to other documents. The basic model for web linking is fairly simple, with unidirectional links connecting to a single page. Links are added in HTML using the anchor tag <a> ... </a> with the attribute href, for example <a href="www.yahoo.com">Go to Yahoo!</a> or <a href="home.htm">home page</a>. These two examples indicate one important way in which hyperlinks differ: the first includes the full address of a page and is known as an absolute link; the second provides a URL in relation to the current page and is, unsurprisingly, known as a relative link. Absolute links are necessary for external sites, where documents are not stored on the same server, while it is possible to use both absolute- or relative-style URLs for internal links to files that *are* located on the server. In practice, it is best to incorporate internal links as relative URLs so that, should a site be moved to another server, it is not necessary to change all the links to pages.

Another distinction between types of links is between static links (the most common type encountered), where the destination is hard-coded into the web page, or dynamic ones, which are generated as the page is viewed, usually by a database. Links can be attached to a variety of forms, the most common being the text link as in the examples above. It is also possible, however, to attach links to graphics, multimedia elements or stylised text buttons created using CSS. For graphics, different parts of an image may be allocated different destinations using the <map> ... </map> and <area> tags; this is known as an image map.

Dynamic web sites

CGI

Despite innovations such as XML and CSS, web designers using HTML still largely rely on static, document-centred design. There is, however, a slow movement towards the more interactive and dynamic, like software applications that process user input, rather than like publishing formats such as print or AV broadcasting. Web programming can be divided into two basic types: client-side, which uses plug-ins such as Flash or scripting languages such as JavaScript to add interactivity on the end-user's PC; and server-side, such as Microsoft's

Active Server Pages (ASP) or the Common Gateway Interface (CGI) specification, which processes information on the server before returning the result to the client's browser.

There are pros and cons for each step: client-side programming is generally much quicker as no round trip to the server to check data is required, and even the frustration of downloading plug-ins has become less problematic as common standards are incorporated into contemporary browsers; on the downside, non-compliant browsers will be locked out of important areas of a site, while it makes more sense to store such things as database information on a server where it can be kept up to date more easily. As such, many of the best interactive sites combine both client- and server-side technologies rather than rely on one or the other.

CGI is the oldest version of server-side programming using the HTTP commands 'post' and 'get' to pass data to the server, so that it can be processed and results returned to the browser. CGI refers to the means of transferring data between client and server rather than the programming language itself, meaning that CGI applications can be written in any language such as C/C++ or Visual Basic, though Perl (Practical extraction and reporting language) is probably the most common because of its excellent web support.

Using CGI, a server can read and write data to disk (saving your name and payment details when you enter an online shopping site, for example), store variables (such as the goods you enter into your 'shopping cart'), and display results that vary according to user input (displaying the list of items you wish to buy, for example, so that you can check they are correct). For CGI programs to work, their files must be executable, that is, they must be able to launch, process data and write out results. Typically, information is entered using a web-based form that offers a means of capturing data from users: such things as text boxes enable visitors to type in data, or they may select from a variety of pre-set choices such as drop-down boxes, radio or check-boxes. This data is then passed to the server for processing using the action and method properties of the form tag, as in <form action= "processform.cgi" method="post">.

CGI programs have a reputation for being slow, largely due to the fact that they predominantly use interpreted languages such as Perl;

that is, instructions to the server have to be interpreted on an ad hoc basis rather than being 'compiled' into a stand-alone executable program. In addition, CGI programs are generally run in a separate memory area to the web server and may incur operating system overheads, as the program has to be run for every user who accesses it. That said, CGI remains a useful way to add interactivity to a site, because it is an open standard with readily available examples and scripts on the Web, for example at www.cgi-resources.com. For more information on CGI, see Jeffry Dwight *et al.* (1996) and Whittaker (2002).

Scripting and Java

Scripting refers to a wide variety of programming techniques, some of which, such as JavaScript or VBScript, work on the client browser, and some of which, such as ASP or PHP, work on the server. The latter technique, often known as 'server-parsed HTML' (SHTML), 'server-side scripting' or 'server-side includes' (SSI), attempts to combine programming with web pages in a format that can be faster than CGI. Such scripting uses templates combining script and HTML that is read, or 'parsed', by the server and output as an HTML file.

Of the various versions of server-side scripting, such as ASP or Allaire's ColdFusion, the main differences are largely those of syntax and personal preference. At its very simplest, SSI can consist of an instruction to the browser to connect to the server for a pre-programmed component, such as a navigation console, as in <!-#include virtual="console.html">. In addition, server-side scripting can use variables from the server, such as time and date, to track information that is not available to static pages, as in the ASP instruction <%date%>, which will insert the server's current date.

The main problem with server-side programming is that it is fairly slow, because of the need to make round trips to the server to verify information. While client-side programming is much quicker, it does have disadvantages, in that pages will not work for a visitor who does not have the appropriate plug-in or has turned off support for scripts. While there are a number of client-side scripting languages, the following comments are restricted to the most popular, JavaScript.

JavaScript was originally developed by Netscape, but was made into an international standard in 1997 by the European Computer Manufacturers Association (ECMA), hence you will very occasionally see JavaScript referred to as ECMAScript. It was intended as an easy-to-use, interpreted language that could be used in small chunks and would be useful for equally small jobs, for example checking forms or adding embellishments such as rollover buttons. While JavaScript does not need to be a complicated process, its 'reusable' quality and wide support means that it is very appealing to designers and so has become a core technology that is worth learning. A good primer in JavaScript is John Pollock's *JavaScript: A Beginner's Guide* (2001).

Another useful component for scripting is a cookie, a small text file incorporating information sent from the server that is stored on a user's computer for later retrieval. Cookies are usually used to store information such as passwords or preferences so that a site can be accessed without having to re-enter such information. Despite some paranoid claims to the contrary, cookies cannot be used to retrieve data from the user's hard drive, although they can be used to track user's movements (something commonly used in banner advertising), so many visitors keep them turned off. For some dynamic effects to work, however, such as noting items that have been entered into an online shopping cart, cookies need to be enabled.

Finally, Java has attracted a great deal of attention in recent years as a programming language that can use the same code across multiple platforms. Developed by programmers at Sun Microsystems in the early 1990s, Oak (as it was then known) was intended to be used in various computer electronics and so had to produce tightly-compiled code. By 1995 it had been adapted for the Internet and renamed Java.

Unlike most languages, Java does not run directly within the operating system of a computer, but rather from a software-driven 'virtual computer' or 'virtual machine'. It is this virtual machine that is specific to the OS (such as Windows, MacOS or Linux), so that any code written once in Java can be run on any platform for which a suitable virtual machine exists. Java has more recently been a cause of controversy: when Microsoft licensed Java from Sun, it 'improved' Java to ensure a faster run time in Windows – but such code would only run on Windows. Sun subsequently refused to allow Microsoft to use Java (and Microsoft has since moved onto its own Internet suite of applications and languages, .NET); it does, however, have some problems in portraying itself as the simple hero to Microsoft's villain. First of all, Microsoft's improvements did make Java run more efficiently, although they undermined the original rationale of Java; second, Sun has not made its language a genuinely open-source platform that could be worked upon by a community of developers. Despite these problems, however, Java was an early indicator of how computer programmers of the future will have to think less about the desktop and more about the network.

Further reading

There are two main starting points for web design and production: the first is to concentrate on key concepts and principles of design, learning the transferable skills that are required to get the most from a wide variety of software and technologies; the second concentrates on learning specific applications. The latter is too wide to cover here – just as there are many programs for web design, image editing and video, so each application has a multitude of books devoted to explaining tricks, tips and good practice. For more general principles, however, see Whittaker (2002), and other good books that include Powell (2000, 2001), Spainhour and Eckstein (1999) and Niederst (1998). There is also a great deal of material and information on the Web, including hotwired.lycos.com/webmonkey, www.bensplanet.com, www.pagetutor.com and www.producing.routledge.com.

Chapter 4

Institutions, ethics and regulation

Introduction

A medium such as the Internet is not spontaneously born from a fertile chaos of communication and technology. While certain aspects have apparently appeared *ex nihilo*, most notably the Web, the popularity of which surprised many commentators in the mid-1990s, in fact these have developed and evolved within a framework of institutions and practices that have contributed to their particular flavour. Even when, as we have seen in Chapter 1, the Internet is positioned as the major new medium of the twentieth century to emerge in a climate of deregulation and free-market economics, for it to work at all there must be at least a set of technological ground rules. What is more, the libertarianism of the Net, although held up as a positive force by many users, has also been a cause of concern to many more: as we shall see in this chapter, this has begun to result in severe reactions in regulatory areas such as copyright and obscenity. As Collins and Muroni (1996) have observed, the increasing dominance of free-market

economics in areas such as new media and telecommunications often requires new policies to deal with unprecedented levels of concentration of ownership or loopholes concerning control of access.

Equally important to issues of official regulation and the performance of modern transnational corporations is how online life is conducted – the question of ethics. Indeed, as writers such as Frost (2000) and Christians *et al.* (1991) have pointed out, ethics are frequently intertwined with regulation and commerce. Ethics are usually treated as equivalent to moral principles, although they are equally concerned with codes of (professional) conduct and, at the danger of oversimplifying, are usually considered philosophically as a question of utilitarianism, the greatest good for the greatest number, or as an issue of duty, as in Kant's categorical imperative, a moral act which I am obliged to follow. Such fundamental principles of ethics are rarely, if ever, transformed by the emergence of new media, but the implications of following an ethical code of conduct must be scrutinised and questioned as new practices and techniques develop. A particularly good introduction to the impact of new technologies on ethics (and vice versa) is Ermann, Williams and Schauf (1997).

Internet administration

Who owns the Internet? Although a common perception of the Internet has been that it is an anarchic place, there are in fact several bureaucratic levels controlling its protocols and development as well as companies responsible for the physical infrastructure. In the UK, a few companies such as BT and AOL control the Internet pipelines entering this country, but even they are provided by a small group of American companies such as AT&T, Cable and Wireless, and Sprint, who own transatlantic cables and communication satellites. A basic starting point for Internet administration and regulation consists of monitoring technical protocols and standards by which the medium works. This is not the only level of interest that governments and institutions display in the Net (far from it), nor is it the only way of answering questions of ownership, but it does explain in part how the Internet is structured.

While telecommunication companies are extremely important to the Net, then, they do not own the protocols and data that are as important to telecommunications as the physical network. As stated in Chapter 1, the Internet was previously administered by the National Science Foundation; although this is no longer the case, any network connecting to the Internet has to submit to standards ratified by the Internet Architecture Board (www.iab.org). This board oversees technical support and reporting committees designed to maintain the protocols for communicating across the Net.

The IAB and other organisations – particularly ones such as the World Wide Web Consortium (www.w3c.org), which provides information on the development of new web protocols – are extremely important in deciding the shape of the Internet. Essentially, these offer archives of information that can help producers determine the future development of the Web. Most of these bodies have their roots in academic and scientific research, although commercial organisations such as Microsoft and IBM play an important role; their work has been important because the Net is a prime example of an open architecture, applying standards that enable different technologies to work together.

The principal non-profit organisations involved with technical administration on the Web include the Internet Engineering Task Force (www.ietf.org) and (Internet Society (ISOC, www.isoc.org), which monitor general Internet standards. Also important is the Internet Corporation for Assigned Names and Numbers (www.icann.org), which handles domain name registration and IP address allocation. Since its establishment, ICANN's role has frequently been a contentious one, as we have seen in Chapter 2: this is not only due to the fact that ICANN generates profits from domain names, but also because those who do not receive the 'real estate' that they want often question how its decisions are reached.

Setting standards

The process of implementing technical standards across the Internet requires a quality control procedure involving some or all of the above groups. The 'standards track' system begins with an RFC (Request for Comments) and progresses through the following stages before becoming an Internet standard: the RFC is circulated to an Internet Engineering Task Force working group and, if accepted, becomes an

Internet Draft that is further discussed by the IETF. Technical discussion now takes as long as necessary to iron out problems (typically six months or longer), whereupon the Draft may become a Proposed Standard. If it is accepted by the Internet Engineering Steering Group (IESG, www.ietf.org/iesc.html), then it becomes a Draft Standard and waits another minimum six months before possibly being accepted as an Internet Standard. During this time it can be discussed by members of other organisations, such as the W3C.

This lengthy process has been used to iron out incompatibilities in the fundamental architecture of the Internet, such as FTP, HTTP and TCP/IP, as well as for other developments such as Internet Printing and IP routing for mobile hosts. While the process of developing standards is rather arcane from the standpoint of most Internet users, RFCs can be useful tools for determining the future shape of the Internet.

Commercial organisations

We shall return to the role played by governments and other regulatory bodies in later sections dealing with topics such as free speech and copyright. Media interest in the Net, however, was largely stimulated in the 1990s, less by its power to transform communication than by the potential to harness such communication for grossly over-inflated profits. By the middle of the decade, reports of astronomical stock flotations provided a clear motive for this interest; five years later the bubble had burst, but technology companies remain immensely important, as part of international and global markets, for developing new ways of business, and also as they contribute to what Castells (1996–7) calls a 'Network Society'.

Netscape – the new model?

We have already seen in Chapter 1 the contribution made by Netscape Communications Corporation to the development of the Web: in this chapter, we shall examine the ways in which Netscape established some of the early paradigms for web business. Founded in 1994 by Marc Andreessen, who had worked on the first graphical browser, Mosaic, at the National Center for Supercomputing Applications, and Jim

Clark, formerly of Silicon Graphics Inc., when Netscape Communications debuted on the capital markets sixteen months after its formation it was valued at over $2 billion with revenues of $100 million. It was this sudden transition from start-up to billion-dollar company that was to kick-start the dotcom phenomenon of the late 1990s.

The main value of Netscape lay in the transformation of a user-hostile environment into something more approachable, and Andreessen has since claimed that his goal was to democratise the Web (Sheff 2000). The simplification of access to the Web was actually a process begun by Mosaic, the producer of which, the NCSA housed in the University of Illinois, tried, but failed, to charge copyright fees on early versions of Netscape. Eventually the NCSA was paid a one-off fee and turned down shares in the company, preferring to distribute Mosaic through its own company, Spyglass; one result of this was that the company founded by Clark and Andreessen, Mosaic Communications, had to change its name to Netscape.

Netscape began producing server and browser software, charging for the former and providing the latter as 'free not free': in effect, the Netscape browser was shareware that required payment for continued use, but Netscape turned a blind eye to the latter in an attempt to make its software as ubiquitous as possible – the lesson it had learnt from Microsoft was that 'whoever gets the volume wins in the end' (Reid 1997: 31). More significantly, from Microsoft's point of view, two years after the launch of Mosaic the Web had come to dominate the Internet and Andreessen began to talk of the Web as a computing platform in its own right, one which would break the Redmond company's Windows monopoly.

In response, Microsoft launched Internet Explorer 1.0 in 1995, based on Spyglass Mosaic; despite the fact that the software was not particularly good, it became part of Windows 95 and saw a sudden change in the company's commitment to the Web, which would be particularly worrying for Netscape as Microsoft could afford to spend a great deal of money on research and development. In addition, Microsoft did not pursue a confusing shareware policy, but instead gave away Internet Explorer for free and signed major deals with AOL, CompuServe, AT&T and Netcom, so that with version 3.0 of both browsers the gap began to close. In August 1996, Netscape complained to the Department of Justice (DOJ) about discounts being offered on Windows 95 bundled with Internet Explorer (Reid 1997).

Unfortunately for Netscape, while it was making money from intranet software and services, Microsoft simply did not need to make money from the Internet during the 1990s, but simply to gain market share in order to secure a long-term strategy. Despite its high market valuation, Netscape could not transform ubiquity in terms of its web browser into profit and, in any case, was losing volume to Internet Explorer. By the beginning of 1998 it reported an $88 million loss and was purchased by AOL in 1999, its most enduring legacy, as Sheff (2000) observes, being the DOJ investigation into Microsoft.

AOL Time Warner

If Netscape provided a business model for the Internet that, for a time, looked set to buck old-economy rules, AOL is a content provider that cut its teeth in the early days of personal computing and, following a merger with Time Warner in 2000, has become a global media corporation.

Founded in 1985 under the name Quantum Computer Services by Steve Case, when the company (with its name changed to America Online) floated on the US stock market in 1992 its market value was $61.8 million and it had ninety-seven employees. This was considerably less than Netscape had achieved in two years, but in this instance the tortoise did not simply beat the hare but devoured him as well; by the time of its merger AOL's market value had risen to $105 billion. Initially, AOL offered proprietary content services such as news, features and chat rooms, concentrating on mass-marketing its product and, to that end, making it as simple as possible. As such, AOL was treated in its early days with a degree of contempt by more expert users, a perception that continues even to this day. And yet, as Chip Bayers has observed, 'for many people, AOL *is* the Internet' (1999: 114). With members rising from just over 180,000 at the beginning of the 1990s to nearly 18 million by the decade's end, AOL was perceived by a number of commentators as being in trouble: by growing at such a rate it could not always provide a reliable service to members and, with the Web offering similar content to AOL for free, its hourly subscription model was jeopardised. Many predicted the death of AOL.

Although the success of the Internet did present problems to AOL, like Microsoft, the company decided to embrace the Net aggressively. It pursued a number of corporate acquisitions, such as Nullsoft (which designed the popular music player, Winamp), CompuServe and, of course, Netscape, while moving to new subscription and advertising models that saw revenues rise rather than fall. Its most audacious move, however, was to initiate a merger with Time Warner, the largest media company in the world following the megamerger of Time Inc. and Warner Communications in 1990 and including traditional media organisations such as *Time* and *Fortune* magazines, CNN, Warner Bros Pictures and Warner EMI Music.

Time Warner had attempted to extend its media empire onto the Web previously and, with CCN Interactive, had achieved some success. However, its most public venture, Pathfinder, had proved to be a failure. Launched in 1994, Pathfinder was the brainchild of *Time* magazine's managing editor, Walter Isaacson (Reid 1997). While Time Warner had demonstrated remarkable initiative in betting on the Web at a stage when its survival was far from assured, Pathfinder proved a drain on resources with no promise of sufficient revenue, so it was soon scaled back. For AOL, however, Time Warner provided huge amounts of content plus broadband cable connections for its subscribers; AOL in return provided established models for generating revenue from the Internet and, when the merger was given the go-ahead by regulators in 2001, it created the largest media company in the world with a combined value of $225 billion (Rose 2000).

Some commentators remarked of the merger in early 2000 that AOL had missed the point, that in the new economy corporations had to be lean to be mean, and that megamergers and acquisitions would simply overload a company, making it too large to respond quickly. In the subsequent crash of technology stocks in late 2000 and 2001, AOL Time Warner's merger has preserved it from much of the fallout that has taken place elsewhere, so that it will continue to be the face of the Internet for many subscribers. While Microsoft has caused major concerns over its apparent attempt to monopolise the Internet, that is a charge that is perhaps more accurately laid at the door of AOL Time Warner.

The Microsoft monopoly

If AOL Time Warner offers a future vision of the Internet, another very public vision has been offered by one William Henry Gates. Microsoft, founded in Albuquerque, New Mexico, in 1975, as an inauspicious two-man show comprising Gates and co-founder Paul Allen, had grown by the end of the last millennium into a company with revenues of $25 billion a year. Although hardly a rags-to-riches story (Gates came from an affluent Seattle family and dropped out of Harvard University), the rise of Microsoft has still been astonishing, outstripping the other commercial giants of America such as US Steel and General Electric in a quarter of the time it took them to become leviathans, a growth fuelled by Microsoft's domination of the operating system market and epitomised by its mission statement, only recently changed, to have a computer on every desktop and Microsoft software running on it (Wallace and Erikson 1994).

The Internet, however, while offering new markets for Microsoft, has also been the cause of its greatest humiliation. As recently as 1995, Microsoft dismissed the Internet as a passing fad: Fred Moody (1995), for example, could publish a book in that year discussing the publication of multimedia enterprises such as *Encarta* without mentioning the Net once, and, while Bill Gates (1995) did consider electronic communication as part of the road ahead, it would be part of a proprietary, Windows-based system produced by the company everyone loves to hate outside Redmond. With the launch of Windows 95, it seemed that Microsoft could do no wrong and that it was only a matter of time before users attracted to the Internet abandoned it in droves for Microsoft's own network, MSN.

When it was clear that this was not going to happen, Gates turned around company strategy in a matter of months. The rather desultory web browser, Internet Explorer, had been released shortly after Windows 95, and Gates devoted massive resources to developing this browser as part of future versions of Windows, while transforming

MSN from a proprietary network service, similar to AOL or Compu-Serve at the time, into a web-based portal. By distributing copies of Internet Explorer freely and building it into Windows 98, Microsoft was determined to dominate the browser market as it dominated the desktop operating system. Tellingly, in Gates's next book, *Business @ The Speed of Thought*, he commented 'It's hard to think of a business category in which the Internet won't have an impact' (Gates and Hemingway 1999: 69).

Microsoft had come under scrutiny for potentially anti-competitive practices in 1990, when the Federal Trade Commission investigated possible collusion between the company and IBM, as well as Microsoft's DOS marketing tactics: after this suit was taken up by the DOJ as a violation of the Sherman Antitrust Act, a compromise was reached via a consent decree, in which Microsoft agreed not to use its operating system to take advantage of rivals. When it announced, however, that Microsoft planned to purchase the finance software company Intuit for $2 billion, the DOJ filed a suit to block the deal, arguing that it would reduce competition (Daly 1997). Attorney Gary Reback had also been gathering information from Microsoft's competitors – Apple, Sun and Novell – that earned him a reputation as the company's most strident critic and, in 1995, he was approached by Jim Clark, who claimed that a team from Microsoft had threatened to put Netscape out of business.

From this simple start began the public humiliation of Microsoft, what John Heilemann has called the 'last great business story of the 20th century and the first great riddle of the 21st' (2000: 262). If Gates and his right-hand man Steve Ballmer had come to see continuing antitrust cases as 'proxy warfare', then the investigation instigated by Microsoft's entry into the browser market threatened to be their Pearl Harbor. Reback joined up with attorney Susan Creighton, to whom fell the task of penning a White Paper detailing Microsoft's rise to power; this was delivered to the DOJ, followed by another White Paper, in which Reback and Creighton contended that Microsoft's plan was to gain a stranglehold over all online commerce. The DOJ began its case late in 1997. During the ensuing investigation and trial, Gates and Microsoft reacted bullishly, but failed to impress federal judge Thomas Penfield Jackson: in May 2001, he ruled that Microsoft had abused its monopolistic position and should be broken into two companies, one dealing with operating systems, the other with applications.

The case against Microsoft had taken many turns, and these did not end with Judge Jackson's ruling. Many expected the company to drag out any division as long as possible through a system of appeals, particularly after the change of government from Democrat to Republican in 2001; some commentators even argued that dividing the company in two would simply create two monopolies where only one had existed before. In a further twist, in the summer of 2001 the US Court of Appeal for the DC Circuit issued a unanimous verdict that Microsoft was not guilty of trying to maintain a monopoly with its Internet Explorer software and condemned Jackson's 'rampant disregard for the judiciary's ethical obligations', accusing him of seeking self-promotion. Nonetheless, while the Court of Appeal maintained that aggressively marketing Internet Explorer did not violate the Sherman Act, the judges did rule that Microsoft's Windows-only agreements with PC manufacturers meant that the company behaved anti-competitively and that it should be held liable for its actions. Tellingly, while Microsoft currently remains intact and enjoys its economic status, the fact that a free piece of software almost brought the software giant to its knees indicates the importance of the Internet to the US and global economy.

The dotcom phenomenon

The importance of the investigation into the world's largest software company coincided with an apparent revolution in the business world. Multinational companies with large workforces, detailed profit and loss plans and big offices – bricks and mortar – were suddenly perceived as dinosaurs incapable of dealing with the rapidly changing global economy, while for some players it appeared that all that was required for success was a good idea and a web site. Dotcom companies received colossal financial investment, with many individuals becoming paper millionaires overnight.

Newspapers, magazines, television programmes and, of course, web sites rode high on the buzz of the so-called 'New Economy' which was making nonsense of 'Old Economy' notions, such as the baseline requirement to sell a service or product for more than its cost. According to the rules of the New Economy, establishing a brand online was everything, even if this required giving away a product (in the form of goods, such as books or CDs or information) for free or at greatly reduced costs (Moon and Millison 2000; Rifkin 2000). By the end of 2000, however, the quest for eldorado had simply become another gold rush: companies such as boo.com and Boxman were closing daily and even the most successful ventures, such as Amazon, Jungle and Freeserve, were accumulating rising debts with no profit in sight.

In retrospect, the supposed New Economy was obeying some very simple Old Economy laws. While the profitability of nearly every dotcom company that was launched in 1998 was far from assured, the considerable amounts of cash that they were provided with very quickly was due, ironically, to the success of the American economy in particular (Heller 2001). Because the US stock markets had been thriving for an unusually long period of time, investors were concerned about a slowdown in the profitability of many established companies, especially those in the computing, electronic and communications industries that had flourished in the 1990s, particularly as businesses such as Intel and Motorola issued profit warnings.

As more and more people began to invest in stocks and shares, this created another problem: too many investors chasing too few stocks were causing to rapidly rising prices. At the same time, economic conditions appeared to support a move towards the new businesses. In the US, for example, President Clinton endorsed a bill in February 1998 that was designed to enable tax-free commerce across the Internet, and, although the EU made threatening noises, it was generally politically agreed that ecommerce required such an environment to flourish. With the rapidly increasing European market for mobile phones and promised Internet connection in the form of WAP services, it seemed that people would be able to connect anywhere at any time – and at a lower cost, following the explosion of unmetered Internet services. In addition, with deregulation of trading, it was easier than ever for individuals to buy online, meaning that they tended to stick with the technology options they knew best.

The end result was a proliferation of disasters: the online toy retailer, eToys, saw its share prices rise to over £57 at the end of 1999, only to rapidly decline to less than a pound a year later; Pixelon, a company claiming to have engineered a more efficient video streaming format, raised $28 million of which $16 million was spent on a launch party; and the famous fashion company, boo.com, also earned notoriety as it had managed to spend £80 million in twelve months, much of that squandered on prolific and expensive advertising campaigns. Internet companies were grossly overvalued (ebay, for example, increased in value by 1,500 per cent in six months) and, as cash flow came not from sales (which were not helped by high-profile stories of credit card insecurities) but from stock flotation and capital investment, the crash would always be a painful one. In the middle of August 2000, Wall Street witnessed some astonishing falls, with a loss of $2.1 trillion on the stock market, with a $1 trillion loss on April 14 that affected all market sectors, including the largest companies represented on the Dow Industrials list. Networking giant Cisco lost 25 per cent of its value, while Microsoft was also worth $200 billion less after the crash. Significantly, the *Wall Street Journal* reported on 19 April that key venture capitalists had sold $22.2 billion of their holdings in February, double the amount of the previous one-month record, and were thus aware that the crash was coming.

Comparisons have been made between the dotcom rush of the late 1990s and tulipomania and the South Sea Bubble; in these latter cases, the valuation of stocks associated with tulip bulbs and land in the New World, accompanied by hysteria as investors sought to cash in, led to panic and disaster as the real value of these overpriced commodities was gradually realised. There is some justice in the comparison, but also a realistic appraisal of the contribution of the Internet to the economy is required: the vast majority of dotcoms indulged in wild speculation, while failing to appraise realistically their requirements. Thus boo.com, for example, was far too ambitious, launching in eighteen different countries with a £35-million system to support those countries in seven different languages. Its gross income, of about £340,000, was as much as it cost to maintain the visuals on its complex web site, which in turn failed to serve consumers who found it too slow or difficult to use. Indeed, at the turn of the twenty-first century, it is the more traditional Old Economy companies that appear best placed to gain from the Internet, so-called 'clicks and mortar' businesses. Companies such as Halifax, Dell, Tesco and IBM are increasingly turning to the Internet to add to their profit line, using existing infrastructure to sell to other businesses as well as consumers. In many cases, these corporations buy up the enterprise and experience of failed dotcoms, but in return are also imposing discipline and realistic plans on ecommerce that are more likely to ensure its future (Heller 2001).

Copyright

As its name implies, copyright is about the right to copy material. It has always been concerned with the form of that material rather than the underlying idea, and in general terms anyone who creates something new is entitled to exercise copyright over that material. What this means is that other people are not able to reproduce that work, whether in the form of words, visual images, or music, without the prior permission of the copyright holder. What it does not mean is that another person cannot rewrite or rework the underlying idea into a new form. A copyright holder may exercise their rights directly, but more typically copyright is transferred to a publisher of the material.

Copyright operates both internationally and at a local level. While there is no general principle of international copyright that works uniformly, there are two major international copyright conventions that lay down certain minimum specifications. These are the Berne Convention of 1886, revised in 1971, and the Universal Copyright Convention of 1952, sponsored by Unesco and again revised in 1971. The minimum international agreement (the Universal Copyright Convention) states that the minimum term of protection for copyright extends twenty years after an author's death, this being fifty years for the Berne Convention. In Britain, the 1989 Copyright, Designs and Patents Act replaced the 1956 Copyright Act, and was further amended by the implementation of EC Directive 93/98 in 1995. Under the terms of the Act and Directive, protection is extended to seventy years after an author's death. In addition, the Act effectively excluded many industrial designs from copyright protection and placed them under a new 'design right' which lasts fifteen years from the first year in which a design is circulated. In the US, the 1976 Copyright Statute (which came into effect in 1978 and was amended in 1988), provides protection for fifty years after an author's death (Cornish 1999).

While the producer of a work has the moral right to be identi-fied as the author (with certain exceptions, such as periodical writing), there are occasions when extracts of works can be reproduced – so-called 'fair dealing'. Copyright allows a producer to prevent others from reproducing substantial parts of their work, but certain conditions apply in which it is held that reproduction does not infringe the rights of the copyright holder. In the UK, for example, these include research, criticism/reviewing, parody or private study. Fair dealing does not apply to all types of copyright (image reproduction, for example), and there are restrictions on the amount of material that can be reproduced, but even the limited amount permissible under fair dealing creates prob-lems when dealing with electronic reproduction and, therefore, certain copyright holders refuse to allow their work to be stored in electronic format at all (Liberty 1999).

Copyright and the Internet

Storing material on a computer network is a very different proposition from copying it via 'analog' means, as from a book or tape. As Negroponte has pointed out, the main difference between digital and analog media is that the former can create an exact replica of the orig-inal without deterioration: copying a book on a photocopier will result in distinct differences between the former and latter and, if the copy is reproduced again, it will typically become harder to read; on a network, the text can theoretically be copied an infinite number of times without deterioration of quality (Negroponte 1995). Put simply, it is much easier to reproduce material across a digital network, such as the Internet, than by using older technologies.

Thus 'digital uses are not equivalent to non-digital uses' (Liberty 1999), and copyright holders are pushing governments to be more explicit with regard to issues such as fair dealing. The European Parliament, for example, proposed the Copyright in the Information Society Bill in early 1999, but this itself introduced problems that were specific to the Internet. The aim of the bill was to enforce copyright regulations, as reproduction of material has become easier than ever.

The bill caused consternation amongst the European Internet Service Providers Association (EuroISPA), however, because in its original form it appeared to exclude all copying, including material held in local caches used by ISPs to store information locally and remove traffic from the wider network (Whittaker 2002).

The ease with which material can be transferred across the Internet, particularly in forums such as newsgroups or chat sites that encourage user participation, has led to certain myths and false assumptions. For example, it is often assumed that, if something does not have a copyright notice, it is not copyrighted. While this was true in the past, it is not the case now in most countries subscribing to the Berne Convention (including the US and the UK): works are copyrighted by default, although this is emphasised by a notice.

Because of the fact that users often do not directly charge for material on the Internet, this again gives rise to the common assumption that it is fine to copy material because the user is not gaining financially. This is not true, although, if a copyright owner does place something in the public domain, that work can be modified by others (for commercial as well as private use). Copyright myths on the Internet also tend to assume that fair dealing extends to all acts of copying, whereas fair use, as we have seen, extends to reviewing, private study and parody – and even in these cases electronic storage may be explicitly disallowed due to the ease with which material can be copied. Likewise, plagiarising another person's work to use as the basis for another text or image is also covered by copyright law under the term 'derivative' work, which remains under copyright to the original creator.

The US Digital Millennium Copyright Act, which implemented treaties signed at the 1996 World Intellectual Property Organization (WIPO) Geneva conference, was passed into law in 1998 after a period of turbulent negotiation: it was supported by the software and entertainment industries and opposed by academics, scientists and libraries. In general, the Act added to existing legislation by making it a criminal offence to circumvent anti-piracy measures or to distribute code-cracking devices or techniques. The liability of ISPs as transmitters of copyrighted information was, however, limited, as was the liability of non-profit institutions, such as universities, when they serve as ISPs.

David Tetzlaff has argued that apparently severe extensions of the nature of copyright in legislation such as the Digital Millennium Copyright Act and the 1997 federal NET (No Electronic Theft) Act are important because of the changing nature of capital: 'the idea of property must be redefined away from possession of material goods towards access to data' (2000: 118). This is a view shared by a number of libertarian commentators, such as Andrew Ecclestone from the Campaign for Freedom of Information (1999) and Herman and McChesney, who argue that much of copyright law is 'arbitrary' and designed for powerful interests: 'Copyright and patents protect monopoly positions, keep prices high, and transfer income from poor to rich countries. The US government aggressively insists upon a protection of intellectual property that provides maximum income to its own industry, while displaying minimal interest in the concerns of anyone else' (1997: 49).

The Internet has also been immensely influential in transforming the attitudes of its users towards copyright in a number of ways outside corporate control, not all of them beneficial. The rise and rise of MP3 and the early boom of dotcoms, which gave away products in order to gain market share, have tended to encourage the attitude of a free-for-all in its most acquisitive sense, but the Net has also encouraged the development of a more positive 'gift' economy of which Linux and GNU are perhaps the best examples. The GNU (for GNU's Not UNIX) project was initiated by Richard Stallman in 1983 as a replacement for UNIX, when the owners of that operating system began charging for software that had previously been freely available. By the beginning of the 1990s, a vast number of applications had been written, missing only the kernel that would enable these programs to communicate with hardware: when this kernel was supplied by Linus Torvalds in 1991, the combined set of kernel and applications became popularly known as Linux.

In the GNU Manifesto (1987), Stallman outlined his philosophy for the GNU General Public Licence (GPL). Free software, explained Stallman, means free as in free speech rather than as in free beer, that is, developers often will charge for their services and products, but for software to develop as quickly and effectively as possible its source code should be open, available to anyone, rather than proprietary, as with operating systems such as Windows or MacOS. The development of the GNU Public License (or 'copyleft' as it is often known) arose due to the perception that material placed in the public domain would often be taken and repackaged in a proprietary format: under the terms of the GPL, 'GNU is not in the public domain. Everyone will be permitted to modify and redistribute GNU, but no distributor will be allowed to restrict its further redistribution. That is to say, proprietary modifications will not be allowed. I want to make sure that all versions of GNU remain free' (cited in Ermann *et al.* 1997: 231). While open-source software does not always replace products from companies such as Microsoft and IBM, the growth of Linux, indeed of the Internet itself, which is also based on open standards, testifies to the importance and capabilities of sharing information.

Case study: MP3 and Napster

In the period from 1999 to 2001, it was in the sphere of music reproduction that copyright issues reached critical mass. MP3 is a popular file format for reproducing sound that enables listeners to experience near-CD quality, but with much smaller file sizes, making it better for transferring across the Internet than older formats. So widespread has the craze for MP3 become that certain search engines reported it as having replaced 'sex' as the number one search term in 1999.

As with home taping on cassette, small infringements of copyright rarely attract attention, but the attempt by certain companies to use the format to build successful ventures attracted considerable concern during 1999 and 2000. Recognising the popularity of sharing music files across IRC, a student at Northwestern University, Shawn Fanning, wrote a program with which users could find and trade music online using dynamic links to computer hard drives that would update automatically when someone logged on to the service. Launching it in July 1999, Fanning gave the program his high-school nickname, 'Napster' (Alderman 2001). The main appeal of Napster was that it connected users together in a peer-to-peer network that did not require them to upload files to central servers: the downside for Napster was that it was not fully peer-to-peer, anyone who logged on being listed on Napster in order to make locating files easier.

While companies such as MP3.com or Emusic had attempted to be company friendly (MP3.com, for example, paid EMI $200 million for copyrighted music used on its site), Napster appeared to sideline record companies entirely. In December 1999, the Recording Industry Association of America (RIAA) initiated legal proceedings against Napster claiming copyright infringement, joined by some high profile (and sometimes unlikely) musicians who felt threatened by the trade of music on the Net, including Eminem, Metallica and Dr Dre. In July 2000, a US district judge ruled that Napster was guilty of infringing copyright laws, as it allowed users to obtain music for free that they would otherwise have paid for. The defendant had argued that an earlier decision by the US Supreme Court that allowed Sony to distribute the Betamax video recorder had set a precedent for such technology, but Judge Marilyn Patel disagreed, commenting that the company had 'created a monster'.

The media giant, Bertelsmann, began a tentative buyout of Napster, and Fanning was employed to rewrite his brainchild in a more legitimate format. Universal Records, however, continued to pursue the original lawsuit against Napster and, after a number of reprieves, the site was temporarily closed in 2001. Once the site began the attempt to police the swapping of copyrighted materials, transforming itself into a subscription service, users stayed away from a site they had once flocked to (peaking at 2.79 billion downloads). The numbers of users, however, indicated the interest in this method of distributing music, and controversy continues as to how much Napster affected sales, with 1999 and 2000 being banner years for the record industry (Alderman 2001). While companies such as Sony, Universal, BMG, Warner and EMI try to work out how they can turn new technologies to profitable use with services such as MusicNet and PressPlay, the failure of Napster has pushed the distribution of copyrighted material under-ground with true peer-to-peer systems such as Gnutella and Freeserve.

Defamation and free speech

One of the fundamental starting points for interest in the Internet is that it is a potentially revolutionary form of communication. With email, web sites, bulletin boards, discussion forums and chat sites, an explosion of communication tools has raised concern about the Internet's potential to spread libellous and slanderous statements, disseminate false information and provide a forum for extremist groups. Furthermore, due to the way that the Internet operates, messages can be posted from anywhere with a lesser or greater degree of anonymity, making it difficult to track down statements that can be passed from server to server very quickly.

At the same time, while the Internet raises a huge number of regulatory and ethical difficulties, it is also true that it has brought to the fore questions about free speech and the rights and abilities of users to participate in open communication. The view of the Internet as fostering a new cyberdemocracy is a naive one and, as Joseph Lockard and others have argued, without universal access free speech on the Internet must largely be a mythical entity (Lockard 1997; Street 1997; Shade 1996). Nonetheless, it has made very public the issue of freedom to communicate and participate in society. A common complaint is that the existing legal system responds too slowly in dealing with regulatory issues thrown up by new technologies, but Laurence Tribe argues that the constitution is actually very flexible with regard to such things as the First Amendment: it is not necessarily that the law requires changing, but that we must reconsider how we implement it (Tribe: 1991).

Free speech and the First Amendment

In the US, the First Amendment to the Constitution guarantees the right of freedom of religion and freedom of expression to all Americans, even those whose opinions may be deemed reprehensible to a community, with the Supreme Court having affirmed that the government could not regulate Internet content any more than in traditional areas of expression. The First Amendment does not provide protection against libel or copyright infringement, nor does it protect speech that threatens or harasses other people, such as an intention to commit an unlawful act against a specific person. The case of *Brandenburg* v. *Ohio* (1969) established a distinction between speech that is 'directed to inciting or producing imminent lawless action' and speech that is not likely to incite such action, usually interpreted via the example that the First Amendment will not protect someone who shouts 'Fire!' in a theatre, thereby causing injury.

Of the various areas where the limits of free speech are applied on the Internet, the most important are pornography and 'adult material', defamation and violence. Regarding the latter, one example where a group has been held responsible for encouraging acts of violence on the Web was that of the American Coalition of Life Advocates (ACLA), responsible for a site called the 'Nuremberg Files', which listed doctors and clinic workers who performed abortions. Names, addresses and pictures were posted on the site, with a line being drawn through the names of those who had been killed: although the site did not explicitly call for the murder of those listed, a jury in 1999 found that the information contained there did amount to a real threat of bodily harm. In March 2001, however, an appeal court ruled that the site was protected under the First Amendment.

While the case of the Nuremberg Files provides a clear example of the attempt to legislate against apparently provocative online content, it is an unusual example in that most cases revolve around issues of race. Content that would be considered racist or anti-semitic would generally be protected by the American Constitution unless it provoked direct action, although prosecutions have been made for racist use of the Net. In 1998, for example, a former student emailed death threats to sixty Asian-American students at the University of California, signing his messages 'Asian hater', for which he received a sentence of one year's imprisonment. The Anti-Defamation League has been involved in exposing the phenomenon of hate speech online, reporting, for example, on the presence of hate clubs on Yahoo! (and working with Yahoo! to restrict access to such clubs). At the same time, while many such incidents are usually resolved with reference to user and service agreements, protection of racist and white supremacist views by the First Amendment is raising a host of legal quandaries online as the Internet provides a new forum for racist groups to reach out and organise (Wolf 2000).

In contrast to the US, many other countries do not provide protection for hate speech and may even actively proscribe against it. It is, for example, illegal to promote Nazi ideology in Germany and it is also illegal to deny the Holocaust in many European countries. This has led to at least one high-profile example of how international laws can come into conflict over the Web, with the prosecution in France of Yahoo! for selling Nazi memorabilia (see 'Case Study: Yahoo!' below). On a more general point, American citizens who post material on the Internet could face prosecution in another country, although the United States will not extradite citizens if the activity they are engaging in is protected by the Constitution. Attempts to deal with hate speech in the US, for example via the 1996 Communications Decency Act (CDA), have generally all been struck down as unconstitutional.

Defamation, libel and slander

While hate speech is a problem for society at large, many individuals have found the Internet more provoking because of defamation of their personal character. Although slander and libel are often used interchangeably, slander is the defamation of a subject by word of mouth, while libel is more serious to a writer or publisher as a charge because it deals with defamation recorded and published to a public audience. For a charge of libel to be effective, a writer must publish an untruth that is damaging to the subject's reputation and recorded in some permanent form, which can be as evanescent as an email or chat posting. In the UK, a distinction is made between libel and fair comment: thus, to say that a certain actor is overweight may be judged as fair comment, but to say that they cannot act because they are too fat could be considered defamatory. In the US, whether the subject is judged as a private or public figure can also come into play, lower standards applying in former cases. The limits of a writer's right to free speech about public affairs were established in the 1964 case *New York Times* v. *Sullivan*, which set out that, where the injured party is a public figure, he or she must prove 'actual malice'. While truth remains protection against libel, however, unsubstantiated rumour can be prosecuted, even if the subject is a public figure.

Until very recently, lawsuits for libel on the Internet were relatively rare, but a number of cases in 2000 and 2001 provided differing, potentially conflicting results, indicating that this is one area where simple understanding of the law will be difficult, particularly in the international arena. Nonetheless, libel lawsuits against online commentators look set to flourish over the coming years. When, for example, Matt Drudge accused White House aide Sydney Blumenthal of wife abuse, Blumenthal sued Drudge for libel even after an apology was published on Drudge's web site (Morris 2001). Confusion over the status of ISPs in libel cases has dogged the Internet from the early 1990s: in 1991, the *Cubby* v. *CompuServe* case saw CompuServe treated as a free carrier, similar to a telephone company, which could not be held responsible for every posting on its servers. Four years later, in *Stratton Oakmont* v. *Prodigy*, the ISP was held responsible, but this was due to the fact that Prodigy specifically maintained that it monitored the content of its bulletin boards in order to market itself as a family-oriented system. One (unintended) effect of this was that ISPs have tended not to monitor content at all, in order to evade responsibility for messages posted by third parties. The UK government attempted to compensate for this in the 1996 Defamation Act, whereby, if the ISP can demonstrate that due care is taken, it will not be prosecuted, a so-called 'Section 1' defence.

In the US, due to the CDA (which became famous in the mid-1990s as part of the debate on online pornography, but actually covered a much wider area of the law), ISPs are immune from prosecution for messages posted by a third party, something that was tested several times. *Zeran* v. *America Online* (1997) established that AOL could not be held negligent in delaying the removal of defamatory messages, while *Lunney* v. *Prodigy* (2000) saw the US Supreme Court rule that ISPs have full protection against libellous or abusive email postings over the Web, after a former Boy Scout served Prodigy with a lawsuit following postings of threatening messages by an impostor using his name. In Britain, the situation has appeared very different: in 1999, a lawsuit was brought against the ISP Demon by Dr Laurence Godfrey concerning material posted anonymously to a newsgroup. It was held immaterial that Dr Godfrey and the poster were not Demon customers and, though the case was settled out of court, it is likely that the ISP would have lost, not because the material was posted, but because Demon failed to act when the presence of the content on its servers was brought to its attention (Whittaker 2002; Hamilton 1999).

Despite fears over the ease with which someone may be defamed by anonymous posters, some commentators have argued that privacy remains an important issue on the Internet (Hilden 2001; Hamilton 1999), and that legislation around defamation may rush to uncover the identity of defendants far too quickly. As Hilden remarks, one of the main uses of defamation laws may not be to extract compensation but to uncover the identity of an anonymous speaker; in contrast to newspapers, ISPs often disclose their users' identities far too quickly and easily. While free speech on the Internet may demonstrate new lows for acrimonious and libellous comment, it also offers the potential for a widening participation in debate denied by more traditional media.

Case study: Yahoo!

In the summer of 2000, the Union of Jewish Students and the International League Against Racism and Anti-Semitism filed a suit against Yahoo! in the French courts, accusing it of allowing users to buy and sell Nazi memorabilia on its increasingly popular auction sites. Such trade is illegal in France and the company's subsidiary, Yahoo! France, had already blocked such sales; the parent company, however, based in the US, initially refused both to block the site and to provide warnings and was, consequently, threatened with fines of up to £100,000 per day.

The sale of Nazi memorabilia is not illegal in the US as it is in several EU states, and Yahoo! spent the next six months attempting to persuade the authorities in France that it was technically impossible to prevent French users viewing Nazi items sold in private auctions. Early in 2001, however, the company agreed to bar the items from auction listings and settled out of court. Ultimately, Yahoo! seemed to change its mind less because of the legal pressure than the constant association that was increasingly linking its portal with Nazis. The company issued a statement that it would refuse items 'associated with groups which promote or glorify hatred and violence', a move that included groups such as the Ku Klux Klan.

US commentators were concerned about the impact of the French ruling for the First Amendment when applied to the Internet. One implication is that material not aimed at a particular population in another country will be subject to that country's laws because of its availability, nor would this necessarily be simply to the detriment of the US: while some countries could threaten sites presenting information on birth control, for example, there is also the possibility that

American courts would be able to pursue foreign web sites that promoted, say, gambling. The impact of the Yahoo! case can be over-stated, however: those who brought the action against the company were not necessarily concerned with the activities of Yahoo! per se, but that sales of Nazi memorabilia broke French law when accessed in France.

Sex, pornography and obscenity

A common means through which new technologies have become popularised is through sexual content. In some respects, this can be seen as the rather anodyne observation that 'sex sells', but, more specifically, certain media, such as video, DVD and the Internet, owe part of their success to an association with easier distribution of adult material. With regard to the Internet, as Claudia Springer has observed, a decade of public information about Aids has also probably contributed to a 'new celibacy', where sex is replaced by computers (Springer 1994). Internet pornography or adult material cannot be separated from the rest of the adult industry, particularly as based in the US and Europe. Regarding the Internet, sex sites have not only proved to be some of the most popular sites on the Web, but have also led the way in terms of ecommerce and business-to-business practice: 'Mechanisms for online shopping, credit card processing, banner advertising, chatrooms, video-streaming and general web marketing were often pioneered by adult site developers' (di Filippo 2000: 125).

While most regulatory and ethical issues are concerned primarily with visual pornography on the Web, sexual content can take a variety of forms. Several years ago there was considerable interest in sex chat, otherwise known as 'tiny sex' or 'compu-sex', which shares features with phone sex lines (Branwyn 1994). In the 1980s and early 1990s, sexual material was typically associated with Usenet, which proved particularly difficult to regulate, especially its 'alt' hierarchy. The alt.sex newsgroup alone accounted for 8 per cent of Usenet readers in 1993, with users downloading and uploading files in categories ranging from the innocuous to the criminal. In one example of how Usenet could work around prohibitions, a Canadian judge imposed a reporting ban on a case involving the sex-related slayings of two young women in Canada by Karla Homolka in 1993; the trial prompted a spate of news reporting in the US, but also a flurry of Net-related speculation, such as alt.fan.karla-homolka, which announced support for Homolka's SM tendencies. This newsgroup was shut down at several universities, but, as John Gilmore remarked, 'The Net interprets censorship as damage and routes around it' (cited in Shade 1996: 24). It is difficult to censor information that can be routinely stored and transferred around the world, so adult material deemed pornographic and illegal in certain states or countries is becoming easier to find for those with Internet access.

Not that it is possible, nor even necessarily desirable, to treat the Net as a completely deregulated zone with regard to sexual matters. While Usenet has frequently served as a forum for the darker recesses of human sexuality, particularly paedophilia, newsgroups that promote or distribute such material are often banned wholesale in many countries. Nonetheless, despite a few extremes, where either public opinion is vehemently opposed to a certain practice, or an individual decides to prosecute material directed against them, the Internet also has thus far seemed capable of routing around many forms of blocking access.

Pornography v. erotica

One problem with understanding sexual activity on the Internet consists in defining what it actually is. Pornography, from *porne* (prostitutes) and *graphia* (writing), has become something of a catch-all term for the user, and can be used to categorise material (typically considered offensive) in a way that tends to bracket off further investigation into such definition. It is a term that tends to be used lazily (as when we talk of a 'pornography of violence'), to indicate a vague excess, even when commercial transactions – or exploitations – based on sex do not take place. Wendy McElroy offers a useful definition of pornography as 'the explicit artistic depictions of men and/or women as sexual beings' (1995: 51). Even this fairly neutral description, however, does not take into account the fact that the vast majority of sexual publication of any form is predicated on commercial exchange, and the inclusion of the adjective 'artistic' simply defers (indeed, extends) the controversy of defining pornography; all this without even taking into account a branch of feminist opposition to pornography epitomised by MacKinnon (1993) and Dworkin (1981), which is questioned by McElroy.

McElroy's definition would perhaps be recognised by most people as a definition of erotica, and indeed a common tactic is to polarise 'good' sexual representations as erotica and 'bad' sexual representations as pornographic. This in turn raises further questions: if one of the functions of pornography is to stimulate direct sexual activity (whether as intercourse or masturbation), is erotica pornographic if it does the same? If it cannot stimulate this way, is it effective in its task, or, to ask the question another way, is morally 'good' erotic art ineffective and thus 'bad' in its depiction of men and women as sexual beings? These questions and others lead John Preston to assert that 'there isn't any workable definition of what is pornography vs what is erotica' (cited in di Filippo 2000: 122). Relying on aesthetic distinctions, for example, again tends to ignore the commercial exchange that is the basis of both pornography *and* erotica.

And yet, outside certain countries that provide access to the Internet but ban users from viewing sites with sexually explicit material, virtually all countries attempt to provide some sort of legal distinction between sexual material that is licit (although not necessarily respectable) and that which is illegal and even considered harmful. In the most liberal of regulatory environments, this may simply be the banning of the depiction of minors in sexual acts; more often, it consists of attempts to distinguish sexual mores and tastes based on public acceptance. This can be notoriously difficult to do: in the UK, for example, the 1959 Obscene Publications Act bans publications that may 'deprave or corrupt', which has sometimes resulted in difficulties for prosecutions when faced with a jury that is indifferent to the supposed harm of a publication (and thus presumably already degraded and corrupted). In the US, the Supreme Court provided a flexible test for obscenity in the 1974 case, *Miller* v. *California*. Following on from this, there were two main reasons for deeming materials obscene: that they depicted sexual acts prohibited under state law, or that they would be considered prurient by the average person applying contemporary community standards. In addition, works could be defended if they were of literary, artistic, political or scientific interest, but the main test of 'community standards' was seen as a means of avoiding the 'absolutism of imposed uniformity'.

Obscenity and free speech

Obviously a compromise between those who wished to abolish obscenity and those who wished to preserve the First Amendment, such as *Miller* v. *California*, would be tested in different states at different times, but the growth of the Internet in the mid-1990s, increased the ease with which it became possible to distribute sexual material between states. In one widely reported case in 1994, *US* v. *Robert and Carleen Thomas*, a couple who ran a bulletin board in San Francisco were convicted by a jury in Memphis of transmitting hard-core pornography through interstate lines when material was downloaded by a postal inspector in Tennessee (who also ordered videos via snail mail). Although the Thomases did not advertise in Tennessee, they were arrested by federal officers: in an earlier incident, the material on their servers was not found obscene, according to the standards of the San Francisco area.

Because sexual material can be accessed by anyone with a phone line, computer and modem, many parents have also been concerned about their children finding pornography on the Net. More seriously, there have been a number of incidents involving child pornography, material that is illegal whether or not it is obscene: in 1995, for example, the Justice Department arrested a number of people as part of an investigation into paedophiles on AOL, while, more recently, paedophile rings such as Wonderland have been investigated and arrests made. More controversially, in a case involving CompuServe, the German manager, Felix Somm, was held responsible for the distribution of paedophile material on the CompuServe network, even though he had no knowledge of such activity, and was given a two-year suspended sentence and fined £33,000 for aiding and abetting the spread of child pornography, which was later overturned by a court in Munich.

The existence of paedophile rings using the Internet has been demonstrated several times, yet reports of such incidents are frequently hyped up by a sensationalising press. Such sensationalism, combined with fear over what children could be accessing on the Internet, led to the Communications Decency Act on 1 February 1996. The CDA, part of the Telecommunications Reform Bill that further deregulated the phone industry, prohibited 'indecent' and 'patently offensive' language and pictures in front of minors, in order to bring the Internet in line with television. Unfortunately for Congress and Bill Clinton, who signed the Act into law, the CDA immediately encountered substantial opposition. Many saw the CDA as unconstitutional and organised a 'blue ribbon' campaign to support free speech and oppose the Act. In addition, there were practical difficulties in implementing the Act: the Internet was not a limited resource like television and indecent sites spread like wildfire. On the same day that the CDA was signed into law, the American Civil Liberties Union (ACLU) sued the federal government as represented by Janet Reno and a temporary restraining order was placed on the Act.

A few well-publicised embarrassments, such as the inability to post material on breast cancer because it could be considered indecent, helped the judges to decide in June 1996 that the CDA was unconstitutional. Other attempts were made to protect minors online, such as the 1998 Child Online Protection Act (COPA), but again this was challenged by ACLU; the Court of Appeals held that the ACLU appeal was likely to succeed in questioning the constitutionality of COPA, because the Act placed web publishers under the most restrictive and conservative state's community standards in order to avoid prosecution. Although the ethics of sexual material on the Internet should not simply be considered as an issue of free speech, this is frequently how it is debated in legal arenas.

Hacking and privacy

Hacking is an activity almost as old as electronic computing itself and is a term loosely used to cover a wide range of activities. The term was first used at MIT and was borrowed from train enthusiasts who 'hacked' trains, tracks and switches to make them perform faster. Hacking soon came to be identified with 'phreaking', breaking into regional and national phone networks in order to make free calls: in one famous instance from the 1970s, John Draper (aka Cap'n Crunch) discovered that a toy whistle given away with Cap'n Crunch cereal generated a signal of the same frequency as the tone used to access AT&T's long-distance switching system. In the 1980s, phone phreaks moved into computer hacking and onto bulletin boards, forming groups such as the Legion of Doom and the Chaos Computer Club in Germany, at the same time that hacking was popularised through the film *War Games* (1983).

Some computer commentators attempt to distinguish criminal activity outside hacking, following Steven Levy's account of computer enthusiasts in his book, *Hackers: Heroes of the Computer Revolution* (2001). In this case, hackers are those who are technical experts who wish to understand systems and software as thoroughly as possible. Hacking in this instance has very little to do with breaking into computer networks, as commonly understood, although such potentially illegal activity may demonstrate the epitome of technical knowledge. Bearing in mind this distinction between legal and potentially illegal activity, hacking tends to be used to indicate the ability to enter and utilise any system. David Tetzlaff (2000) provides some useful distinctions between hackers and crackers (who use their skills to break encryption codes), to which may be added 'script kiddies' (who rely on readily available tools and scripts to access computer networks), and 'warez pirates' (anyone who regularly trades in illegal copies of copyrighted material). Despite the fact that they are at the bottom of the food chain, script kiddies are probably the most damaging group in that it is increasingly easy to bring down a web site, steal information from just about any computer connected to the Internet or prevent legitimate users from accessing their data (Dr-K 2000).

Despite the concentration on hacking as criminal, it remains a contested activity, one that has given rise to its own 'hacker ethic' or 'hacktivism'. These two terms are not necessarily synonymous, although they do often overlap: at its simplest, the hacker ethic may consist of a desire for technical expertise. Slightly extended from this is the notion that all information is free, and thus without the need for intellectual property, security and privacy, a view that Spafford (1992) considers 'naïve and unrealistic'. In such a view, one justification of hacking is that it provides a valuable service in demonstrating security flaws, utilising idle systems or, as Paul Taylor (1999) points out, developing the very skills that led to the formation of the computer industry in the first place. 'Hacktivism' is usually a more socialised form of the 'hacker ethic', concerned to use technological skills to effect social and even political change. It may justify itself as a means of closing the gap between the technological haves and have-nots and operating on parts of the Internet such as peer-to-peer and IRC channels and newsgroups away from an increasingly commercialised Web (Tetzlaff 2000), or even as a youthful counter-culture frequently allied with such movements as anti-globalisation protests (Ross 1991). Those opposed to hacktivism precisely because of its *juvenile* nature, such as Richard Power (2000), often see such justifications as hypocritical.

Information war, digital crime and viruses

In his book *Tangled Web* (2000), Power charts how the move to online services has resulted in a less secure world as companies and institutions struggle to keep up with the progress of technology. While the myth of the hacker often focuses on the (usually teenage) individual freelance, Power also notes how industrial espionage, organised crime and even disgruntled employees can wreak most havoc. Thus, for example, Kevin Mitnick, who was convicted of stealing software from Digital Equipment Corp. in 1989, was the first hacker to become a household name, while, nearly a decade later, ex-CIA official Harold Nicholson was accused of spying for Russian intelligence between 1994 and 1996. Similarly, Clifford Stoll has provided a famous account of how he traced a spy who was selling military information to the KGB, his detective work later leading to the arrest of three West Germans (Stoll 1989). More recently, during the Kosovan conflict in 1999, Serbs saw the World Wide Web as 'a unique instrument for waging their own "information warfare" against NATO countries' (Taylor 2000).

Information warfare may take the form of propaganda, espionage (commercial or political), or even the targeting of other web sites. The most common forms of attack consist of port-probing and Denial-of-Service (DoS) or Distributed Denial-of-Service (DDoS). In addition to the TCP/IP addresses that connect computers across the Net, ports are used to access particular services such as File Transfer

Protocol and Hypertext Transfer Protocol servers: thus a request sent to 179.137.12.58 will reach one particular machine but, typically, will be directed to the FTP server if it is addressed to port 21 or the HTTP server if addressed to port 80. As there are 65,535 potential ports, many of which are not secured, DoS attacks overrun servers with continuous streams of data that appear to be normal network messages but to which the server cannot respond. The result of such an attack is that the server cannot process such information and keels over: when a Denial-of-Service is distributed across a network hundreds of DoS attacks take place simultaneously, generating enough malformed packets of data to bring down major servers, as happened with Yahoo! and Amazon in 2000 (Power 2000).

Another form of digital crime is often associated with viruses. While some may consider writing a virus as no more than a demonstration of technical expertise, it is also the case that such programs can cause considerable damage. A virus is a self-replicating file, one that can duplicate itself and infect other files, and that carries a 'payload'; such payloads can be relatively benign, such as simply displaying a message, but many are much more harmful, causing data loss or even rendering the hard drive inaccessible by wiping BIOS (Basic Input-Output System) or drive settings. Worms are a specific form of virus that copy themselves to other systems by using networks and email, while Trojans are non-replicating programs that usually carry hidden but potentially devastating effects while pretending to perform another task. Trojans such as Back Orifice from the Cult of the Dead Cow can be used to open ports and provide remote access to a system.

Viruses first came to public attention in 1988, when a graduate student at Cornell University and the son of a chief scientist at the National Security Agency (NSA), Robert T. Morris Jr, released a worm onto ARPAnet which spread to 6,000 systems. Andrew Ross suggests that the Morris case is significant in demonstrating a peculiar relationship between institutions and hackers: although Morris received three years' probation, the Cornell Report admitted his brilliance and described his virus as a juvenile act with no malicious intent. Thus the academy used the affair to strengthen its own moral and cultural authority: it reprimanded Morris on *its* terms, without reference to external authorities (Ross 1991). The number of such virus attacks rose from 7 in 1988 to 30,000 in 1991 and, following the release of Windows 95 and the wider take-up of the Internet around the same time, virus attacks have become increasingly prevalent, with an estimated 50,000 at large in 2001. Some of the most highly publicised viruses, such as the Love Bug, Melissa and AnnaKournikova have spread themselves quickly via email.

Surveillance and the state

Despite the dangers from hackers, viruses and digital crime, such events constitute only a small part of the potential security problems of Internet usage. Most people using any form of communication will assume that anything they transmit will, in most cases, remain confidential. Only in exceptional cases would they expect messages to be intercepted and read – for example, a phone tap may be established or letters examined to locate criminals, such as those involved in drug trafficking, kidnapping or terrorism. With regard to media such as letters, it is indeed fairly difficult to inspect a suspect's mail without them becoming aware, but the principle that the state has a right to intercept such communications is far from new: state monopolies for the transport of mail were granted in the eighteenth century to enable governments to track subjects more easily, with the Geheime Kabinets-Kanzlei in Vienna, for example, dedicating considerable resources to reading diplomatic mail and cracking cyphers.

Such surveillance remains difficult, however, in contrast to electronic forms. Telephone communications, mobile and fixed line, are subject to interception, while in many countries all email and other Internet-related messages are scanned on a regular basis. While telegraph and telephone services were, as with the mail, largely maintained by monopoly services, until the latter part of the twentieth century such activities were still labour-intensive and so were mainly synonymous with police states that maintained large, secret bureaucracies. Even in the UK and US, however, major intelligence services were established during the Second World War to monitor coded radio messages, most famously at Bletchley Park, where Alan Turing and others worked on cracking codes produced by the German Enigma machine. The UKUSA Treaty of 1947 joined these countries with Canada, Australia and New Zealand to form a single intelligence network that would monitor the Communist bloc (Davies 1996).

Throughout the decades following the War, such organisations had grown considerably, with a secret budget for the NSA estimated at $4 billion in 1990. With the collapse of communism in the early 1990s, they turned their attention to other forms of crime in addition to the traditional task of monitoring foreign nations. Particular interest with regard to electronic surveillance emerged in the 1990s, when the European Parliament accused the US government of employing Echelon, a network used to eavesdrop on a variety of media, for industrial espionage against European companies. Echelon, the existence of which has never been formally admitted by the US, was developed after the War and is believed to monitor all email and Internet-based communications, as well as traffic carried by the Intelsat and other satellite networks, radio broadcasts and cable communications. Echelon trawls through every message to which it has access, indexing these and then searching for keywords, with an estimated two million messages being searched every hour; attempts have even been made to use speech recognition to trawl phone calls automatically.

While Echelon led to friction between the US and the EU, European countries, including the UK, France, Germany and Spain, had participated in the International Law Enforcement Telecommunications Seminar (ILETS) in 1992, whereby the FBI initiated a set of standards for monitoring and intercepting communications: an International User Requirement standard (IUR 1.0) was ratified by the European Parliament and an update proposed in 1998, though this was rejected when the story was leaked to the German press. From 1992 until 1998, the capability for surveillance was maximised with the minimum of public scrutiny. While awareness of electronic observation by the state has increased, new initiatives such as Carnivore in the US and the Regulation of Investigatory Powers Act (RIP) in the UK have extended governmental and commercial rights to spy on citizens and employees. The UK government has argued that RIP was an attempt to regulate activities of companies that did not have transparent policies on the monitoring of employees, but the Home Office has also considered proposals from the National Criminal Intelligence Service to keep records of all Internet and telephone usage for seven years, something that civil liberties groups have argued convenes the Data Protection Act and possibly Article 8 of the Human Rights Act. Carnivore, a controversial project established in 1997 and designed to allow the FBI to 'wiretap' the Internet, was given provisional permission at the end of 2000 to conduct further research, although this was opposed by the ACLU and ISPs.

Surveillance by the state, therefore, is widespread and intrinsic to government practice, as indeed it has been for several centuries. Modern technologies and the proliferation of electronic communication have made the task easier in many respects, although the sheer volume of information presents its own problems. As a declassified CIA document cited on the cryptome.org web site makes clear, 'there is a strong presumption in today's intelligence setup that additional data collection rather than improved analysis will provide the answer to particular intelligence problems' (www.cryptome.org). In addition to such surveillance, the subject of rights for consumers in the face of increased electronic commercial monitoring raises important issues around civil liberties, with the use of cookies (small text files stored on a computer) and logs of visits regularly employed to build up profiles of visitors to sites.

Some writers, such as Mary Williams, argue that, while 'computerization has a tremendous potential for destructive invasion of privacy ... this potential can be kept in check with a combination of legislative and technical devices' (cited in Ermann *et al.* 1997: 16), a viewpoint that can seem naive in the light of continued pressure by governments to remove issues of data surveillance from any form of public scrutiny. Some, such as Dorothy Denning (1993), argue that computer-mediated communication should not weaken law enforcement, and that the rights of a society to combat crime tend to outweigh those of individual privacy, but many Internet commentators tend towards a more libertarian line, arguing that such data collection threatens innovation and communication in a free market (Rotenberg 1993) or compromises more fundamental rights of citizens (Mylott 1984; Rachels 1975; Liberty 1999). In 2001, the UK Information Commission, for example, announced that it was targeting businesses that did not comply with EU regulations such as the Data Commission Act, amidst concerns that companies were simply collecting too much information on individuals.

Encryption

Although, as we have seen, computerisation enables easier monitoring of electronic communications, it is this same computerisation that has placed obstacles in the path of total state surveillance. Interception is at its most effective when dealing with unencrypted messages, but the proliferation of ever more complex forms of digital encryption has greatly hindered such operations.

Encryption renders messages unintelligible to anyone without the appropriate key, and cryptography, from *kryptos* (hidden) and *graphia* (writing), has been used since the days of ancient Egypt (Kahn 1972). The best and most widely used form of digital encryption uses a pair of mathematically related keys, or numbers, rather than a single password, one of which is private, stored on the sender's computer and imprinted on every encrypted email, while the other is a public key that is freely distributed. Of public key encryption methods commonly in use, the first requires a digital certificate provided by a third party, rather like a passport or driver's licence. Digital certificates, also known as digital IDs, are available from companies such as VeriSign (www. verisign.com) – the public part of a certificate is usually sent as a signature with a message and is then used to decrypt further messages from the author. The algorithms used to create cyphers are measured in bits, with higher-bit cyphers being more difficult, if not impossible with current technology, to crack.

Before the advent of cheap personal computers, effective digital encryption was only available to governments and was not illegal in most Western countries other than France until the end of the 1990s. In 1998, the US State Department, acting on advice from the NSA, classified encryption software as munitions, the exports and imports of which were to be controlled. Because of the activities of individuals who referred to themselves as 'cypherpunks', such software had become a political dilemma, as it was seen to compromise the security aims of UKUSA participants. A disarmament activist, Phil Zimmerman, had written a free encryption program, Pretty Good Privacy (PGP), in the early 1990s, which was later posted to web sites by anonymous cypherpunks, making it theoretically available anywhere in the world to users with an appropriate Net connection. Zimmerman was subjected to legal action and threatened with imprisonment, although charges were eventually dropped (Bowden and Akdeniz 1999).

Because of the potential for ecommerce, encryption was becoming an important business topic, to which the US government had to respond by authorising the use of a deliberately weakened cypher (40-bit DES) for commercial use and by attempting to promote an NSA-devised hardware encryption scheme in 1993: consisting of a chip called Clipper and a software algorithm known as Skipjack, the government would be able to access encrypted information using a master key applicable to every Clipper chip, a process known as key escrow. Objections centred on the fact that, while key escrow would enable the government to spy on legitimate civilians, criminals would almost certainly employ a system such as PGP to evade detection, thus undermining the rationale for mass surveillance in the first place. The Clipper initiative had failed by 1998, when encryption software was placed on the ITAR (International Traffic and Arms Regulation) list of restricted items (Bowden and Akdeniz 1999), though by 2000 cryptographic tools had been quietly removed from that list. It remains a felony to export such applications to certain countries, notably Iran, Lybia and Iraq, but the US government monitors which sites provide digital encryption rather than preventing them from being downloaded.

Case study: Operation Sun Devil and the EFF

By the end of the 1980s, hacking had come to be perceived as a major threat to corporate America. While the decade had begun with the romantic image of the teen hacker in *War Games*, the arrests of Kevin Mitnick and West German spies, as well as the release of the first major virus to affect large networks, were events seized upon as evidence of the nefarious implications of computing. By this time, major institutions were making heavy use of computing and were increasingly networked, making them vulnerable to what increasingly appeared to be a form of terrorism, all of which led to the formation of Operation Sun Devil in 1988.

In 1990, after collecting information, government agents, law officers and security personnel cracked down on hackers in a flurry of arrests between January and May. As related by Bruce Sterling in his book *The Hacker Crackdown: Law and Disorder on the Electronic Frontier* (1992), one hundred and fifty agents confiscated a large number of computers, information and software, their targets including figures who went under the names of Phiber Optik, Acid Phreak and Knight Lightning, as well as Steve Jackson and Craig Neidorf. Acid Phreak was accused of crashing AT&T's computer system and causing damage costing $1 billion, but was never charged, while Jackson, whose offices were ransacked during the operation, filed charges and was later awarded $50,000 in lost profits. In perhaps the most ridiculous incident, Craig Neidorf was accused of publishing a document stolen by another hacker from Bell South, whereas the supposedly confidential document was actually freely available from the company.

Sterling believes that Operation Sun Devil was a wake-up call to the computing community at the beginning of the 1990s, throwing into sharp relief the paranoia that had grown during the late 1980s. An immediate consequence of the heavy-handed operation was the formation of the Electronic Frontier Foundation (EFF) by John Perry Barlow (of the Grateful Dead) and Mitchell Kapor (the founder of Lotus Development), who put forward $200,000 for the EFF's initial fund to support Jackson's suit against the Secret Service (Moschovitis *et al.* 1999). The EFF (www.eff.org) has attracted some controversy over its support for a particularly individualistic stance towards technology, conjuring up in particular the frontier of the Wild West, but throughout the 1990s it has served an important function in keeping civil liberties near the top of the agenda in any discussion about the Internet.

Further reading

Ethics and regulation are major topics in media studies, and unsurprisingly there are a number of titles that have appeared dealing with how these issues affect the Internet. One title that is beginning to show its age, but which still asks relevant questions about ethics and technology, is Barbour (1992), while Ermann *et al.* (1997) is an excellent collection of essays dealing with many aspects of computer ethics. Such standards often play an important role in the gathering of information by journalists, and the issues that this raises are dealt with by

Hall (2001), who looks specifically at online journalism, and by Frost (2000).

Regulation of the Internet is an often thorny topic, but some useful material is contained in Collins and Muroni (1996), Dyson (1998), Liberty (1999) and Gauntlett (2000); the web site www.gigalaw. com is also very useful for information on Internet regulation. Specific topics include privacy, discussed by Davies (1996) and Lyon (1998) for example, or rights of access to the Web, as in Rifkin (2000). Unsurprisingly, discussion about who controls the Web frequently leads to questions of hacking and hacktivism, whether as a criticism of such activities as irresponsible, as in Power (2000), or supporting them to some degree, as in Sterling (1992) and as in Levy's classic 1984 book that has just been reissued in a revised edition (2001).

Regarding the business of the Internet, there are a large number of books, many of which are, frankly, worthless: following the collapse of the dotcom market during 2000, the vast quantities of titles exhorting readers to build Internet businesses for the twenty-first century are probably best left unread. There are, however, some interesting titles about the IT businesses that laid the foundations for the Net explosion at the end of the last decade, such as Carlton (1997), Cringeley (1996), Jackson (1997) and Wallace and Erikson (1994). In this rapidly changing field, however, it is also worthwhile consulting business magazines and the Internet (such as ZDNet and Wired News) to keep up to date with commercial developments. Amongst the magazines, although it frequently allows its enthusiasm to escape its control, *Wired* is still one of my personal favourites. Other relevant business titles include *PC Advisor*, *PCW* and *.NET* in the UK, and *PC World*, *PC Magazine* and *InfoWorld* for the US (and, under franchise, many other parts of the world).

Chapter 5

Cyberculture I

Society, community and
cyberspace

Introduction

An increasing number of writers and theorists dealing
with media, culture and communication are turning
their attention – unsurprisingly – to the Internet. More
than just a study of the physical medium, its history,
technologies and use as a communication tool, such
theorists are concerned with how digital media and
technologies are transforming our identities, our social
relations and the spaces in which we live. A common
tendency for such studies brackets them together under
the heading of 'cyberculture': we will explore the
meaning of this term further in this chapter, but it is
useful in emphasising the study of new media as a
cultural phenomenon.

The study of cyberculture is concerned with questions about who we are and the world we live in as
affected by digital technologies. It has been the seedbed
for some of the most interesting and significant work
regarding these questions and, as such, the final two

chapters of this book are devoted in some detail to issues arising from the cultural study of the Internet. The division of topics in these final chapters is intended to segregate such cultural studies into those that deal with social or communal questions, and those that deal more with the configuration of the individual, but such division of labour is always, at some point, arbitrary and there is considerable cross-fertilisation between these two chapters.

Studying cyberculture

Cyberculture, as used here, is a portmanteau term for a wide range of subjects and methodologies related to, but not restricted to, the Internet. It is typically wider than web studies or Internet studies, although also less specific than each of these and, unfortunately, more at the mercy of vagaries of fashion. As a term it obviously owes a great deal to cyberpunk, the sub-genre of science fiction that emerged in the 1980s and the history of which serves as a warning to anyone engaged in the study of cyberculture: cyberpunk had, by the 1990s, become somewhat passé, only to achieve a renewed lease of life with the release of the film *The Matrix* at the end of the last millennium.

Cyberculture, then, is a word that enjoys (or suffers from) the perception of being close to the cutting edge of cultural studies simply by the addition of the prefix 'cyber'. It is a rhetorical flourish that makes the subject more memorable and it is in this spirit that I have employed the label in these final chapters. At the same time, cyberculture is an aspirational definition: as David Bell writes in his introduction to *The Cybercultures Reader*, cyberculture attempts 'to understand the ways in which cyberspace as a cultural phenomenon is being experienced and imagined' (Bell and Kennedy 2000: 3). Cyberspace refers not simply to the medium of the Internet, but all the virtual worlds that affect our perceptions as subjects, identities created by our environment, language and social interactions: cyberculture is more specifically the study of *technoculture*, the interaction between humans and their technologies, which, since the invention of the wheel, fire-making and writing, have not simply achieved specific material aims, but also formed and transformed the physical, social and cultural fabric of the world we live in.

The use of 'cyber' as a prefix stems from cybernetics, a term coined by Norbert Wiener in 1948 to describe the field of control and communication theory, particularly the flow of information in mechanical, electronic and biological systems. This in turn is derived from the Greek *kubernetes*, or 'pilot', indicating the ability of cybernetic systems to regulate themselves, to 'navigate' processes as new information becomes available. As Timothy Leary (1991) observes, *kubernetes* becomes *gubernates* in Latin, from *gubernare*, to control or govern, and he sees in this translation a basic ideological conflict between the freewheeling pilots of the Hellenic world and the centralised regulation of the Roman imperium, the former at the centre of his utopian view at the end of the twentieth century.

The discipline of cybercultural studies (including, for the moment, more specific variants such as web and Internet studies) was dominated in its earliest years by a rather glib postmodernising tendency based on the work of Deleuze, Guattari, Baudrillard and others that, for all its claims to maintain a critical distance from its subject, adopted rather too enthusiastically the over-hyped claims of new media proponents. A good example of this is virtual reality: I remember all too well a host of newspaper, magazine and journal articles in the early 1990s that accepted that we would regularly be making virtual trips to Mars or engaging in cybersex by the end of the century before asking whether or not this was a good thing; at the beginning of the third millennium, we are either still waiting or, more typically, have continued with our old pursuits. David Silver (2000) offers a very good overview of cyberculture studies from 1990 to 2000, in which he notes three main phases to the discipline: a descriptive, popularising phase in the early 1990s, followed by a more theoretical (but still largely enthusiastic) period and, finally, an opening up of cyberculture to much more critical methods and theories by the end of the decade.

There is, then, in the early years of the twenty-first century, much less consensus about the impact and effect of new media and technologies. Nina Wakeford remarks that 'currently there is no standard technique, in communication studies or in allied social science disciplines, for studying the Web' (2000: 31). This is a good thing: the hyperenthusiastic consensus of early cyberculture studies ultimately made for dull and disappointing reading, particularly for anyone coming from a background in other disciplines where one would expect argument and controversy. For a brief period of time, a requirement for anyone engaging in critical Internet studies appeared to be the handing in of their passport for inspection by a one-party state. One of the most appealing aspects of contemporary cyberculture research is that it works less as abstract theory in search of a model, but rather begins from how people use the Internet before theorising computer-mediated communications. There are dangers with such approaches, especially as empirical research can very easily slip into unproblematic positivist assertions on the nature and status of the evidence used, but they have reinvigorated the study of cyberculture that appeared to be in danger of eliciting only negative cynicism in response to its claims for a magical 're-enchantment of the world' (Herman and Swiss 2000).

Cyberspace

Before continuing to discuss aspects of cyberculture based on notions of community, identity, gender and race, it is worth stepping back and considering how the Internet – or more particularly, cyberspace – has affected some of our fundamental notions of location, topography and perception.

As Margaret Wertheim observes in her book, *The Pearly Gates of Cyberspace* (1999), we have conceived space in radically different ways throughout history: in the Middle Ages the world was conceived as embedded in the centre of a concrete physical space that interfaced with a higher spiritual world or series of planes; and throughout the early modern period the world was transformed by a renaissance of perceptions of perspective, as well as new discoveries in space, first across the globe and then in the outer regions of the solar system. In the nineteenth and twentieth centuries, space came to be perceived as relativistic (Einstein), epistemological (Kant), psychological (Freud) and social (de Certeau) but, according to Wertheim, the important transition from a medieval to a modern world view was that we shifted from a conception of ourselves as embedded in spaces of both body and soul to one set in physical space alone.

Cyberspace draws upon these modern definitions of space, but is also held to be different, whether as emblematic of the fragmented, postmodern condition or providing a new spiritual dimension that has been missing since Columbus sailed the Atlantic and Leonardo da Vinci mapped out the distant plains and mountains of Italy. The starting point for any definition of cyberspace has to be William Gibson's 1984 novel, *Neuromancer*, which coined the term as well as initiating the genre of 'cyberpunk'. In an often-quoted passage, Gibson describes cyberspace as 'a consensual hallucination experienced daily by billions of legitimate operators . . . a graphic representation of data abstracted from the banks of every computer in the human system' (1984: 67).

As Katherine Hayles points out, cyberspace did not spring from *Neuromancer* as Athene from the brow of Zeus, but rather emerged from a complex history of technological innovations, including cybernetics, virtual reality and sociological and epistemological reactions to new forms of physical and urban space, as well as being a familiar staple of science fiction throughout the century (Hayles 1996). Nonetheless, Gibson's novel crystallised the idea of a space combining architecture, data traffic, psychosocial and epistemological frameworks, along with dystopian effects mixed with utopian possibilities.

Space and place

A ground-breaking book in the theoretical discussion of cyberspace was published by MIT Press in 1991: entitled *Cyberspace: First Steps*, and edited by Michael Benedikt, its contributors could not completely account for the reality of the World Wide Web that was emerging from its embryonic stage as the book was published, but it established some of the physical, social and metaphysical paradigms through which cyberspace continues to be discussed today.

A commonplace of discussions around cyberspace is to establish it as contradictory to physical embodiment that has its roots in Euclidean geometry reified by Enlightenment physicists such as Descartes, Newton and Leibniz. This 'real', or 'physical', world is (often simplistically) contrasted to relativistic space that in turn contributes to a cyberspace enriched by symbolic codes and information theory. More subtle accounts of this relationship concentrate on how different models of space affect our perception of that world around us: thus Euclidean space, the three-dimensional void through which matter could move and which achieved its triumph as a common-sense view of space only with Galileo in the sixteenth century, was consolidated as a theoretical model of the real world by Descartes, which was mapped out, ironically, by a free-roving 'virtual eye'. Thus the revolution in thinking about space that occurred in the seventeenth century, culminating in Newton's mechanistic model of the universe, was the result of a new way of looking at the world that took place in the sixteenth century (Benedikt 1991; Wertheim 1999).

Although this model of physical space underwent a further revolution in the twentieth century due to Einstein's theory of relativity (building on an interest in non-Euclidean geometry from the 1860s on), as several commentators have observed it has remained extremely persistent as a 'common-sense' world view, primarily because it is so effective at describing the vast majority of phenomena that we encounter. More significant, perhaps because more noticeably changeable over time, are our conceptions of metaphysical space. Aristotle had not simply rejected the notion of space as a void but, equally importantly, moved from questions of simple physics, such as the nature of space, to metaphysical considerations of the nature of the prime mover of the heavenly spheres. Probably the most important philosopher to consider the relationship between space and epistemology was Immanuel Kant. For Kant, space is a precondition of human knowledge (rejecting Newton's conception of space as a substance), providing one of the categories by which we perceive objects: objects are perceived as products of the perceiver's imagination. One of the reasons that we recognise objects as not identical is because they do not occupy the same space: the space of representation is, therefore, intimately connected with our mental representation of space.

Cyberspace theorists such as Oswald (1997), Benedikt (1991) and Heim (1991) have sought to problematise classical conceptions of space, drawing particularly on post-structural and postmodern writers such as Foucault, Baudrillard, de Certeau, Deleuze and Guattari. Thus, it is increasingly common for those discussing cyberspace to remove space from being simply the geometricisation of symbolic mathematics and resituate it within structures or webs of political and economic power, which are deterritorialised and reterritorialised by the relationship between subject and dominant economic and political groups. At the same time, perceptions of geometric space have been revolutionised by fractals, complex geometric shapes that commonly exhibit the property of self-similarity. Even when these developments in mathematics are taken into account, however, space is not simply a mathematical abstract, the void of three dimensions through which matter moves, but also that in which we *live* and, while such experiences may be described by simple laws, the end results are part of a complex system. Benedikt, drawing on Karl Popper, discriminates three types of world: the physical, the subjective and the structural.

> For Popper, in short, temples, cathedrals, market places, courts, libraries, theatres or amphitheatres, letters, book pages, movie reels, videotapes, CDs, newspapers, hard discs, performances, art shows . . . [are] the physical components of objects that exist more wholly in *World 3*. They are 'objects', that is, which are patterns of ideas, images, sounds, stories, data . . . patterns of pure information. And cyberspace, we might now see, is nothing more, or less, than the latest stage in the evolution of *World 3*, with the ballast of materiality cast away – cast away again, and perhaps finally.
>
> (Benedikt 1991: 4)

Benedikt's final assertion on the immateriality and final purpose of *World 3* evolution would appear to verify Robert Markley's assertion that the rhetoric of cyberspace removes itself from history and resists critical examination by the mystifying use of extremes of technical language, the discursive aspirations of which are criticised by Kevin Robins as utopian and largely non-verifiable (Markley 1996; Robins 1996). Benedikt does restate his hypothesis more accurately, that cyberspace does not *re*place objects but *dis*places them; nonetheless, his rhetoric shares the wilder optimism of many thinkers and writers at the beginning of the 1990s who saw the virtual reality of cyberspace as a possibility that would emerge from its chrysalis of hype at any moment.

Virtual reality

An important component of cyberspace is the notion of virtual reality (VR), which has often owed more to science fiction than fact. In his novel, *Idoru* (1996), William Gibson relates an 'alchemical' marriage between a male rock star and a woman who doesn't exist. The 'idoru' of the title, Rei Toei (a pun on the Latin *res*, or thing), is a virtual media star, a Japanese hologram who is special because she evokes emotion as much as admiration for her realistic design. Claims for virtual reality often extend it to many different kinds of representation of space, extending as far back as early cave paintings, and a desire to control such space. Rheingold has argued that our fascination with computers is part of a desire to use 'mind amplifiers', or 'power tools for the mind' that allow us to range from the microscopic and even the subatomic to the universal, creating models outside our everyday experience that can be explored (Rheingold 1991). While the common perception of virtual reality is of a fantasy environment, paradoxically VR research has more often been motivated by the need, identified by Francis Bacon, for tools to verify fallible human experience: Rheingold's 'mind amplifier' has its roots in the 'augmentative machines' (such as the telescope) referred to in the *Novum Organum* that could dispel the false 'idols' of knowledge.

VR enthusiasts at the turn of the 1990s, such as Jaron Lanier (the CEO of VPL Research who was commissioned by the NASA Ames research centre to create a data glove), Howard Rheingold and Frederick Brooks (director of the 360 operating system for IBM), tended to overestimate the possibilities of virtual reality. Rheingold has traced the history of virtual reality back to the 'Sensorama', invented by Morton Heilig in the 1950s. Heilig was a Hollywood cinematographer who responded to the 3D, stereophonic craze in movies at the time by working on a model for a screen with a 100 per cent field of vision, 180 degrees horizontally and 150 degrees vertically – such a screen, thought Heilig, would approximate how a person looks on an object in real life.

The real breakthroughs in VR, however, began to come in the 1970s at MIT, where engineers and scientists such as Nicholas

Negroponte and Ivan Sutherland worked on the 'Architecture Machine Group', adapting technology to human needs by such things as voice recognition and visual cues. Arch-Mac, as the group came to be known, produced a VR media room called 'Dataland', full of wall-size screens and monitors to track and display responses to eye movement, voice and gesture, an immersive VR environment rather than an invasive one. The notion of an environment that can respond to human actions was also at the heart of the work of Myron Kreuger, who invented the term 'artificial reality' to describe his interactive computer art shows in the 1970s. These works, such as VIDEOPLACE and CRITTER, created interactive artificial reality laboratories that could also follow people around.

While this work was entirely experimental, important developments that still determine many of our ideas about VR came out of NASA's Ames Research Center in the mid-1980s. It was at Ames that Scott Fisher from Arch-Mac and Atari built the second head-mounted VIVED (visual environment display) that also used a glove to manipulate visual images. The first, stand-alone, headset was designed by an electronics buff in Leicester, Jonathan Waldern, between 1981 and 1984. 3D sound, another important feature of immersive environments, was also developed initially at Ames. The role of NASA also indicates the importance of VR to the military, with significant work being done by the US Air Force at this time at the Human Interface Technology Lab in Seattle to create simulators to help train pilots. At the same time, Jaron Lanier, who claims to have coined the term 'virtual reality', began work on suits and gloves that would provide feedback for users (Rheingold 1991; Sherman and Judkins 1992).

One of the most important features of simulation is the attitude, or 'intentional stance' of the user. In the words of Allucquere Rosanne Stone, users require tokens – also known as 'affordances' – or handles to link the real and virtual environments, such as visual and audio clues, as well as physical feedback (Stone 1991). Such tokens may be relatively crude, although innovations in computer science seek constantly to refine the affordances provided by VR. One important principle is stereoscopic illusion, based on the difference in the angle of vision between each eye, so that alternating images can be transmitted from slightly different angles to each eye. In addition to 3D vision and audio (where sounds are reflected at different angles to the ear), another technique employed by VR is 'haptic' perception, or tactile responses to events: pressure sensors in the skin give the same type of response to any application of force, with sensations of pain or pleasure being determined by frequency.

Two other important distinctions in VR occur between simulation and modelling and immersive and invasive VR. Both modelling and simulation involve building a model of a real system with a computer program, but the difference lies in whether the user observes the model or experiences it. Regarding immersion versus invasion, the distinction lies in whether users bolt technology onto their bodies (the invasive model) or surround themselves with an 'augmented' reality that responds to actions, such as machines that power up when someone enters a room.

The digital city

Perhaps the ultimate immersive environment that questions common sense assumptions around space is the notion of the 'digital city'. As virtual reality and cyberspace employ architectural references, as well as requiring the economic resources that come from highly urbanised societies, many commentators have begun to explore the ways in which technology configures our cities. Such research often draws upon postmodern theory, such as Baudrillard's writings on simulacra, something not particularly surprising considering its use in describing the work of architects, such as Robert Venturi and Charles Jencks, from the late 1960s onwards (Docherty 1993).

Baudrillard begins *Simulacra and Simulation* (1994) with a reference to a Borges story in which the cartographers of an empire continue work on a map for so long that the political entity no longer exists. For Baudrillard, the sign has closed into a self-referential loop and, although the mind may be deceived into believing that the sign refers to something real outside the system, this is illusion: instead, what is being generated is a simulacrum. When human subjectivity itself is absorbed into this network of self-replicating digital systems, when there is no 'outside' to refer to, we live in the 'hyperreal', the best example of which is Disney: visitors to Disney, argues Baudrillard, travel there in order to convince themselves that the rest of the world is real, that they live their daily lives outside the simulation. This notion, which was pursued with greater irony in *America*, is a vision of the future as hyperreal: 'You should not begin with the city and move inwards to the screen; you should begin with the screen and move outwards to the city' (Baudrillard 1988: 56).

In the field of architecture, this deliberate confusion of space and its sign systems shares similarities with the dictum of Cedric Price, that an architectural solution may not necessarily be a building but might lie in social policy or practice. Likewise, cultural critics such as Michel de Certeau (1984) argue that we should think of the city less as a concept and more as an 'urban practice', something that cannot be totalised as a map, plan, building or model, but only experienced by the 'pedestrian rhetoric' of flows, traffic and displacement. Such thinking, influenced further by the writings of Gilles Deleuze and Félix Guattari on nomadising space in *Anti-Oedipus* (1972) and *A Thousand Plateaux* (1988), as well as Foucault's work on the use of institutional space to discipline bodies, has had an immense impact on critics exploring the way that urban space informs and is informed by cyberspace. Michael Oswald (1997), for example, has compared the virtual spaces of LucasFilms' Habitat to equally virtual malls, such as that at West Edmonton. Probably the most sustained work, however, comes from William J. Mitchell, who has explored the manifold ways in which new technologies are transforming our social, psychological and political relations in urban centres:

> The network is the urban site before us, an invitation to design and construct a City of Bits (capital of the twenty-first century), just as, so long ago, a narrow peninsula beside the Maeander became the place for Miletos . . . This will be a city unrooted to any definite spot on the surface of the earth, shaped by connectivity and bandwidth constraints rather than by accessibility and land values, largely asynchronous in its operation, and inhabited by disembodied and fragmented subjects who exist as collections of aliases and agents. Its places will be constructed virtually by software instead of physically from stones and timbers, and they

141

will be connected by logical linkages rather than by doors, passageways, and streets.

(Mitchell 1995: 24)

It has become a commonplace, then, to talk of cyberspace in terms of a transcendent topography – virtual or 'liquid' architectures. Yet there is a major difference between Mitchell's conceptual city of bits and de Certeau's urban practice. While it has long been recognised that urban spaces are infiltrated by flows of information, capital and people that regularly transform their solid geometries of stone and mortar, the consensual hallucination of cyberspace is frequently dominated by a surviving Western myth, the New Jerusalem that will survive the mutability of this world. Cyber-utopianism, as Margaret Wertheim points out, is frequently inadequate: 'while contemporary exponents of the Renaissance tradition see cyberspace as a potentially heavenly place, harking back to the earlier medieval tradition, there is every potential, if we are not careful, for cyberspace to be less like Heaven and more like Hell' (Wertheim 1999: 298).

The Internet, the public sphere and virtual communities

Oswald (1997) has discussed in detail the connections between virtual and 'Cartesian' urban spaces, drawing upon the theories of Paul Virilio (1991), Deyan Sudjic (1993) and Michael Sorkin (1992) to explore the ways in which space is tied up with our perception of it. Thus, for example, the *agora* of classical times was a space outside the city's grid and one used by strangers, encouraging commerce and communication. This *agora* was not a fixed space, therefore, but one closer to malls, such as the huge site in West Edmonton (the size of one hundred football pitches), than to government institutional structures. As Meaghan Morris remarked in her essay 'Things To Do With Shopping Centres' (1998), analysing spaces such as these indicates that this is a culture we live 'through' rather than 'alongside'.

Concerns about the role played by capitalism as represented by these malls and other, monolithic commercial spaces, have often figured in the language of the 'public sphere'. This term, derived from the German *Öffentlichkeit* in Jürgen Habermas's *The Structural Trans-formation of the Public Sphere* (1989), originated with Greek notions of citizenship centred on the *polis* (city), whereby discussions and prac-tices took place publicly and openly in an area devoted to trade and discussion, the market place, or *agora*. More than simply a place to buy and sell goods, the *agora* was the locus for the transfer of infor-mation, customs and gossip, often a field or open space on the edge of the city where citizens of the polis could meet and mix freely with travellers from neighbouring lands. According to Habermas, this combination of private trade with public discussion began again in the seventeenth century, centred on the coffee houses and salons of Europe where citizens would gather to read newspapers, consult financial information and discuss aesthetics, religion and politics. As the confidence of the middle classes grew, so their demands for the formalisation of these public spaces increased, at the same time that governments sought to control and moderate opinion via public insti-tutions. Writers such as Brian Connery (1997) and James Knapp (1997) have sought to relate explicitly new electronic media such as news-groups and chat sites to this notion of the public sphere, arguing that these technologies provide a new forum in which private individuals may discuss civic issues.

At the same time, theorists and fiction writers or film-makers often express fears about the impact of the Internet on the public *agora*. Dorothy Nelkin (1994), for example, has argued that the steady accu-mulation of larger and larger databases could lead to the erosion of democratic freedoms, while Philip Bereano (1984) observes that tech-nology has always been primarily a tool of the powerful. Frequently questions are asked about the capacity of a democratic society formed in the aftermath of the Enlightenment to control and regulate the Net, both by libertarians as an argument for less regulation, and by those who wish to preserve a status quo. As Laurence Tribe (1991) suggests, however, obituaries of the US Constitution may be premature: although it may appear anachronistic in relation to new technologies, it has long been concerned with the definition of public, social and personal practices, which operate along relational as well as geographical and topographical lines.

143

Online communities

Much ink has been spilled in recent years over the contribution of the Internet to so-called 'online' or 'virtual communities', with many commentators disagreeing over the vices and vicissitudes of online communal life, or whether such a thing even exists. Shawn Wilber (1997) points out that 'virtual community' is a much-abused phrase of which we should be more critical. Wilbur points out that there is not one notion of community, but several: community shares links with communication, though we rarely reduce it to that outside the Internet; it also involves an element of 'immersion' and usually geographical location, though we have long become used to communal experiences shared by mail or telephone; and, most significantly, since the rise of television in the 1950s we have become aware of a virtual community, such as people watching the Olympics or World Cup. As Wilbur observes, although multiple and even contradictory definitions of virtual community are problematic, they are also more useful than a single 'elegant' definition.

Probably the most influential proponent of positive arguments for the power of online communities is Howard Rheingold, whose 1995 book *The Virtual Community: Finding Connection in a Computerized World* sought to capture the Zeitgeist at the beginning of the online media boom. For Rheingold, using the WELL (Whole Earth 'Lectronic Link) as his archetypal example, '*Virtual Communities* are social aggregations that emerge from the Net when enough people carry on those public discussions long enough, with sufficient human feeling, to form webs of personal relationships in cyberspace' (Rheingold 1995: 5). The biggest breakthrough of virtual communities for Rheingold and for many users is that they transcend physical limitations of geography (and, to a lesser extent, the body); as well as the dubious advantage of being able to conduct an argument without being punched on the nose, the main benefit of community online is that people are able to communicate with like minds regardless of the accidents of physical location.

Rheingold has often been accused of a certain naivety with regard to the Net and the communities it forms, and, indeed, of pursuing the kind of blinkered, technological evangelism responsible for the hype of the Internet in the late 1990s. To be fair, ad hoc groupings of the type described by Rheingold have been growing over the last decade, for example amongst academics and fans who use the Internet as a primary mode of communication, though how such means of communication are made qualitatively different by the use of the Internet, and whether such groups are *communities*, are moot points. It is also significant that Rheingold's best example of the use of the Internet to form a virtual community, the WELL, is one that still remains tied, however loosely, to a geographical location around the San Francisco Bay area: it seems that people still like to meet face to face occasionally, as they have done since the growth of similar communication with pen pals. Michele Wilson (1997), in particular, has argued that the complete withdrawal from an embodied, political and social reality can simply result in notions of community becoming no more than an abstract ideal or even being abandoned altogether in favour of nostalgic simulacra.

Perhaps one of the most commonly experienced types of online community is in the arena of fandom. Susan Clerc (1996) has written on the formation of online fanzines as a primary means of communication, and how such communications may be gendered. Online fan forums, points out Clerc, tend to divide into two main types, following the growth of fan conventions elsewhere: guest-based forums tend to be more official, where institutions involved in the production of fans' materials organise the discussion of that material; fan-based forums, by contrast, are run by and for fans, although 'official' members such as actors or producers may also participate. Clerc notes the ways in which such forums tend to police themselves (for example, to prevent members insulting a guest) and reactions to sexual or pornographic content; the emergence of rules and conventions, which are similar to those for online gaming (MUDs or MOOs; see 'Online games' below), can be seen as one indication of the possibility for forming one type of limited community online.

Writers such as Randal Woodland (1995) and Nina Wakeford (1997) have shown how sexual communities around the gay community can form online, while Ananda Mitra (1997) demonstrates some of the interesting ways in which nationalist groupings from the Indian subcontinent can be recreated online as 'imagined communities' that may reflect and co-opt, but do not simply duplicate, the absent home-land. Some of the most disturbing elements of online communities and communication are discussed by Susan Zickmund (1997), who discusses how the Internet has transformed the radical right in the US, bringing together isolated individuals and groups across America. For Zickmund, the creation of such communities is dependent on what Wittgenstein called the 'language game', with Usenet newsgroups being particularly important to the formation and dissemination of a group identity. Indeed, she observes, 'antagonists' who enter such forums to attack racist groups are important as catalysts to the clarifi-cation of positions and ideals.

Online games

While race-hate groups represent an extreme system of language game, other forms of (sometimes more wholesome) play are very common on the Net. Computer games are almost as old as electronic computers themselves: ever since *Spacewar* was written by Steve Russell for the DEC PDP-1 mini-computer at the turn of the 1960s, games have been responsible for demonstrating hardware and software as well as tech-nological innovation (DEC requested a copy of *Spacewar* so that they could show off the capabilities of the PDP-1 to prospective customers). At the same time, games are often dismissed as a 'fringe' concern of computing or, indeed, as a vice that entraps the unwary young (and not-so-young). The explosion of arcade games at the end of the 1970s and early 1980s caused by *Space Invaders* led to calls for regulation of the 'menace' in the UK Parliament in 1981, as well as concerns in American psychology studies that such games were addictive or led to a lack of social skills. As Leslie Haddon remarks, however, 'very traditional fears about "deviancy" and working-class, male youth underlay some of the apparently new alarm about video games-playing' (Haddon, 1999: 319) (See also Herz 1997 and Cawson *et al.* 1995.)

Games, like the Internet itself, have strong connections with the military, whether it is the development of flight simulators from the US Airforce's SIMNET (acquired by Lockheed Martin in 1996) or the use of id's *Doom* for R&R by marines. As such, many of the concerns around games have linked the 'deviancy' of working-class youth with the ever-present threat of male aggression even though, as Haddon points out, statistics on actual male–female usage are hard to come by. What is not in doubt is that the average age of users has increased throughout the late 1990s, as players who first encountered games via arcades in the 1980s graduated to PlayStations and PCs in the 1990s. In addition, many of the giants of computer gaming, such as Electronic Arts and Infogrames, predict that their future profits will be generated online.

Online games have been around for years, but commercial interest in online gaming was sparked in 1993 when a free demo of id's violent, first-person shooter *Doom* was released onto the servers at the University of Wisconsin: such was the demand for the game around the world that the servers shut down within hours and *Doom*, a game promoted as shareware on magazine cover discs and across the Internet, became a giant hit. *Doom* was significant, not only for using the Internet as a distribution channel, but because it introduced a networking, player-against-player feature known as the deathmatch. Networked players could compete against each other, a factor that contributed to the game's long-term playability: once a player learnt how artificial characters reacted, a game would become tedious, so it incorporated the ability to compete against equally wily and unpredictable humans. The Internet was also important to the success of *Doom* because its open design meant enthusiasts could design their own add-ons to the game and distribute them online. This is why, according to Herz, 'the online *Doom* community transcended the mere sharing of cheat codes to become a virtual kustom kar kulture' (1997: 89–90). Pitting networked players against each other has become increasingly important to a vast array of games, whether first-person shooters such as *Quake* and *Half-Life*, strategy games such as *StarCraft* or *Civilization*, or role-playing games (RPGs), such as *Asheron's Call* or *Ultima Online*, following the traditions of MUDs.

MUDs (Multi-User Domains, or Dungeons) and MOOs (Multi-User Domain, Object-Oriented) have frequently been invoked as examples of virtual communities. Yet, while such spaces may contribute to no more than fairly innocent gaming pleasures, one famous incident known rather melodramatically as 'the Bungle Affair' and written about by Julian Dibbell in the *Greenwich Village Voice*, indicated how social conditions could form in reaction to an apparently traumatic event. Several members of LambdaMOO, a long-running, text-based MOO, found that a character called Mr Bungle could telnet in and take control of their characters, forcing them to commit lewd acts. Several participants of the MOO wished to erase the player's account, while others argued for a libertarian stance (Dibbell 1994). Habitat, a MUD produced by LucasFilm and Quantum Computer Services in 1986, was the world's first electronic environment inhabited by avatars: as with LambdaMOO, Habitat quickly developed in ways unforeseen by its creators, leading to the first virtual murder when an avatar couple were mugged (Oswald 1997).

The use of virtual worlds for illicit or unexpected purposes is nothing new. What is unprecedented is the widespread success of games such as *Ultima Online* and later imitators such as Verant Interactive's *EverQuest* or Microsoft's *Asheron's Call*, *EverQuest* being the largest online game with 270,000 subscribers a month by mid-2001. Yet, despite the growth of online RPGs and first-person games, Internet play is still something of a niche market, and predictions of a massive uptake of online gaming failed to materialise in 2000–1 (Poole 2001). Of the two million copies sold of *Half-Life*, for example, it has been estimated that only 100,000 users regularly play online, while free or low-cost subscription servers such as Barrysworld and Wireplay were cut back or closed down. Two ways in which online gaming is predicted to expand are through consoles and the growth of more casual 'family' activities, such as card games or bingo across the Internet. Nonetheless, even this area has suffered setbacks: while online games for the Dreamarena network, such as *Phantasy Star*, sold very well, Sega's decision to halt production of the Dreamcast console in 2001 placed the future of such games in doubt; similarly, Microsoft drew back from early bullish predictions about the future of networked gaming for its Xbox.

One of the most successful and fascinating examples of online gaming is *Ultima Online*, launched in 1997. The *Ultima* series of games, set in a fictional kingdom of Britannia, was devised by Richard Garriott in the 1980s, growing into a distinct and sustained alternative world. Unlike first-person or strategy games, but like many other RPGs,

Ultima Online is set in a 'persistent' universe so that, when players are not online, the game continues around them. This has added advantages for Electronic Arts, the publisher of the game, in that it encourages users (who pay $10 per month) to return to the game on a regular basis, many playing on a daily basis and averaging twenty-one hours a week online, some individuals even clocking up a hundred hours a week in the *Ultima* universe. Garriott has remarked on the surprising success of the game: Origin, the game's developer, only expected to sell 10,000 copies, but had 50,000 applications to test the game in beta, and by 2000 there were over 185,000 players on twenty-one servers around the world, generating £13 million per year.

The game is so detailed that a complex internal economic system has sprung up. Unlike more traditional RPGs, players can adopt any role within this medieval universe, including fishers, miners and blacksmiths as well as the more usual spectacular fare such as warriors and wizards. This has meant that soldiers may protect miners while the latter dig for iron ore that is then sold on to smiths for conversion into weapons. The game aroused controversy in its early years because of the practice of 'player-killing', whereby more experienced (and thus more powerful) characters would prey on greener players. Such experiences, as well as aggravations over slow or undeveloped servers, led a group of players to hack into the game's servers and parade their avatars naked around Garriott's online castle in protest at their perceived ill-treatment.

'Digital poverty'

If online gaming represents one of the more enjoyable aspect of virtual communities, the consequences of non-participation can be extremely disturbing. Nicholas Negroponte, in an article in the *New York Times* in 1997, issued a dire warning to what he called the 'digitally homeless': 'To be non-digital now is truly a new form of illiteracy. If you're a stubborn adult who insists the digital revolution is just some throwaway fad like a hula hoop, you're simply not going to have a full life' (1997: 1). It is worth bearing in mind Negroponte's audience: his readers, as he made quite clear in the article, could not be considered 'poor' in any conventional sense, but had simply failed to embrace the wonders of the 'digital revolution' promoted by writers such as Negroponte as the cure-all for late capitalism's ills – what Clifford Stoll (1995) has called 'silicon snake oil'.

What, however, of those excluded access to the digital revolution, those who do not register on Negroponte's new media radar? Even Bill Gates seems to have recognised that computers will not solve all the world's problems, when he announced that the foundation set up by him and his wife would concentrate on providing food and clean water to the world's poor. As several commentators, such as Jeremy Rifkin (1995) and Ian Barbour (1992), have observed, the spread of information technologies has not been accompanied by any obvious collapse in distinctions between rich and poor; indeed, there is plenty of evidence to suggest that the divide between the two will only increase. For most information workers, new technologies mean the decentralisation of work away from union intervention into factory conditions in the Third World, such as high surveillance, physical restrictions, and exhausting and repetitive work (Pearson and Mitter 1994).

One response to the perceived dystopia of new technology is to insist on our essential humanism. This is, for example, the route taken by Mark Slouka in his book, *War of the Worlds* (1995), and by Sven Birkerts in *The Gutenberg Elegies* (1994). Slouka, responding to what he, not entirely unreasonably, characterises as the digital fascism of West Coast technological capitalism ('You will assimilate, and have a nice day'), argues that the combination of postmodernist ideologies and cyberspace is resulting in the dispossession of our bodies as 'meat on the fringe', of our identities, and of those who fail to succeed in this 'digital hive'. Birkerts is similarly critical of the combination of deconstructive philosophies and technological applications, claiming that the pursuit of depthless self ignores the fact that there may be a difference between knowledge and information.

It is easy in some respects to see writers such as Birkerts and Slouka as reactionary, positing an essentialist humanism in response, not simply to the developments of technology, but also to advances in contemporary critical and cultural theory from which simplistic notions of artist as genius have been banished. In addition, as both writers are fully aware, to seek to banish technology (which includes the ability to make fire and the wheel as well as silicon chips) from our lives is both impossible and undesirable. Yet their critiques of a tendency towards simplistic postmodernist techno-evangelism can be seen as repeating the observations made by Fredric Jameson (1991) when he referred to postmodernism as the cultural logic of late capitalism.

Several writers have developed the socio-historical critique employed by Jameson with regard to capitalist societies by paying special attention to technology. Gary Chapman, for example, has argued that placing technology in a socio-historical context provides richer interpretations than the simpler transactional models routinely employed. Typically, transactional models of our relationships with computers concentrate only on the input and output of machines, reducing us to the status of Marcuse's 'One-Dimensional Man' and resulting in the acceptance of a '"technological imperative" that compels us to automate wherever and whenever possible' (Chapman 1994: 302). Thus, for example, we concentrate merely on the *features* of hardware and software, not whether and how computers may affect our society.

The dangers of one-dimensional thinking are that, by using computer technology to reduce pain and automate production, we lose our capabilities to engage with and analyse the social world around us, becoming cocooned in what Arthur and Marylouise Kroker (1996) call the 'bunkered self'. Michele Willson (1997) makes a similar point when she observes that the idealisation of virtual communities is resulting in a paradoxical 'thinning' of the complexities of human interaction in a social and embodied community.

Techno-Luddism

One response to such cultural 'thinning' has been to seek a more fundamental rejection of technology. 'Luddism' is often a semi-abusive term applied to those who cannot, or are unwilling to, engage with new technology. And yet there are some, particularly in the context of a wider anti-globalisation movement, who maintain a more positive attitude to what Ross (1991) calls 'technoscepticism'. Taking their lead from the organised frame-breakers, followers of Ned Lud, who operated in the textile industries of England during the early nineteenth century, some radical anti-globalisation protestors share more in common with the Zapatistas (see 'Cybercolonisation' below) than a technologically benighted old aunt or uncle, rejecting technologies because of their impacts rather than because they break commonly accepted traditions.

Neil Postman (1990) talks of technology as a 'Faustian bargain' that increases the sense of the individual at the expense of the communal, particularly since the invention of the printing press, which inaugurated the information age. Computers have increased the powers of large-scale organisations and high-level scientific researchers, but not necessarily workers, who find their private lives intruded into more and more. Not that the winners can be sure of the purpose of their technology, or how it will be used. Postman cites the example of the clock, invented by Benedictine monks who wished to devote themselves to God; today, the main use of the clock is in the service of mammon. Likewise with information: Gutenberg invented the press to extend the power of the Holy See, whereas in fact it extended the Reformation. Prior to the fifteenth century, information was scarce and valuable: ninety years after Gutenberg's invention there were eight million books in print, rising to some 300,000 new titles a year (including the one in your hands). To demonstrate the dangers of information overload, Postman conducts a humorous experiment with colleagues, in which he lies to them about stories in papers they have not read. Most people are willing to believe, or at least not disbelieve, so, as Orwell suggested, we are as naive as our ancestors in the Middle Ages, and we just use science to cover our ignorance instead of religion.

> What started out as a liberating stream has turned into a deluge of chaos. . . . Everything from telegraphy and photography in the nineteenth century to the silicon chip in the twentieth has amplified the din of information . . . We don't know how to filter it out; we don't know how to reduce it; we don't know how to use it. We suffer from a kind of cultural AIDS.
>
> (Postman 1990: 134)

An extreme example of reaction against technology is the case of the Unabomber. Between 1978 and 1995, a terrorist with a grudge against computer technology sent a series of sixteen bombs that killed three people and injured twenty-three. The Unabomber, as the American press dubbed this terrorist, concentrated on people involved in science and computing, although one of his bombs in 1995 killed a forestry lobbyist and he also caused chaos two months later by threatening to blow up a Los Angeles airliner. In June of that year, the Unabomber sent a 35,000-word manifesto, *Industrial Society and the Future*, to the *Washington Post* and the *New York Times* and said that, in return for publishing it, he would no longer use his bombs to kill people. After printing extracts, the *Post*, on 19 September, published the entire manifesto in a pull-out section jointly funded by the *Times*.

Following leads provided by his brother, David, after publication of the manifesto, 53-year-old Theodore Kaczynski was arrested as the suspected Unabomber on 3 April 1996 and tried in November. At the home of Kaczynski, a reclusive former mathematics professor, authorities found 22,000 pages of writings that provided the backbone of the government's case, with a day-by-day account of his hermit existence, including references to four of the bombings and their consequences. Kaczynski, who had studied for his Ph.D. at the University of Michigan and taken an associate professorship at Berkeley, retreated to Montana in 1971 and lived in a shack he built himself on his 1.4-acre property, attempting to return completely to nature. Kaczynski's manifesto demonstrated his commitment to a survivalist and individualist worldview that opposed all forms of modern industrialisation and corporate life. Nor was this a view particularly favourable to the Left, which Kaczynski held responsible for softening up men and women to acceptance of the machine age of the nineteenth and twentieth centuries. What is perhaps most remarkable about the career of the Unabomber, however, is that, despite the narrow range of his ideology, terrorism and extremist lifestyle, there was not inconsiderable sympathy for his views expressed by many Americans who felt that technology had come to dominate their lives excessively.

Cybercolonisation

As we saw in Chapter 1, the spread of the Internet has been a key factor in the process of globalisation, the nexus of financial, economic, political and cultural trends that aid the spread of multinational media and transnational corporations. Unlike the spread of European colonies and empires that took place against the backdrop of a struggle for power on the Continent from the sixteenth to nineteenth centuries, and unlike the ideological cold war that dominated the world for much of the twentieth century, it is often assumed that new global flows of trade, peoples and ideas take place in an increasingly homogenised environment. Events in Afghanistan at the end of 2001 may have shaken some of these assumptions, but the crude belief remains that atheist, Christian, Muslim, Jew, Hindu or Buddhist will all drink Coca-Cola and snack at McDonalds.

The threat of global monoculture, however, has generated resistance and revolt in cyberspace as well as bland acceptance. Perhaps the most surprising example was that of the Zapatistas: the Zapatista National Liberation Army (EZLN) suddenly attracted attention when it seized four towns in Chiapas, the southernmost state of Mexico, which is homeland to the indigenous Mayan population. Because it was rich in resources, the Mexican government had begun to privatise the region, a move generally seen as enabling it to exploit those resources as part of the North American Free Trade Agreement (NAFTA). While much of the rest of the world had paid little attention to the plight of the peoples of Chiapas, this was one of the first revolutionary movements to make successful use of the Internet both to organise grass-roots protest movements around the world and to publicise events taking place in Chiapas. The importance of the Net to the Zapatista movement can be overstated: it was the willingness to engage in armed struggle that brought the Mexican government to the negotiating table, but the revolutionaries also realised the potential of decentralised global communication provided by the Internet and used it more effectively than their opponents.

Cultural pluralism v. cultural imperialism

Outside specific struggles (such as that described above), the collapse of the Berlin Wall, ease of travel and a 24-hour society tend to suggest that we live in a unitary world of space and time; yet any newspaper or television bulletin will confirm the vast disparities between the haves and have-nots of this world. In the decades immediately after the Second World War, the period when old political imperialisms began to crumble and the term 'the Third World' came into use to describe the geographical distinction between the rich and poor, international communication models tended to emphasise developmental aid, a one-way transition of media and capital from the developed to the developing world. As Annabelle Sreberny-Mohammadi (1996) observes, the sense of deepening dependency enforced by this model led to a criticism of 'cultural imperialism' during the 1970s and 1980s. By the next decade, with the rise of greater free trade in media as well as other commodities, the cultural imperialist arguments that had previously raged in the UN tended to give way to models of cultural pluralism, particularly taking into account the impossibility of returning to a 'pure' and 'authentic' (that is, non-Western) culture. Nonetheless, cultural pluralism tends to neglect the tensions in media globalisation: for Sreberny-Mohammadi, a good example of this is the disparity in distribution of television receivers, with 23 per 1,000 inhabitants in non-Arabic African countries compared to 800 per 1,000 in North America in 1992 (1996: 182). Such disparity had hardly changed – if anything, had deepened – by the end of the 1990s. Unesco statistics for 1998, for example, indicated that the Democratic Republic of Congo had the lowest 'teledensity' in the world, with one phone line for 1,318 people, and all of Africa and most of central Asia and South America compared badly to western Europe, North America and Australasia.

In a remarkable essay on technology as a force for cultural imperialism, 'alt.civilizations.faq: Cyberspace as the Darker Side of the West', Ziauddin Sardar explores the Internet as a motif of what he calls 'Janus-faced' Western civilisation, projecting on the one hand innocent civilisation while on the other masking the inner, psychotic reality. While Sardar's polemic is sometimes undermined by its emphasis on the colonising power of the West as an apparently singular phenomenon (could the same projection, for example, not be found in Islamic conquests of previous centuries?), nonetheless, for the past two to three centuries Europe and North America have been predominant powers and cyberspace can easily be seen as a new frontier for domination. Indeed, Sardar, pursuing a line of thought provided by Fanon and other post-colonial theorists, considers it the ultimate such frontier in that it can be seen to extend ad infinitum; what is more, cyberspace *does* have victims, as it erases non-Western histories. Anything outside the West eventually will only exist as a digitised hologram.

More than this, cyberspace is the practice area for new military weapons, and VR constantly betrays its military origins and the West's obsession with using technology to conquer new territories. Since its military genesis, cyberspace has become the preserve of big business, promoting crime as well as the gold rush: the 'cyberspace frontier, then, is set to follow the patterns of the old West' (Sardar 1996: 22). It is hardly surprising that, in the face of an ideological struggle between Islam and the West, resistance to the Internet is often strongest in Moslem countries.

And yet the opposition of West and East, centre and periphery can be too simplistic: if Islamic countries have opposed the Internet, then pockets of resistance have equally often been found in Europe (such as in France, which for a long time not only did not care for American-English but also had its own highly developed Minitel system). At the same time, former colonies have frequently outper-formed their parent countries: Brazil, for example, has long broadcast much more television in Europe than Portugal, and, if the US domin-ates the world in terms of Hollywood films, the same cannot always be said of its television, which is often reworked for domestic audi-ences (Sreberny-Mohammadi 1996; Tunstall and Palmer 1991). In North America, Telemex has used its monopoly of the Mexican phone service to set its sights on companies north of the border (Kandell 2001), while David Sheff and others have suggested that China's slow take-up of the Internet could even be to its advantage, enabling it to learn from others' mistakes while not being saddled with out-of-date infrastructure, rather as Britain and other early industrialisers were in the twentieth century (Sheff 2001).

Jon Stratton argues that the cultural territorialisation conducted in the name of cyberspace has its origins in the nineteenth century and the telegraph, increasing the speed of communication to such an extent that 'the time taken to cross the geographical space decreases' until 'that space is decontextualized and replaced by a distinctly non-geographical hyperspace' (1997: 254–5). The telegraph functioned in the service of capitalist exchange, enabling the valued of commodities to be compared across markets; in the late twentieth century, the hyper-spatial market becomes ideal for trading in money itself. Cyberspace, then, offers 'electronic hyper-deterritorialization' (Stratton, 1997: 258), what Arjun Appadurai (1990) refers to as a 'global cultural flow'. Global capitalism, according to Appadurai, is not binary positionalities such as centre–periphery, but a series of flows: whereas previous colonies created by nation states were organised along centre–periphery lines dominated by the imperial centre, global flows are a consequence of the capitalist dynamics of nation states but place pressure on old territorial definitions, particularly across the Internet and money markets. Whereas the nation state sought homogeneity within its borders and differentiation from other states, Stratton argues that the Internet elides such formations.

Various theorists have explored the complexities of multicultural communities on the Internet. Ananda Mitra (1997), for example, has shown how different Indian communities bring with them cultural differences formed in geographical locations to newsgroups on the Internet, while Madhavi Mallapragada (2000) has followed the traces left by the diaspora of the subcontinent on the Web and in the US. The Internet is also widely used by socially marginal groups, such as different races who have experienced near-extinction at the hands of Euro-American settlers – for example, the Shoshone-Bannock tribe (Trahant 1996) or Cherokee (Arnold and Plymire 2000). Such studies often raise the question of whether the medium of the Internet has a tendency to promote or destroy indigenous cultures: compared to other media such as television or radio, the Net certainly provides a space for alternative traditions and, according to Trahant, is actually closer to the oral and pictographic forms of communication employed by native Americans and has even contributed to 'a stunning recovery' of the Cherokee tribe as part of democratic and material equalisation, particularly via gaming profits (Arnold and Plymire 2000: 192). As Chela Sandoval (1995) observes, centuries of repression and the technologies of colonisation form a new agency and consciousness in the oppressed, what she refers to as the basis of a new cyberconsciousness. Ironically, therefore, an understanding of oppression often provides the willing-ness to adapt to new technologies, even to use them against their original intentions. The culture that emerges through contact with the Internet is not necessarily the same as before, and there may be much to lament in that which passes away, but by the same token when cultures are treated as museum pieces they are probably already dead: some communities will reject the Internet as an extension of American imperialism, but others will find new ways to flourish.

Race and the Internet

Throughout much of its history, the Internet has been the preserve of white, middle-class males: by the end of the 1990s, Internet use had begun to spread to a multitude of other groups. Nonetheless, as such use still largely depends on access to expensive and difficult-to-use equipment, groups that have traditionally been underprivileged have faced additional barriers. As Oliver and Shapiro (1997) pointed out with reference to economic life in the US, often-cited examples of an expanding black middle class neglect the fact that African-Americans often accumulate much greater debt – and fewer assets – than other races in their efforts to improve their economic situation. Likewise, the vision of the Pax Americana and liberal tolerance in the States has been questioned by Lowe (1997), who describes repeated acts of rejection against Chinese, Mexicans and Vietnamese during the twentieth century. As Franz Fanon sought to explain, the attempt to set up post-colonial societies has often been undermined by the feelings of inadequacy and dependency experienced by black people after centuries of colonisation; as histories and cultures alternative to a European world-view were steadily destroyed, so the new states that emerged after the Second World War often felt that there was no option but to follow the model of the nation state. Fanon's ideas have been expanded by theorists such as Homi Bhaba (1994), who has sought to ally postmodern and post-colonial projects, and Edward Said (1994), who traced the roots of European imperialism and our relationship with a once-colonised world.

One of the claims made for the Internet, particularly following the advent of the Web, was that computer-mediated communication would render participants equal in terms of race (as well as gender and disability). The simple line was that, as with other elements contributing to identity politics, users would pick and choose racial characteristics without regard to offline prejudices. Lisa Nakamura (1995) has examined the way that race is written on role-playing sites such as LambdaMOO: players 'pass' their identity in such games, a phenomenon we shall explore in more detail in the next chapter. Racial passing is not something specific to online cultures: Randall Kennedy (1999), for example, comments on the long-perceived stereotype of the 'white negro' in the US, whose physical appearance means he or she can present him- or herself as white, but whose 'black' lineage makes him or her a negro in a racist society.

Nakamura makes the important point regarding race on the Internet that the borders and frontiers of cyberspace, which had previously seemed so amorphous, take on a keen sharpness when the enunciation of racial otherness is put into play as performance. Certain stereotypes (such as the 'exotic' Asian female) are acceptable insofar as they do not challenge the unspoken 'natural' sense of self as white. For Nakamura, race is a 'bug' in such virtual spaces, an unwanted and problematic difference that new technologies are meant to erase: the fact that it is unwelcome means that cyberspace can be as discriminatory and prejudiced as any national space, but also provides race with the potential for subversive sabotage.

While a great deal of media attention directed towards the Internet has tended to concentrate on race-hate sites, African-Americans have also begun to utilise it more positively. Black Quest (blackquest.com) and @fronet (www.afronet.com), for example, offer educational material and black interest news as well as links for business and a wide range of issues (such as families, literature, work and digital living). While @fronet serves as a portal for African-Americans, providing links for things such as discussion boards and African-American literature, it is not restricted to black interests: under the family section, for example, items for discussion deal as much with providing safe guidance to children when surfing the Web. At the same time, the site has a clear interest in outlining how the Internet can be used to provide resources for black communities and identities, with links to the Blacklist for Black Consumers (users.javanet.com/~yvonne) or slave narratives (xroads.virginia.edu/~hyper/wpa/wpahome.html), as well as the web pages of Congress members such as Jesse Jackson and Julia Carson.

Certain sites indicate the ways in which the Internet can be used positively as a tool for activisim. The Blacklist for Black Consumers, for example (strapline: 'Don't take our disposable income for granted!') lists businesses and locations users should avoid. Similarly, the Black Sisters and Brothers United Network (www.blackunitynetwork.com) is dedicated to raising black consciousness and, as its title implies, networking activists and individuals. Both sites are part of the Afro-American web ring (www.soulsearch.net/aawr), with a variety of participating sites covering politics, religion, leisure and IT interests, as well as basic commerce in anything from fashions to foodstuffs.

The growth of racial of cultural communities that position themselves as separate to a dominant European model are not restricted to African-Americans. We have already seen some of the ways in which Native Americans use the Internet as an alternative forum to broadcast and print media, and other examples are INDIANnet (indiannet. org) and INDOlink (www.indolink.com) for Indians, Kurdmedia (www.kurdmedia.com) for the Kurdish community and FuturePinoy. com (www.futurepinoy.com) for Filipinos. Such activities and sites, however, do not detract from the hegemonic nature of the white Web: unsurprisingly the most popular sites excluding search engines, according to Netmation (netmation.com), which tracks server activity, remain those of corporate multinationals such as Pathfinder (AOL Time Warner), Microsoft and Sony.

Further reading

The cultural study of the Internet has generated a large number of books and papers on computers, society and space, of which only a few are indicated here. An excellent starting point is *The Cybercultures Reader*, edited by David Bell and Barbara Kennedy (2000), while David Gauntlett's *Web.Studies* (2000) also serves as a good primer for many of the issues raised in this chapter.

Benedikt (1991) is one of the few books on cyberculture to have survived a decade and still contains some chapters on the formation of cyberspace that are worth consulting. Some more up-to-date information is contained in Bell and Kennedy, while Mitchell (1995) is thought-provoking about how the Internet may affect urban spaces;

however, probably the best text on cyberspace as a social, psychological and technological formation is Wertheim (1999).

There are a number of texts on society and the Internet: Rheingold (1995) kickstarted much of the debate around virtual communities, but has been superseded by many other writers. Anyone serious about studying the impact of new technologies on society and culture must consult Castells (1996–7), but other useful books include Dery (1994), Markley (1996), Shields (1996), Fidler (1997), Jones (1997), Porter (1997) and Herman and Swiss (2000). Many of these texts deal not only with virtual communities, but also questions about the public sphere and cybercolonisation, more useful information on which can be found in Sardar and Ravetz (1996).

Chapter 6

Cyberculture II

Identity, sexuality and
popular culture

Introduction

As we have seen when discussing race on the Internet
in the last chapter, issues of communal definition
frequently cross over into more personal areas of identity politics, while, in the topics to be outlined in this
chapter, the personal is often the political, a site for
various transactions between communities, ideologies
and societies. Over the following pages, we shall
explore some of the ways in which technoculture and
thinking about the Internet influence concepts around
individual psychology, gender, sexuality and the formation of subcultural styles.

Online identities

The basis for much thought on how the Internet is
changing our identity lies in some sort of technological
determinism, that media such as chat rooms and web
sites, or technologies such as computers and mobile
phones, influence our perceptions of ourselves and

163

how we are perceived by others. Indeed, in the century since Freud published *The Interpretation of Dreams*, deterministic notions of our sense of self have tended to prevail even in areas that explicitly reject Freudianism, such as behavioural psychology and genetics, as well as other disciplines such as Marxist politics and different schools of sociology. In these and many other fields we take it for granted that our environment has an important part to play in defining identity. As we saw in Chapter 1, technological determinism is frequently encountered when discussing the 'natural history' of the Internet and computing, but it also rears its head in discussions of human evolution: 'soft' determinism indicates probabilities rather than definite cause and effect and, in current media discussion, frequently owes a great deal to Marshall McLuhan (1962), who outlined how the print revolution of the fifteenth century enabled European reformations and renaissances in the midst of a 'Gutenberg galaxy' and began a transformation of the human nervous system into an extended information processor.

The relation between users and computer technologies in the 1960s and 1970s tended to concentrate on usability testing and notions of whether computers could display signs of artificial intelligence. Theorists also began to move into areas of psychotherapy, including Kenneth Mark Colby *et al.* (1966), Herbert Simon (1969) and Joseph Weizenbaum (1976). Important work in the 1980s and 1990s was conducted by the psychologist and sociologist, Sherry Turkle, who published results of her experiments on such things as the impact of computers on child development in *The Second Self: Computers and the Human Spirit* (1984), and summarised many theories of the effects of technology on identity in *Life on the Screen: Identity in the Age of the Internet* (1995). Turkle's main argument is that we are increasingly comfortable with taking things at 'interface value', accepting representations of reality for the 'real'; indeed, in line with much post-structuralist or postmodernist thinking over the past four decades, the real has simply become a boundary open to constant negotiation. At the same time, we often use this culture of simulation to reflect on the human, so that Turkle believes that the fear of computers as thinking machines that was prevalent in the 1970s has, by the 1990s, become a pragmatic acceptance that computers may be able to think but remain just machines: we no longer cling quite so romantically to a definition of the human as that which is capable of thought. At the same time, our relationships with computers become more subjective: we attribute personalities and reactions to them.

A surprising feature of much popular rhetoric on how computers shape our identities is the ease with which we separate our minds and bodies, what several commentators (Stone 1991; Foster 1993; Dery 1996) refer to as the 'Cartesian trick', after René Descartes whose philosophical method led him to doubt everything but the existence of a *cogito*, a thinking mind. For some writers, such as Stone, while we cannot forget the body, online communication is translating and refiguring that body into a post-human form, literally in the case of the performance artist Stelarc, who attaches external and internal prostheses to his body and hooks himself up to the Internet as a very apparent external nervous system (Stelarc 1998). For others, such as Mark Dery, Anne Balsamo (1996) and Deborah Lupton (1995), this post-human rhetoric is in bad faith: 'Sheathed in an impregnable exoskeleton, the Stelarcian cyborg is powerful but not empowered, a pharaonic monument to the mummy-like body withering inside it. . . . What is needed here is a politics of post-humanism' (Dery 1996: 165). Power in Stelarc's (and McLuhan's) musings tends to disappear, for they do not ask who builds the machines and so forget how bodies are encouraged or coerced into constructing instruments in a social space; when we treat the body like a machine we also forget that this is simply an analogy and that, in fact, we are embodied.

Perhaps the most spectacular demonstration of the objectification of the human body by new technologies is the Visible Man project (www.nlm.nih.gov/research/visible/visible_human.html). This project, presenting a dissected body that has been sliced and photographed to provide one of the most complete records of the human body ever, uses the corpse of an executed murderer, Joseph Paul Jernigan. Jernigan, a burglar who murdered a house owner, was executed in Texas in 1993, but regulation of his body did not end with his death. Jernigan held an organ donor's card: execution by poisoning made him unfit for conventional medicine but suitable for the Visible Man project. As Lisa Cartwright (1997) has observed, however, his role as a perfect cadaver came because he was stripped of his rights as a citizen by the state in accordance with processes that are usually discussed by experts behind closed doors, rather than in the public domain.

Passing and identity theft

An old joke about online identity features two dogs seated before a computer terminal: 'The good thing about the Net', says one dog to the other, 'is that no one knows you're a dog'. 'Passing', or taking on alternative identities based on differences in gender, race or more subtle characteristics, is not an uncommon phenomenon on the Net. For some commentators, it is precisely the ability of computer-mediated communication to obscure our common identities that renders this medium so exhilarating, while for others passing indicates the schizophrenic culture of the Internet and is the basis for more psychologically damaging, even criminal, hoaxes. Certainly the investment that is sometimes made in alternative online identities can be extreme, with participants spending hours every day on bulletin boards and in chat groups pretending to be someone else. Sometimes this may indeed be for criminal purposes, and several high-profile cases have focused on paedophiles pretending to be younger males and females in order to strike up friendships. More common, and considerably less harmful, is the vast number of online gamers who build up avatars of themselves in MUDs such as *Ultima Online* or *EverQuest*.

Perhaps the most interesting examples of passing, however, are those where a person devotes large amounts of time to constructing an identity that is not fantastic and is intended to delude not merely a chosen target but everyone who encounters it and often for long periods of time. One of the most famous early cases documented by Allucquere Rosanne Stone (1991) was that of 'Julie', a disabled woman who built up a wide support network through her use of computers but who was, in fact, a male psychiatrist. Many people were angry at being deceived but others, according to Stone, had quickly become used to the notion that online identity was a fluid thing. While such intense passing in the 1990s appeared to be an almost entirely male phenomenon (and probably indicative of masculine obsessions and anxieties), in a two-year period up to May 2001, thousands of visitors to the weblog, or online diary, of Kaycee Nicole followed the brave and touching account of a young girl's struggle with cancer: when members of the discussion forum metafilter.com followed up the story, however, there was no record of the young girl living in Kansas and local schools knew nothing of her. Kaycee and her mother were the inventions of Debbie Swenson, who extended the virtual lives of these two characters beyond the Internet so that, for example, the administrator of her web site, Randall van der Woning, believed that he had spoken to them on the telephone. As he recounted to journalists at the time, 'I opened my heart, and I gave of my time, money, energy, and emotional resources to help someone else. And in the end, I was burned for it' (cited in Dunne 2001: 26).

The Kaycee Nicole story illustrates some of the ways in which social and emotional interaction takes place online. Van der Woning was a Canadian living in Hong Kong, Kaycee, her mother and Swenson inhabitants of Kansas. While it may be easy to mock the apparent ease with which users are fooled by these false identities, the factors that make them possible are predominant in a large part of contemporary communication, whether by letter, telephone or, increasingly, email. As Stone remarks, based on her research into telephone-sex and VR workers, there are many times when we construct *tokens* that are recognised as representative objects of our desires, whether sexual satisfaction using verbal tokens or 3D bodies via code tokens. Tokens are condensed and need to be interpreted so that an important feature is their 'warrantability': our willing suspension of disbelief is based upon their ability to be verified. On the Internet and in virtual reality, however, Stone argues that 'warrantability is irrelevant, spectacle is plastic and negotiated, and desire no longer grounds itself in physicality' (1991: 106).

For Stone, then, certain identities are performative, arising from the attempt (after Judith Butler) to produce 'intelligible bodies' that will be understood according to a series of hyperreal signifiers. And yet, as Steve Dunne remarked of Kaycee Nicole, while we recognise that our social lives involve a series of masquerades and performances, many users of the Internet are less inclined to read personal writings critically: we still expect online communications to be unmediated in email and certain web genres in a way that we do not expect of other written forms of communication.

While passing has generally been restricted to games and forums such as newsgroups or chat sites where any potentially traumatic effects may be restricted, another new phenomenon that is far from harmless is identity theft. Drawing upon the fact that most of our communications and transactions are highly mediated, criminals may locate a fairly comprehensive description of an individual in order to engage in illicit activity, typically to take out loans or credit cards in the name of that individual but never make repayments. The victim may know nothing about the crime until they in turn attempt to take out a loan, discovering that their credit rating has been affected dramatically; financial and insurance companies involved have been unwilling to accept that such activities take place, arguing instead that victims of identity theft are attempting to evade responsibility for their actions, but the crime has recently begun to attract a great deal of attention. In one highly publicised case, Abraham Abdallah was accused of stealing the identities of Steven Spielberg, Oprah Winfrey and George Soros, using the Internet and his local library in Brooklyn to enter the financial accounts of more than two hundred people on the Forbes list of the richest in the US (Tran 2001).

Identity theft rose by over 3,000 per cent between 1999 and 2000, with nearly 26,000 cases reported in the US. Such activities do not depend on the Internet – fraud has often been perpetrated using receipts left in stores, restaurants or even discarded as rubbish. Nonetheless, a host of online databases has made it much easier to track down relevant information more comprehensively than ever, and identity theft is increasingly popular because it is perceived as low-risk. What this twenty-first century crime points to is the increasingly shadowy world that constitutes identity and that, as communities attenuate and fragment, appeals to essential characteristics and personality make less and less sense: we emphasise our individuality at the same time that we have become more reliant on institutional organisations and databases to validate who we are in order to participate in a consumer society (Lockard 1997).

Artificial intelligence

If passing is – for the moment – an activity engaged in by people extending online the sort of performances we take for granted in a wide range of social occasions, the thought that machines may be able to pass for humans has, traditionally, been a subject arousing much greater anxiety. In May 1997, the supercomputer Deep Blue defeated the reigning chess champion, Garry Kasparov, the first such defeat in a regulation championship (Khodarkovsky and Shamkovich 1997). At the time, many commentators saw this as a significant step in the evolution of machine, or artificial, intelligence. Marvin Minsky, however, the professor at MIT who first built a 'neural network' capable of learning in 1951, remarked that, while 'we have collections of dumb specialists in small domains, the true majesty of general intelligence still awaits our attack' (cited in Stork 1996).

The complexity of constructing an artificial intelligence (AI) is due very much to that of defining a general theory of intelligence, although a very simple test of AI has existed since 1950, when Alan Turing outlined what has since become known as the Turing Test in his paper 'Computing Machinery and Intelligence'. This test consisted of an 'imitation game', in which a person would communicate with a computer and another human being via a terminal: if the person was unable to distinguish which respondent was human, Turing suggested that the computer could be regarded as intelligent.

The Turing Test has been criticised a number of times for failing to be a real test of intelligence, most famously in John Searle's example of the Chinese Room (1982). Searle uses the analogy of a room containing one person and a large number of boxes, each of which has a specific Chinese character depicted on the side. On one wall are two slots, through one of which the person receives slips of paper; once they have matched each slip of paper to one of the boxes and taken out a corresponding note, the room's inhabitant pushes this note through the second slot. To someone outside the room, argues Searle, it would appear that the person inside the room could understand Chinese, as correct replies came in response to the questions on the first slip, yet this is not the case. Yet, while computers may not possess self-consciousness, Minsky (1982) has also suggested that humans do not possess complete consciousness: for example, we find it difficult to explain how we recognise what we see, how we choose the words we speak or how we make generalisations. At least since Freud, even in the human brain intelligence has not been recognised as the same thing as consciousness.

Minsky and other theorists, such as Hans Moravec (1999) and Ray Kurzweil (1999), have explained the conditions under which machine intelligence can progress. The example of Deep Blue's chess game against Kasparov is indicative of recursive procedures, that is, all possible answers to a problem (such as possible chess moves) are called and the best one selected. Recursion works best with problems with clearly defined answers, but not all problems are defined this way and so a great deal of work has involved neural nets that emulate the computing structure of the human brain: each input representing a problem to be solved is randomly connected to other simulated neurons and, as wrong answers come through, the responses from these are weakened while those from correct inputs are strengthened. Such neural nets have shown themselves to be powerful enough to emulate a wide range of human pattern-recognition faculties and even learn. As James Bailey (1996) has remarked, we have tended to consider rational thought as the pinnacle of human mental achievement, but if by this we mean logical processing then we are likely to be left far behind by computers. Bailey points to alternative measures of human intelligence, such as Schopenhauer's definition of intelligence as the power of the will, drive and emotions.

Regardless of whether recursion and neural nets are capable of generating 'true' intelligence (regardless of consciousness), it is likely that we will, in the very near future, come to regard computers as intelligent, what is referred to by psychologists as our 'intentional stance'. Such assumptions come into play with regard to pets and other animals without reference to any objective measure of their intelligence or consciousness, and a computer that is able to pass the Turing Test is likely to emerge on the Internet. In 1990, Hugh Loebner offered a prize of $100,000 to the first computer system to pass the Test and, each year, $2,000 is offered to the most human-like computer. Thus far such systems work best when the human interrogator hits a pre-programmed phrase, but tend to have difficulties in sustaining coherence across long conversations. This has not prevented a proliferation of AI programs appearing on the Internet: the 'Eliza' programs provided one of the first attempts to understand natural language and can be accessed at www-ai.ijs.si/eliza/eliza.html; some more recent (and successful) examples include ALICE (www.alicebot.org) and Minsky's Start System (www.ai.mit.edu/projects/infolab/start.html). A comprehensive list of 'chatterbots' is maintained by Simon Laven at www.simonlaven.com.

While AI research from the 1960s through to the 1990s tended to concentrate on the search for a useful definition of intelligence, probably the most significant feature of AI online is that avatars, agents and bots erode any essence of personality and identity as intrinsically human. As we have seen with the phenomenon of passing, there is a strong element of artifice in many online identities, a performance principle that we have acclimatised ourselves to in social situations writ large; likewise, many of us have probably often been engaged in conversations in chat rooms and bulletin boards with fellow human beings who would fail the Turing Test in any reasonable world. While computer software and hardware may fail stringent tests of intelligence for some time to come, it is very likely that we shall treat the agents and bots that collect and collate information for us online as companionable in the very near future.

Popular cyberculture and postmodernism

Historically, 'popular' culture has referred to oral and folk, as distinct from 'high' literate, culture and, by the early twentieth century, was often considered alongside or confused with 'mass' culture. Its study has changed greatly, particularly following the work of sociologists, such as the Chicago School, and cultural studies theorists, such as Richard Hoggart and Raymond Williams in the 1950s. After this, the study of everyday experience, style and culture was taken much more seriously and, more recently, postmodernist fascination with popular culture has seen within it the possibility of subverting or inverting cultural elites.

During the twentieth century, it became clear that, for industrialised countries, the earlier relationship between popular and oral culture was a problematic one, and communication theorists and sociologists began to distinguish the various components of a mass society, such as the distinctions between mass communication (reaching many individuals) and the mass media (such as the radio and press, designed for mass production but not necessarily reaching large numbers of people). Early theories on the relationship between the mass media and popular culture tended to focus on theories of uses and gratifications, that is, empirical research into how people used the media and to what effect. Such uses range from the very simple (to be amused) to the more complex (to feel part of a community, or to see authority figures exalted or deflated); it is not always possible to gain a consensus view of a particular use or gratification provided by a popular form, but this approach is important for directing us away from notions of intrinsic (and often poorly theorised) aesthetic or ethical values (Berger 1998).

As the study of popular culture has become more legitimate, many of the old certainties of modern industrial societies have begun to break down: whereas members of the Frankfurt School were very critical of the 'culture industry' as anti-Enlightenment (Adorno and Horkheimer 1972), the pervasiveness of popular media culture has made it central both to people's lives and to the study of ways of communication and constructing meaning (Strinati and Wagg 1995). By the 1990s, the television set had found its way into 98 per cent of British homes, and by 2001 over half the British population said that they used the Internet in some shape or form. If contemporary theories of popular culture question easy assumptions about the relationship of such a culture to the elite establishment, it should not be automatically assumed that popular culture is intrinsically subversive. Simon During (1977) has usefully defined what he calls the 'global popular' formats, such as Hollywood blockbusters, which originate as part of corporate globalisation but which are also genuinely popular *because of*, not in spite of, their often reactionary nature in support of authority.

Such observations should warn us against the dangers of assuming that mass participation in the Internet is to be rejoiced in, and that the ability to communicate without an intermediary such as a publisher or television company is politically radical. Nonetheless, in the decade since the Internet has become a mass medium it has been taken up for genuinely popular uses; in many cases, this is a transfer of production and distribution techniques developed in other mass media – sports channels, or the use of webcasts to transmit episodes of the British TV show *Big Brother*. On the other hand, the Internet is also a mass medium in which two-way communication can be facilitated in a way that has not been available to those media that supplemented and supplanted oral culture, such as print and broadcasting (Millard 1997).

Pop memes

One of the most interesting things about the Internet is the way in which crazes spread, flourish and fade with an apparent life of their own. One way of thinking about these communication complexes is as *memes*, a term devised by the geneticist Richard Dawkins to refer to cultural units of replication such as songs or recipes. The notion of memes also owes something to the linguist Hjelmslev's classification of *monemes*, or significant units of meaning, for example the term 'mare', which consists of the monemes horse and female (Barthes 1973). Like a gene, a meme can 'mutate', typically through accidental miscommunication or invention and innovation.

Examples of memes have included the Hamster Dance (www.hamsterdance.com), Jennicam (www.jennicam.org) and 'Mahir', a Turkish man whose home page 'Welcome to my home page!!!!!!!!! I kiss you!!!!!' tickled the collective Web fancy. A more recent example that also demonstrates how memes can spread across the Net is the case of *Zero Wing*, a game developed for the Sega Genesis console in 1990. As a platform, the Genesis had been most successful in Japan and *Zero Wing* was one disposable space opera game that had some success before being completely forgotten – until the spread of email and the Web. The narrative of *Zero Wing* included cut scenes and stills in a Manga cartoon style, accompanied by a series of captions that had been very badly translated from the original Japanese. It was this text that contributed to the transient success of *Zero Wing* as a cult phenomenon:

In A.D. 2101
War was beginning
Captain: What happen?
Operator: Somebody set us up the bomb.
Operator: We get signal.
Captain: What!
Operator: Main screen turn on.
Captain: It's you!!!
Cats: How are you gentlemen!!
Cats: All your base are belong to us.

It was this final phrase, 'All your base are belong to us', that became the keynote of the phenomenon, a tribute to the globalised and ironic nature of the Internet as a communications medium. As well as being pasted into emails and web sites, the phrase 'All Your Base' appeared on doctored images, posters and advertising. As Rich Johnston remarked in *The Guardian*, this craze was all the more remarkable for involving neither gratuitous sex and violence, but was simply an in-joke that, for a short space of time, became 'one of the most requested [phrases] on internet search engines across the world' (2001: 4).

'All Your Base' began life in the middle of 2000 as a textual joke that then began to mutate in a number of ways at the turn of 2001. Appearing on message boards such as Tribalwar.com and Popbitch. com, variations included Bart Simpson writing it on the Springfield Elementary blackboard, and President Bush's face appearing next to the phrase. Its repetition in *Invasion of the Gabber Robots* by Laziest Men on Mars made that track one of the most popular downloads on Napster for a brief while, and web sites distorted the slogan, as 'All Your Turkey Basters Are Belong To Us' or 'All Your Base Are Belong To Darius'. The phrase and image from *Zero Wing* even made the front cover of *Time*.

Johnston has commented on the speed with which the 'All Your Base' phenomenon emerged and disappeared: this was not engineered by a marketing department (the struggling Sega announced that its Dreamcast line was to be discontinued just as it was receiving the best publicity in years for a console, albeit one ten years out of date);

at the same time, as fellow *Guardian* writer Charlie Parker remarked on his site www.tvgohome.com, overt reference to this particular meme did not help those in the media who tried to hijack the craze to parade themselves as cool. Businesses and the media have attempted to use the way in which the Internet transmits these Chinese whispers, what is now known as 'viral marketing' but what used to be called 'word of mouth'. It can be very difficult, however, to control the spread of information across the many-headed (and multi-mouthed) Internet.

Postmodernity and the Internet

Over the past decade, many commentators on the Internet have emphasised its fragmentary nature in contrast to other mass media. If the Net is looked upon as a medium that carries the potential for creating a new civil franchise, then typically it is less the single, coherent society envisaged by modernism and more the multiple communities that can, for convenience, be labelled postmodern. Postmodernism is a controversial term: for some it is simply a historical period that follows modernity (associated with the period from the Enlightenment to the mid-twentieth century); for others, such as Jean-François Lyotard (1984), it is a 'condition' associated with the fading of progressive modernity, the end of totalising explanations or 'grand narratives'. For critics, definitions of postmodernism are so varied that the term can be used to mean anything, and Fredric Jameson (1991) has argued that, rather than replacing modernism, it is actually the cultural dominant of late capitalism as an advanced form of modernism. Against this, sociologist Todd Gitlin offers a working definition of postmodernism as that which 'self-consciously splices genres, attitudes, styles' and relishes 'the blurring or juxtaposition' of forms, stances, moods and cultural levels (1989: 52).

If there is such a thing as postmodernism, then, it is characterised by a blurring and fragmentation of boundaries. On the level of mass media, we are less likely to watch or listen to national networks on television or radio, but instead pursue niche media on cable, satellite and, indeed, the Internet. Some have even argued that this fragmentation is intrinsic to modern media. David Lyon (1998), for example, has suggested that, as organisations seek as much information as possible to minimise risk, according to complexity theory more information makes systems unstable and chaotic.

Ien Ang (1996) has built this into a theory of postmodern audiences: most current communication theory seeks to reduce complexity, using models that privilege the sender and the *efficiency* of communication; even alternatives such as those proposed by John Fiske (1987) maintain a binary opposition between sender and receiver, one that is simply reversed to privilege the audience. For Ang, communication must be based on notions of radical uncertainty and indeterminacy of meaning. One consequence of this is that, as postmodern capitalism seeks greater information for hegemonic purposes, it ironically makes its system more unstable. One such instability is planned obsolescence, the exploitation of the pleasure principle to drive productivity, not simply by limited needs but potentially limitless desires and wants. At the same time, then, that capitalist postmodernity creates an integrated global village, its audience appears more fickle because the matrix of possible responses becomes ever more heterogeneous.

The negative side of such postmodern fragmentation is the collapse of any sense of community, the isolation of individuals who may be more easily manipulated to pursue manufactured desires. This is not necessarily a process that can be controlled by the multinational corporations releasing those desires: a common complaint about Hollywood is that 'no one knows anything', and the same is often true of the Web. Viral memes that demonstrate a life of their own can in some cases be initiated by big business, but for every successful site that generates hype there are dozens of failures. Another fear expressed about this homogenisation is that users of the Internet will only congregate with those who share similar tastes and opinions, taking over what was previously the function of national ideologies. As Jon Stratton (1997) observes, the nation state sought homogeneity within its borders and differentiation from other states, but the Internet elides the formation of nation states. Instead, audiences and communities fragment into competing or co existing subcultures, few if any of which can claim real dominance over cyberspace.

Cybersubcultures

In the 1980s, a number of participants on Usenet, who wished to engage in forms of communication from simple chat and gossip to intense debate around areas of personal interest, discovered that there was no easily identifiable place for discussion threads in the established hierarchy of comp, rec and soc newsgroups. The way forward was to establish an entirely new, portmanteau category, alt, which very quickly became the largest (and often the liveliest) collection of groups. Alt, for alternative, was seized by the media in the mid-1990s as the perfect expression for some of the cultural formations of the Internet: alt.culture. Although computer enthusiasts were gradually moving to a more central stage in society, reflecting the increasing importance of information technology, computers and the Internet to economic, political and social life, large swathes of the computer-using community were still perceived as somehow subcultural.

What is a subculture? It is to be distinguished from the 'public', the collective body of responsible citizens engaged in rational debate via democratic channels and communicative organs, such as the press and certain forms of broadcasting, as outlined by Habermas especially; it is also different to the 'masses', those politically manipulated and irrational groups explored in particular by the Frankfurt School. A subculture is probably most easily identified as a community, although one that is contingent, impermanent, less closely tied to kinship relations and geographical proximity, and this indeed was the way in which subcultures were initially studied by sociologists at the University of Chicago between the 1930s and 1960s. Subcultural theorists, particularly those identified with the Birmingham Centre for Contemporary Cultural Studies (CCCS), established in 1964, drew upon Marxism and the Frankfurt School to emphasise the disaffection, resistance, style, rituals and youth of subcultural movements, for example in the work of Dick Hebdige (1979). Although later writers criticised the CCCS for privileging style and youth over substance and for neglecting how far resistance could be manipulated, exploited and even created by the media (Cohen 1972; Clarke 1981; Stratton 1992), in the second half of the twentieth century subcultures came to be identified with social groups that are in some way deviant from the perceived norm, are indeed subaltern, subordinate or subterranean (Gelder and Thornton 1997).

Technology, particularly as it provides channels for communication and consumption via music, film and television, often has an important part to play in the formation of subcultures, and the Internet has provided a particularly rich ground for so-called cybersubcultures. Arturo Escobar (1994) argues for the importance of establishing an 'anthropology of cyberculture', one based on (after Paul Rabinow) theories of *biosociality* and *technosociality*, that is, how the production of life, society and nature may be affected by biological and technological interventions. As Foucault argued that modernity brought with it particular arrangements of life, labour and language, Escobar suggests that these are still being modified by cyberculture, enhancing the transformation of the world away from a sphere of the socius (as existed in medieval societies) to one based on production and therefore the appropriation (and destruction) of nature in the service of deterministic laws. The effects of such transformations have an impact on industrialised society that, since the days of the Chicago School, has been seen as responsive to sociological, anthropological and ethnographic analysis.

Arthur and Marilouise Kroker (1996) have described the danger of a schizoid personality created by new technologies as the 'bunkered self', amenable to modern technosocial criteria of production that substitute interaction with others for digital, global communities without people. Less pessimistic, and closer perhaps to the real work of defining subcultures, are the slightly tongue-in-cheek categories outlined by Deena and Michael Weinstein (1997): 'Cyber-hippies', for example, look to the Net as a means of overcoming human failings, liberating imagination in cyberspace where the Net is the 'nervous system of heaven'. Of the other subcultural groups, 'Net defenders' do not value the loss of humanity, but see the potential of the Net as that which makes possible voluntary, 'anarcho-democratic' communities, an idealism and utopianism refuted by Marxists; Net defenders may place the Net in a social capacity, but remain bourgeois individualists, while 'Net Marxists' seek to engage the Net in a revolutionary praxis rather than simply criticising from the sidelines like more traditional Marxists. In contrast to Marxists, 'Net promoters' dismiss communism as a failed agenda and also cyber-hippies as irresponsible counter-culture types: capitalism and cyber-populism will provide empowerment, a positive agenda rejected by 'hacktivist' and nihilistic cyberpunks who will just use what they can get.

Outside such attempts to categorise overall ethnographies of Internet usage and subcultures, much valuable work has been done on the microeconomic scale, studying small groups such as fan news-groups and zines (Clerc 1996), feminist-oriented sites (Bassett 1997) and those aimed at sexual subcultures, such as gay and lesbian sites (Wakeford 1997; Woodland 1995; Foster 1993), as well as some of the more disturbing groups dedicated to promoting race hate or other forms of discriminatory activity (Zickmund 1997; Whittaker 2000). As with a great deal of work elsewhere on subcultures and segmented audi-ences, empirical research into specific activities and groupings is frequently more illuminating than large-scale attempts to define mass social trends and operations.

Alternative sexualities and cyberqueer

Some of the key areas for subcultural formation include aspects concerning cultural production, such as music, film, written texts or games, which may be closely allied to fandom, political or pseudo-political activities (including issues such as religion) on what have traditionally been identified as left or right, and sexual groupings. There are some key dangers in identifying activities by, for example, gay and lesbian Internet users as belonging to a subculture, particularly when this sees homosexuality as something intrinsically subcultural. Yet the movement towards cultural and community groupings that fulfil the definition of a subculture as a 'population segment', in the rather neutral language of Arnold Green (1946), is helpful when distin-guishing such groups from other sexual activities on the Net that may not necessarily have any communal features, such as the distribution of pornography or 'tinysex'. Theorists such as Laud Humphreys (1970) and Jeffrey Weeks (1987) have used concepts around subcultures to provide a home for homosexual studies.

One of the reasons for using queer theory to distinguish sub-cultures on the Net is because it has become increasingly concerned with sexual and identity politics, with a much clearer articulation of the identity of individuals and groups against a heterosexist norm. Obviously, sexuality is key to this particular formation (which is not necessarily true of other subcultures) and Nina Wakeford (1997), for example, has criticised cyberqueer studies for concentrating on the sexual at the expense of the economic and political. Nonetheless, despite their infancy, cyberqueer studies have seized on the Internet as a serendipitous example of how alternative communities can flourish outside dominant norms.

Randal Woodland (1995) has observed how Internet chat rooms, bulletin boards and web sites can function as a kind of 'third place' for gay men and women, an informal public place, distinct from both home and work, as envisioned by Ray Oldenburg. Of the online services Woodland discusses, such as ModemBoy, AOL and LambdaMOO, some retain tight control and others are more anarchic, but all use spatial metaphors to indicate purpose and ethics, such as Locker Rooms (ModemBoy) or 'private' areas (AOL); such metaphors constitute (often unspoken) rules about the types of discourse that are permitted or constrained, to the extent that a service such as AOL, which officially prohibits sexual activity online, permits it tacitly in private. Woodland sees the initial impetus in 'queerspace' as the need to set up a 'safe' environment, and that, while these places may be transitory, the ability to express identity freely does lead to the shaping, testing and transformation of individual and communal identities.

Cyberpunk

While the subcultures discussed above are of interest to this book because they use the Internet, all pre-date it and can easily be conceived of as groups outside of and extrinsic to the Net. The same is not necessarily true of cyberpunk: cyberpunk, which combines elements of genre, lifestyle and subculture, did not exist before the Internet and one of its defining features is a close association with cyberspace, a term that was coined by William Gibson, an author frequently associated with cyberpunk.

The term cyberpunk was first used by Bruce Bethke in his 1982 story 'Cyberpunk' and was picked up by Gardner Dozois to describe a literary movement centred on writers such as Bruce Sterling, Rudy Rucker and, most famously, William Gibson, whose novel *Neuromancer* 'definitively shaped' cyberpunk. As a subgenre of science fiction, cyberpunk deals with systems of technology, economics, sociology and politics in which multinational corporations control densely populated urban environments that owe much to late twentieth-century Japanese society and the west coast of the US, as well as to SF films such as *Metropolis* and *Blade Runner*. Usually set in an usually unspecified near future, the 'punks' of these technological systems are nearly always on the edge of legitimate society, and are more often than not hackers who use their technological skills to survive in the interstices of these urban futures. Stylistically, cyberpunk fiction owes much to other types of generic writing, such as the western and crime novel, as well as to other SF forms: using devices such as nearly recognisable brand names to orient the reader in an almost explicable environment, Gibson himself has commented that the techniques he sought with *Neuromancer* and early stories such as 'Johnny Mnemonic' owed a great deal to the novels of Ian Fleming and Raymond Chandler. At its worst, cyberpunk forms a subgenre that is easy to pastiche, as the writer Orson Scott Card has remarked: 'Splash some drugs onto brain-and-microchip interface, mix it up with some vague sixties-style counterculture, and then use really self-conscious, affected language, and you've got cyberpunk' (1990).

Prototypes of cyberpunk include Alfred Bester's *Tiger! Tiger!*, the cut-up novels of William Burroughs, and new wave writing of the 1960s and 1970s, such as that of Samuel R. Delaney and J.G. Ballard. Cyberpunk is also frequently referred to as a version of postmodern fiction but, more significantly, has also been envisaged as a lifestyle and even a political movement. Bruce Sterling was at the forefront of this development: as well as helping to shape the literary movement through his influential anthology *Mirrorshades* in 1986, Sterling (1992) has argued that the role of technology in determining all aspects of our world must be engaged with and utilised or resisted. Norman Spinrad (1990) has also argued that the appeal of much cyberpunk is that it provides a survival of the romantic impulse combined with science and technology. Ironically, then, a movement that appears to embrace posthumanism offers a humanist counter-insurgence, probably most clearly in the work of Gibson (Sterling's novels, by contrast, are probably closer to the machine and certainly welcome the future world more enthusiastically); such resistance owed much to the hacker ethic promoted by writers such as Steven Levy.

While hacktivism can easily be overstated as a means of political resistance and subversion, subcultural tendencies may still be important in providing a *protopolitical* language: 'If hackers lack a "cause", then they are certainly not the first culture to be characterized in this dismissive way: the left in particular has suffered from the lack of a cultural politics capable of recognizing the power of cultural expressions that do not wear a mature political comment on their sleeves' (Ross 1991: 260). Like both Romanticism and hacking, however, cyberpunk unfortunately seems to espouse a certain kind of machismo – a geek machismo in this case – with there being few female writers in the genre (notable exceptions being Pat Cadigan and Elizabeth Hand, author of *Winterlong*), and the genre has been accused of pandering to masculine fantasies, particularly in its depictions of heavily fetishised women (Springer 1996; Nixon 1992; Foster 1993).

Significantly, many authors who were viewed as central to cyberpunk announced its death in the 1990s: like the earlier version of punk music, it appeared that the genre had to self-implode once it became more mainstream. Certainly the term has become a fetish and cliché and it certainly is no longer fashionable to announce that one is a cyberpunk. One typical exception, always in search of a craze to latch on to, was Timothy Leary (1991), who argued that cyberpunks were 'pilot-people', guiding us to decentralised self-reliance. And yet the death of cyberpunk appeared to be rather premature by the end of the decade, following the release of *The Matrix* by the Wachowski brothers. Drawing upon the style, imagery and plot devices of Gibson's and Sterling's fiction, as well as more disparate elements such as *Terminator*, *Blade Runner*, kung fu movies and *Alice in Wonderland*, *The Matrix* wore its cyberpunk and postmodern heart on its sleeve. Ultimately, the futuristic gloss covers a very conventional messianic, even Christian, narrative of one hero redeeming his world: cyberpunk may not be dead, but its existence as a fringe subculture must be called into question.

Cyberfeminism

Women and the Internet

The relationship of women with technology has often been perceived as a problematic one. In a world where boys and toys go together like a horse and carriage, and in a domain emphasising skills in hardware or software engineering (which have until recently remained the preserve of men), women are usually assumed to be the losers.

This is not, however, automatically the case. Although most inventors and engineers associated with the computer revolution have been men, women have also been involved with computers since their inception. When Charles Babbage wished to publicise his Analytical Engine, it was Ada Lovelace, the daughter of the poet Lord Byron and Annabella Milbanke Byron, who translated and extended an essay by the Italian mathematician and engineer Luigi Federico Menebrae (Plant 1997; Woolley 1999; Swade 2000). Grace Murray Hopper, a mathematician and lieutenant in the Naval Reserve, coined the term 'bug' to describe computer malfunctions while working on the Mark I, before going on to devise the first compiler, a program that translates commands from English into machine code. Before the widespread use of electronic computers, a 'computer' was usually a person or bank of people performing calculations by hand, many of whom would be women. Indeed, Sadie Plant has argued that, far from being backward in the use of computer technology, the demands of the Internet for linguistic and communication skills, as well as multitasking, are better fulfilled by women (Plant 1996).

At the end of 1998, International Data Corporation (IDC) predicted that women would overtake men as users of the Internet in the United States in the following year (from only 3 per cent in 1995), a prediction that was repeated for the United Kingdom in the middle of 2000. The validity of such predictions are highly suspect, based, for example, on the growth of computers sold into homes, as well as the extension of the Internet into a wider range of jobs, and revised statistics placed the ratio nearer 35 : 50, with under-eighteens separated into another category accounting for approximately 15 per cent. Nonetheless, a report by the computer company Hewlett Packard and *Working*

Woman magazine in 1999 claimed that women were more enthusiastic about technology than men, and the National Organization of Women (NOW) indicated that many of its members viewed new technologies as a primary means of enhancing employment opportunities.

Although technology and women's perceptions of technology may be changing, the process is not a straightforward one. Despite the closing of the gender gap in terms of technology use, the number of women pursuing careers in the higher echelons of the computer and Internet industries still lags behind that of men. A Women in Technology conference at Santa Clara, California, in 2000 attempted to boost the number of women engaging with science and technology, but a report commissioned by the AAUW Education Foundation Commission on Technology, Gender, and Teacher Education reported that girls were critical of a culture based on dull programming classes and violent computer games.

Not that feminist issues around the Internet and technology are restricted to the question of access, important as this is. The growth of telecommunications and digital media during the final decades of the twentieth century has also prompted many feminists to use the Internet as a model for debating issues about identity, communication, power and sexuality, not only as a testing ground for theories, but also as a means of re-envisaging gender roles in the twenty-first century.

The feminism in cyberfeminism

Cyberfeminism has developed against a backdrop of wider post-feminist debates, which in turn have evolved from the positions taken up by liberal and radical feminisms from the 1960s onwards. Feminism has been a particularly rich source of criticism and philosophy in a wide range of fields such as literary and cultural theory, sociology and politics.

The eruption of 'second wave' feminism in the 1960s may be seen to have worked in two broad groups. Liberal feminism protested against the failure in the US to deliver to women promises of independence, autonomy and fulfilment made after the Second World War, for example in Betty Friedan's 1963 book *The Feminine Mystique*.

Such feminism may be defined as a concern with equality, but critics of liberal feminism have pointed out that equal pay has not been achieved in the intervening decades, and that the perception of 'affirmative action' as reverse discrimination can lead to a backlash (Jagger 1994). Radical feminism is concerned less with equality and more with emphasising the diversity and difference of women's experience, and sees oppression of women under patriarchy, in public and private life, as the most widespread form of domination, as in Kate Millett's *Sexual Politics* (1969), Germaine Greer's *The Female Eunuch* (1970) and Eva Figes's *Patriarchal Attitudes* (1970).

Post-feminism, which has aroused considerable controversy due to the fact that it is sometimes marked by a withdrawal from sexual politics (as in Friedan 1981 and Greer 1984), also has a more positive aspect that claims its grounds as part of postmodernity, drawing particularly on the work of French psychoanalytical feminists, such as Hélène Cixous and Luce Irigaray, as well as other post-structuralist and postmodern theorists, such as Michel Foucault, Jacques Lacan and Gilles Deleuze. Such post-feminism seeks to deconstruct typical boundaries of identity, arguing not for an equality of gender, but for the fragmentation of ideals and narratives of the body that have included definitions of gender (Braidotti 1994).

Regarding new technology, while a particularly strong ecofeminist movement developed in the latter part of the twentieth century that strongly opposed the environmental damage caused by industrial society, cyberfeminists such as Sadie Plant and Donna Haraway argue that histories of women's liberation and technological development are 'woven together', and that their subjectivity can transform the development of technology (Plant 1996, 1997; Harraway 1991). Plant has been criticised by Judith Squires (1996) as offering an apolitical version of feminism, and Claudia Springer (1996) has offered one of the strongest critiques of a depthless and far-from-liberatory cyberfeminism, demonstrating how sexual stereotypes survive even in cyberspace. An interesting recent attempt to negotiate the discourses initiated by Plant and Haraway is in the work of Nina Wakeford (1997), who concentrates on the social experience of women using the Internet to create their own spaces and networks.

Cyborgs, monsters and women

The notion of the discontinuity of identity, brought into focus by post-industrialisation and new technologies, can be linked to one of the most influential theories of cyberculture in recent years, that of the cyborg. Although post-human notions of the body and human identity have circulated with regard to films such as *Blade Runner* and *Terminator* (Bukatman 1994; Pyle 1993), the theory has had its widest repercussions in relation to cyberfeminism, particularly following the publication of Donna Haraway's 'A Cyborg Manifesto' in 1991. Haraway positions herself as a socialist-feminist offering an ironic myth of the 'blasphemous' cyborg, a monstrous hybrid that refuses to obey traditional boundaries, whether sexual, organic or social. While admitting that cyborgs are the 'illegitimate offspring' of a patriarchal military, Haraway finds them the most useful figures to deconstruct patriarchal myths of social, biological and gendered order. What is more, as technology extends throughout our lives so that we cannot escape its domain, whether as pacemakers installed to save our lives or pens to sign our names, there is a sense in which we are all cyborgs (Haraway 1991).

Haraway uses post-colonial critiques of feminism and Marxism to demonstrate that these theories have become monolithic, ignoring difference in their desire to identify solidarity against oppression. In contrast, she uses Chela Sandoval's argument that 'women of colour' produce analyses of power that are not totalising as the basis for her own discussion of the role of cyborg feminism, as well as drawing on Irigaray's analogy of women as flows and webs of meaning. Women, suggests Haraway, are assigned places in the 'integrated circuit', the webs of power that extend through the world, but can use networking to permeate bodies, identities and space, building their own circuits: 'Networking is both a feminist practice and a multinational strategy – weaving is for oppositional cyborgs' (1991: 307).

While critics such as Springer and Squires have attacked what they perceive to be the apolitical 'cyberdrool' of Haraway and Plant as offering a meaningless, utopian vision of feminism, Sandoval returned the compliment to Haraway by developing further the use of cyborg feminism as a 'methodology of the oppressed', a way of combining cyberfeminism with post-colonial theories of hybridity to resist globalised capitalism. Colonised peoples in the Americas and elsewhere, argues Sandoval, are already cultural hybrids who speak 'the cyborg speech of McDonalds ... [and] have already developed the cyborg skills required for survival' (1995: 408).

A somewhat different approach has been taken by Allucquere Rosanne Stone, who argues that the desire for mastery over machines is an anxious retreat into virtual space away from the lost sexualised body of the mother. The seductiveness of this space is the myth of unlimited power (over the mother's body), and this is the envy of the mother's body that, when translated into machines, Stone calls 'cyborg envy'. The practice of cyberspace disembodies but also re-embodies as we 'penetrate' the screen and put on the female body. 'In all, the unitary, bounded, safely warranted body constituted within the frame of bourgeois modernity is undergoing a gradual process of translation to the refigured and reinscribed embodiment of the cyberspace community' (Stone 1991: 109). Thus, as society attempts in modernity to produce intelligible bodies (after Judith Butler), so there is increasingly the opportunity for the *illegible* body, the boundary subject. But this corporeal form still exists – we cannot live by the old Cartesian trick of forgetting the body.

Grrrls on the Web

While many web producers are more concerned with the power of the female dollar when designing for the Internet, feminists have been using the Internet for research, communication, organising and activism. At its simplest, this consists of mailing lists to keep women (and men interested in feminist issues) in touch with each other and current events. Members of NOW can subscribe to an Action and Legislative Update list at now-action-list@now.org, for example, while those engaged in environmental campaigning will find much of interest at the Ecofeminist list ecofem@csf.colorado.edu. Other lists include information on abortion rights, rape, women's health and gay and lesbian news; for a full list, see Joan Korenman's compilation at www.umbc.edu/wmst/forums.html. Another useful source of information is the moderated soc.feminism newsgroup; soc.women and alt.feminism probably receive more traffic but, because they are not moderated, also receive a substantial amount of hostile postings.

As with many other groups, feminists have found the Web particularly fertile ground for information and communication. As well as sites such as NOW's www.now.org and women.com, Barbara O'Leary set up the Virtual Sisterhood as 'a global women's electronic support network' (www.igc.apc.org/vsister/vsister.html) and Carla Sinclair's NetChick is an elaborate virtual space for work, entertainment and communication (www.cyborganic.com/people/carla). As Wakeford remarks, perhaps the most significant feature of the proliferation of such sites is that they 'do not exist in isolation but are themselves electronically linked' (1997: 354).

NetChick points to a recent phenomenon that has attracted considerable attention: 'Grrrl' sites. Originating in music and subcultural scenes, sites such as Geekgirl (www.geekgirl.com.au) and Cybergrrl (www.cybergrrl.com) are 'what Riot Grrrls are to music and the Guerrilla Girls are to art' (DeLoach 1996). The relative ease of web production has resulted in a proliferation of Grrrl zines on the Net, many of which share some common features. The first is a celebration of technology, an acceptance of previously derogatory terms such as nerd and geek that were earlier associated more with men; and, second, they appear to be ambivalent or even hostile to what they perceive as the traditional rhetoric of feminism. While many Grrrl sites may be criticised for the same apoliticism ascribed to post-feminism in general, they also point to problems in attempting to prescribe a homogeneous women's movement, demanding a radical reconfiguration of the relationship between women and technology that is at the heart of cyberfeminism.

Further reading

As recommended in Chapter 5, Gauntlett (2000) and Bell and Kennedy (2000) provide two of the most contemporary primers for discussions of cyberculture, but there are also a number of books and collected essays that the reader may wish to pursue when dealing with online identities, cyberculture and cybersex. Regarding online identities, a good starting point is Sherry Turkle (1984, 1995), although some more entertaining postmodern applications of identity politics can be found in Featherstone and Burrows (1995), Dery (1994, 1996) and Gray (1995). Useful texts that contain chapters on how new technologies can configure and transform identity include Dery (1994, 1996), Markley (1996), Shields (1996), Holmes (1997), Jones (1997), Porter (1997), and Herman and Swiss (2000). For a discussion of artificial intelligence, the reader is advised to consult Stork (1996), Kurzweil (1999) and Moravec (1999).

Cyberpunk fans and critics should consult McCaffery (1991), while an excellent reader for gender studies online can be found in Wolmark (1999). Other useful texts dealing with cybersexuality, particularly from a feminist perspective, include Springer (1996), Plant (1997) and Balsamo (1996).

Appendix I
Glossary

ADSL Asymmetric Digital Subscriber Line, which offers much faster connections across standard copper phone lines.

Andreessen, Marc (1972–) Worked on the first graphical browser, Mosaic, while based at the National Center for Supercomputing Applications (NCSA) and then went on to found Netscape Communications with Jim Clark in 1994.

AOL America Online, the largest commercial online service in the world, which merged with Time Warner in 2000. AOL Time Warner has become the largest media corporation to dominate the Internet.

ARPANET Advanced Research Projects Agency Network, the prototype computer network established in 1969 that laid the foundations for the Internet.

AVI Audio-Video Interleaved, a video format developed by Microsoft.

Banner advertising First developed by the Hotwired site, banner ads quickly became a standard-sized format for web-based promotions.

BBS Bulletin Board System, originally computer-text message boards that could be dialled into via a modem, and now used mainly to refer to a wide variety of forum or discussion formats on the Internet.

Berners-Lee, Tim (1955–) Inventor of the World Wide Web while working at CERN (European Nuclear Research Centre), Geneva, 1990–1, he established the World Wide Web Consortium (W3C) in 1994 to develop universal standards for the Web.

Bitmap A type of graphic in which the image is described pixel by pixel. Bitmap graphics tend to produce better photographic images but with larger file sizes.

Browser A program for viewing web pages: the earliest of these were text-based applications such as Lynx, but, since the release of Mosaic in 1993, they have nearly all been capable of displaying graphics. The browser market is currently dominated by Microsoft's Internet Explorer followed by Netscape Navigator.

Bug Any computer glitch or malfunction. The term supposedly has its origins in the story that an early programmer, Grace Murray Hopper, found a moth in one of the first computers.

CD-ROM Compact Disc, Read Only Memory, similar to an audio compact disc but capable of storing between 640 and 700 Mb data that can be used by a computer.

CGI Common Gateway Interface, a standard used to pass data dynamically between servers and clients, so that it can be processed on the server and sent back to the web browser as meaningful information.

Chat A synchronous form of communication (as opposed to asynchronous forms, such as email), where the correspondent's messages appear instantly on the screens of all participants.

Codec Compressor/decompressor, an algorithm or equation used to encode video and audio, typically by using a frame of video and noting only where subsequent frames differ, or by discarding information not audible to the human ear.

Cookie   A small text file sent from a web server and stored on a visitor's hard drive. Cookies provide pieces of information, such as dates or reference numbers, which can be recalled on later visits.

Cracker   Often used to distinguish between 'good' and 'bad' hackers (in that crackers break into systems to perform illegal activities). Strictly speaking, a cracker is someone who breaks encryption codes, to distribute software as warez, for example, or to gain access to credit card information.

CSS   Cascading Style Sheet, an extension to HTML that is used to control the style and position of elements of web pages, such as text.

Cyberpunk   A sub-genre of science fiction that originated with Bruce Bethke's 1982 story 'Cyberpunk' and that draws much of its inspiration from William Gibson's novel of 1984, *Neuromancer*. The term is also often used to refer to technological subcultures.

Cyberspace   A term coined by Gibson in *Neuromancer* to refer to the conceptual space created by new technologies, and often used as another term for the Internet.

Cybersquatting   The practice of buying domain names so that they can be resold to companies for a profit.

Digital   The storage or transmission of data in a form of discrete symbols, usually translated from electronic or electromagnetic signals as binary zeros and ones (from the simplest state of a switch as off or on).

Directory   A database of web sites, such as Yahoo!, which is indexed and maintained by individuals rather than by software.

DNS   Domain Name System, a hierarchical system of routing IP addresses: a server looks up an address to check whether it matches a computer on the local network and, if not, passes it up the ladder to a server holding more detailed domain listings. Before DNS, every server had to store a list of the IP addresses of every computer attached to the Internet.

Domain A web site's location, with endings such as .com or .co.uk that specify commercial (the latter associated with a geographical location), government (.gov), educational (.edu), non-profit organisation (.org) and internet-related (.net) sites, amongst others. In 2001, ICANN released a new set of domain names including .pro for professional users and .museum for museums.

DVD Digital Versatile Disc, originally Digital Video Disk, a high-density storage medium, which, as its two names suggest, was first developed for video but has since come to be used for other forms of data. Although roughly the same physical dimensions as CD-ROMs, DVDs can store much more information.

Ecommerce The generic term given to using the Internet (and particularly the Web) for commercial purposes. Various commentators have predicted that ecommerce will change the way we do business in our daily lives, though this has yet to materialise for most people.

Email Electronic messages sent via the Internet, usually as text but increasingly incorporating more diverse elements such as images, sound and even video. The 'killer app' of the Internet.

Ethernet The most commonly employed networking standard used to connect computers with each other.

Ezine An online-based magazine or newsletter, usually found on the Web, that may be produced by corporate organisations or share features with print-based fanzines.

FAQ Frequently Asked Questions, a list of the most common queries for a newsgroup, web site, software program, and so on. When using a new application or joining a new group, it is considered good practice to consult any FAQs before posting or emailing queries that may have been answered several times before.

Flame The practice of sending provocative (and usually abusive) messages, typically via email or newsgroup postings.

Flash A popular format for vector graphics, animation and interactive design.

FTP   File Transfer Protocol, a method of transferring files between computers on the Internet.

Gates, Bill (1955–)   Co-founder of Microsoft with Paul Allen, and its Chief Executive from 1975 to 2000, he is currently Chairman and Chief Software Architect, as well as, usually, the richest man in the world depending on the value of Microsoft shares.

GIF   Graphic Interchange Format, a commonly used image format, which uses a palette of limited colours to keep down file sizes and which can be used with transparency and animation.

GNU   A recursive acronym for GNU's Not UNIX, an alternative to UNIX developed under the guidance of Richard Stallman in the 1980s and 1990s as part of a free software movement. Applications developed under the GNU project are usually found as part of the Linux/GNU operating system.

Gopher   Developed at the University of Minnesota, Gopher was a precursor to the Web designed to allow users to locate information on the Internet via a system of hierarchical menus.

GPL   GNU General Public Licence, the copyright notice (often called copyleft) that enables users to change open-source code, as long as they do not transform such code into proprietary software. Unlike public domain material, which can be taken and incorporated into proprietary systems, code available under the GPL must also be made available for other programmers to make potential changes.

GUI   Graphical User Interface, a visual front end for computer programs and operating systems.

Hacker   Originally derived from the activities of model train enthusiasts who would 'hack' their models to improve performance, a computer hacker was anyone who sought to understand a system as thoroughly as possible. Increasingly the term has come to be used to mean someone who gains access to computer systems without the owner's consent (or even knowledge).

Hits   The number of requests made for files to a web server, such as HTML files, images and Java applets. In the early days of the Web, hits were taken to indicate the numbers of visitors, whereas in fact they are very different figures.

HTML   Hypertext Markup Language, a simple tagging language used to format pages so that they can be displayed in a browser. HTML tags use angular brackets < > to indicate such formatting information.

HTTP   Hypertext Transfer Protocol, the series of rules governing the passing of files across the Internet.

Hyperlink   A graphical or textual link that connects one document to another on the Internet.

Internet   The worldwide network of networks that grew out of ARPANET and other systems during the 1970s, 1980s and 1990s. The Internet connects millions of computers and their users around the globe, comprising services such as email, the Web, newsgroups and chat.

Internet Explorer   A web browser released by Microsoft in 1996 and based on an earlier version of Spyglass Mosaic. Subsequent development saw IE overtake its main rival, Netscape, by the end of the 1990s, which in turn led to a monopoly investigation by the Department of Justice due to its inclusion or 'bundling' with Microsoft's operating system, Windows.

ISDN   Integrated Services Digital Network, a series of communication standards that provides faster communication and more efficient links across a digital network than standard phone lines.

ISP   Internet Service Provider, a company that provides access to the Internet by allocating IP addresses to users at home or at work.

Java   A programming language developed by Sun Micrososytems (and called Oak in its first incarnation). The main virtue of Java for application development is that it can be written for multiple operating systems.

JPEG   Joint Photographic Experts Group, a compression standard for images that results in small file sizes for images containing up to 16.7 million colours.

Linux   Invented by Linus Torvalds in 1990, this is often used to refer to an alternative to, and increasingly more popular server operating system than, Windows. Linux is, strictly speaking, the kernel, the drivers that communicate between software and hardware, with the operating system consisting of this kernel and GNU applications. Linux is part of the 'open source' movement, meaning that, not only can it be downloaded and distributed for free, but its source code is fully available to anyone for modification.

LISTSERV   The most popular of the servers that maintain mailing lists for automated distribution of email topics.

Metasearch   A search engine that builds its results by scanning the indexes of other search engines.

Microsoft   Founded by Bill Gates and Paul Allen in Albuquerque, New Mexico, in 1975, Microsoft has grown into the world's largest software company and is responsible for Windows, Internet Explorer and Office, amongst other applications.

Modem   Modulator/demodulator, a device that converts digital signals into analog signals (and vice versa) that can be communicated across a telephone line.

Mosaic   The first widely available graphic web browser.

MP3   MPEG1 Audio Layer 3, an audio format that compresses sound by between 4 : 1 and 12 : 1 by discarding information that is inaudible to the human ear. MP3s have become a popular format for distributing music across the Internet.

MPEG   Moving Pictures Expert Group, the organisation responsible for international standards for the compression of streaming video and data. MPEG is commonly used to refer to a type of highly compressed video used in DVDs and on the Internet.

MUD   Multi-User Domain, sometimes referred to as MOO, Multi-User Domain, Object-Oriented. MUDs are online role-playing environments that, until recently, tended to be text-based but that are becoming increasingly visual. MOOs are less common, still tend to be text-based, and allow users to interact with programmable objects.

Netscape Navigator   The browser developed by Marc Andreessen and the main product of the company he co-founded with Jim Clark, Netscape, which led the dotcom phenomenon before being bought by AOL. Netscape Navigator is the main competitor to Microsoft's Internet Explorer.

Newsgroups   A public form of bulletin board, typically found on Usenet, where users can post messages that are widely read and responded to.

NTSC   National Television Standard Code, the US standard for video and television broadcasts.

Opera   An alternative browser to Internet Explorer and Netscape Navigator.

PAL   Phase Alternate Line, the European standard for video and television broadcasts.

PHP   A recursive acronym (one that refers to itself), PHP stands for PHP: Hypertext Preprocessor, that is, a scripting language used to generate pages dynamically.

Plug-in   Software that is used to extend the functionality of an application, typically a browser, enabling it to view certain file types or communicate with other users.

Portal   A web site that aims to be the starting point for all Internet-based activity, such as email, web browsing and news. Typical portals are MSN and Yahoo!

QuickTime   A video format and application developed by Apple.

RealAudio/RealVideo   Audio and video standards developed by Real.com that provide streaming material as quickly as possible.

Search engine   A search facility that indexes web sites using 'spiders' or 'robots', applications that scan pages to build databases of content.

Server   A computer that provides client machines with shared resources, such as printers, files or web pages.

Spam   Junk email sent to multiple recipients simultaneously and that is usually unwanted and unsolicited mail.

Streaming media   A common term for a variety of audio and visual materials that are transmitted continuously (hence streamed) from a server to a client device.

TCP/IP   Transfer Control Protocol/Internet Protocols, the main collections of rules (or protocols) used to enable computers to communicate across the Internet.

Telnet   A protocol allowing users to log in a remote computer and use it as their own.

Torvalds, Linus (1970–)   Creator of Linux, the kernel of a free UNIX clone, while a student at Helsinki University, and spokesperson for the free software movement.

UNIX   An operating system developed jointly in the late 1960s and early 1970s by General Electric, AT&T Bell Laboratories and MIT. Used to support telephony systems and networking systems, UNIX gradually became the backbone of the Internet, supported by its later imitator, Linux.

URL   Uniform Resource Locator (occasionally Universal Resource Locator), the individual address that is used to locate files on the Web.

Usenet   Established at Duke University in 1979, Usenet is the largest collection of newsgroups arranged into hierarchical groups such as rec., comp., alt. and misc. Although not strictly part of the Internet, Usenet is largely accessed via ISPs.

Vector graphics   Unlike bitmaps, vector graphics describe an image in terms of the positions of elements, their direction and shape. They usually produce smaller file sizes than bitmaps and, although they tend not to be useful for photographic reproduction, they can be scaled to any size without pixellation.

Web   World Wide Web, the collection of sites that use HTML and HTTP to connect to each other and that are accessed via a browser.

WELL   Whole Earth 'Lectronic Link, an online community established in 1985 for the San Francisco area that has since grown into an international forum.

WYSIWYG   What You See Is What You Get, a phrase used to refer to visual editors that display what the page should actually look like as you work on it.

Yahoo!   A directory founded by David Filo and Jerry Yang in 1994 and one of the first collections of links to useful sites on the Web. Yahoo! has since grown into a major portal offering a range of services, such as news, shopping and email.

Appendix II
Useful sites

The following is a selective list of sites that readers may find useful for further information on topics covered in this book. A more comprehensive list is maintained at www.routledge.com/internetbasics/resources.htm.

Search engines and research

411 Locate (www.411locate.com) – useful for finding names and addresses in the US.

Ask Jeeves (www.ask.com) – directory that responds quite well to natural language searches.

Bigfoot (www.bigfoot.com) – useful for finding names and addresses in the US.

Bookmark (bookmark.iop.org/alerts.htm) – provides updates on new releases.

BOOKNews (www.booknews.co.uk) – provides information on new publications.

Dogpile (www.dogpile.com) – one of the better metasearch engines that trawls through other sites.

Euractiv (www.euractiv.com) – database of events and information in the EU.

Fast (www.alltheweb.com) – quick search engine that is used by many other sites.

Google (www.google.com) – the best search engine on the Web, particularly as you can search images and newsgroups.

Infobel (www.infobel.com/uk/) – useful for finding names and addresses in the UK.

MedNet (www.mednets.com) – database of medical information.

Northern Light (www.northernlight.com) – particularly useful site for students as it links to reports and articles.

Search Engine Colossus (www.searchenginecolossus.com) – list of online search engines and databases.

Switchboard (www.switchboard.com) – useful for finding names and addresses in the US.

Whowhere (whowhere.lycos.com) – useful for finding names and addresses in the US.

Yahoo! (www.yahoo.com) – the first directory and still one of the best for structured searches of information in a particular area.

Yell (search.yell.com) – useful for finding names and addresses in the UK.

Zetoc (zetoc.mimas.ac.uk) – list of tables of contents from journals, based on the British Library's electronic data.

Internet administration and technical specifications

Association of Internet Professionals (www.association.org) – for technical professionals working with the Internet.

CIO.com (www.cio.com/metrics/) – various online statistics from Cio.com.

Digital Divide (www.digitaldivide.gov) – US government initiatives to overcome 'digital poverty'.

Domain Wars (www.domainwars.com) – information on administration and registration systems on the Net.

History of the Internet (www.netvalley.com/intval.html) – a history of the Internet with links to other relevant sites.

How the Internet came to be (www.bell-labs.com/user/zhwang/
vcerf.html) – contribution by Vince Cerf.

International Telecommunication Union (www.itu.net) – Geneva-
based organisation that agrees such things as modem standards.

Internet and Web history (www.elsop.com/wrc/h_Web.htm) –
histories and biographies.

Internet Corporation for Assigned Names and Numbers
(www.icann.org) – body responsible for domain name
registration.

Internet Engineering Task Force (www.ietf.org) – body responsible
for Internet Standards.

Internet Society (www.isoc.org) – promotes Internet development.

World Wide Web Consortium (www.w3c.org) – body responsible for
technical standards across the Web.

Web development and new media

Adobe (www.adobe.com) – tools and resources for online design.

Ben's Planet (www.bensplanet.com) – a complete HTML reference
guide.

Big Info (www.biginfo.net) – complete webmaster resource web site.

Helpdesk (Web.canlink.com/helpdesk) – HTML support.

HTML Primer
(www.ncsa.uiuc.edu/General/Internet/WWW/HTMLPrimer.
html) – beginner's guide to HTML.

Internet Content Rating Association (www.icra.org) – information on
rating sites for sex, violence and bad language.

Killer web sites (www.killersites.com/core.html) – tips from *Creating
Killer web sites*.

Macromedia (www.macromedia.com) – tools and resources for
online design, including links for Flash and Shockwave.

NetMechanic (www.netmechanic.com) – monitors errors on your site
with an HTML validator.

Page Tutor (www.pagetutor.com) – lots of tutorials for HTML,
JavaScript and CSS.

Web Developer (www.webdeveloper.com) – links to other sites
providing information and guidance.

WebMonkey (hotwired.lycos.com/webmonkey) – a good web
developer's resource.

Web Production for Writers and Journalists (www.producing.
routledge.com) – links and tutorials for web producers.

Web Reference (www.webreference.com) – FAQs, articles and
resources for web design.

Web Wonk (www.dsiegel.com/tips) – tips for designers and
writers.

News and media

Asia Pacific Front Page (www.asiamedia.ucla.edu) – daily publication
of the Asia Pacific Network.

BBC.co.uk (www.bbc.co.uk) – online services for BBC broadcasting
and publishing.

CNN (www.cnn.com) – online news from CNN.

Electronic *Telegraph* (www.portal.telegraph.co.uk) – site for the UK
Telegraph newspaper.

Financial Times (www.ft.com) – UK financial newspaper.

Guardian Unlimited (www.newsunlimited.co.uk) – site for the UK
Guardian newspaper.

International Herald Tribune (www.iht.com) – international
European news.

Libération (www.liberation.fr) – French daily newspaper.

Los Angeles Times (www.latimes.com) – one of the main US
regional newspapers.

Lycos News (www.lycos.com/news) – serves AP and Reuters
stories.

Le Monde (www.lemonde.fr) – French daily newspaper.

Moreover (www.moreover.com) – provides a broad range of (not
always immediately up-to-date) news sources.

News Is Free (www.newsisfree.com) – offers less mainstream news
stories.

New York Times (www.nytimes.com) – one of the main US regional
newspapers (registration required).

Nordwest Zeitung Online (www.nwz-online.de) – major German
regional newspaper.

The Onion (www.onion.com) – the reason why the Web was
invented: a previously neglected periodical that has become
probably the funniest online site.

Pravda (english.pravda.ru) – English version of the Russian daily
newspaper.

Suddeutsche Zeitung (www.sueddeutsche.de) – major German
regional newspaper.

The Times (www.the-times.co.uk) – site for the UK *Times* newspaper.

TotalNews (www.totalnews.com) – serves the BBC and *Washington
Post*.

USA Today (www.usatoday.com/) – site of the popular US daily.

Wall Street Journal (public.wsj.com/home.html) – premiere US
business journal (subscription required).

Washington Post (www.washingtonpost.com) – one of the main US
regional newspapers.

Cultural and media studies

Association of Internet Researchers (aoir.org) – group devoted to
cross-disciplinary Internet studies.

Centre for Cultural Policy Studies (www.warwick.ac.uk/fac/arts/
Theatre_S/cp/index.html) – hosted by the University of
Warwick.

Computer Industry Almanac (www.c-i-a.com) – information on a
wide range of computer statistics.

CTheory (www.ctheory.com) – cultural and critical theory edited by
Arthur and Marilouise Kroker.

Cultural Studies Online (www.culturalstudies.net) – links and
resources.

Information Observatory (www.unesco.org/webworld/observatory) –
hosted by Unesco.

Internet Studies (www.isc.umn.edu) – Internet Studies Centre at the
University of Minnesota.

Internet Studies (www.it.murdoch.edu.au/~cec) – Centre for
Ecommerce and Internet Studies at Murdoch University.

New Media Studies (www.newmediastudies.com) – David Gauntlett's
new media site.

Unesco (www.unesco.org/culture/) – United Nations Educational, Scientific and Cultural Organization.

Victorian Web (65.107.211.206/victorian/victov.html) – more than just Victoriana, this is an excellent resource for research.

Yale Internet Studies (www.ycis.yale.edu) – the Yale Center for Internet Studies.

Bibliography

The following bibliography is divided into two parts: the first lists books, papers and sites dealing with the Internet, computers and technology, while the second part lists titles cited in the text that are concerned with more general aspects of media and cultural studies.

Internet studies

Abbate, Janet (1999) *Inventing the Internet*, Cambridge, MA: MIT Press.

Alderman, John (2001) *Sonic Boom: Napster, P2P and the Battle for the Future of Music*, London: Fourth Estate.

Anderson, Alan Ross (ed.) (1964) *Minds and Machines*, Englewood Cliffs, NJ: Prentice-Hall.

Arnold, Ellen L. and Plymire, Darcy C. (2000) 'The Cherokee Indians and the Internet', in David Gauntlett (ed.), *Web.Studies*, London: Arnold, pp. 186–93.

Aronowitz, Stan (1996) *Technoscience and Cyberculture*, London and New York: Routledge.

Bailey, James (1996) *After Thought: The Computer Challenge to Human Intelligence*, New York: Basic Books.

Balsamo, Anne (1996) *Technologies of the Gendered Body: Reading Cyborg Women*, Durham, NC: Duke University Press.

Barbour, Ian (1992) *Ethics in an Age of Technology*, London: HarperCollins.

Bassett, Caroline (1997) 'Virtually Gendered: Life in an On-line World', in Ken Gelder and Sarah Thornton (eds), *The Subcultures Reader*, London and New York: Routledge, pp. 537–50.

Bayers, Chip (1999) 'Over Seven Million Served', *Wired* 7.10: 112–40.

Bell, David and Kennedy, Barbara (eds) (2000) *The Cybercultures Reader*, London and New York: Routledge.

Benedikt, Michael (ed.) (1991) *Cyberspace: First Steps*, Cambridge, MA: MIT Press.

Bereano, Philip (1984) 'Technology and Human Freedom', *Science for the People* November/December: 132–43.

Berners-Lee, Tim (1999) *Weaving the Web*, London: Orion.

Birkerts, Sven (1994) *The Gutenberg Elegies*, Boston and London: Faber and Faber.

Bovik, Al (ed.) (2000) *Handbook of Image and Video Processing*, London: Academic Press.

Bowden, Caspar and Akdeniz, Yaman (1999) 'Cryptography and Democracy: Dilemmas of Freedom', in Liberty, *Liberating Cyberspace*, London: Pluto Press, pp. 81–124.

Branwyn, Gareth (1994) 'Compu-Sex: Erotica for Cybernauts', in Mark Dery (ed.), *Flame Wars*, Durham, NC: Duke University Press, pp. 223–35.

Brown, David (1997) *Cybertrends: Chaos, Power and Accountability in the Information Age*, London: Penguin.

Bukatman, Scott (1994) *Terminal Identity: The Virtual Subject in Postmodern Science Fiction*, Durham, NC: Duke University Press.

Bush, Vannevar (1945) 'As We May Think', *Atlantic Monthly* 176(1), 101–8.

Card, Orson Scott (1990) *Maps in a Mirror: The Short Fiction of Orson Scott Card*, New York: TOR.

Carlton, Jim (1997) *Apple: The Inside Story of Intrigue, Egomania and Business Blunders*, London: Century.

Cartwright, Lisa (1997) 'The Visible Man', in J. Terry and M. Calvert (eds), *Processed Lives: Gender and Technology in Everyday Life*, London: Routledge. Reprinted in David Bell and Barbara Kennedy (eds), *The Cybercultures Reader*, London and New York: Routledge, pp. 619–23.

Castells, Manuel (1996–7) *The Information Age: Economy, Society and Culture*, 3 vols, Oxford: Blackwells.

Cawson, Alan, Haddon, Leslie and Miles, Ian (1995) *The Shape of Things to Consume: Delivering Information Technology to the Home*, Aldershot: Avebury.

Chapman, Gary (1994) 'Taming the Computer', in Mark Dery (ed.), *Flame Wars*, Durham, NC: Duke University Press, pp. 297–319.

Clerc, Susan (1996) 'Estrogen Brigades and the "Big Tits" Thread', in L. Cherny and E. Reba Wise (eds), *Wired Women: Gender and New Realities in Cyberspace*, Seattle: Seal Press. Reprinted in David Bell and Barbara Kennedy (eds), *The Cybercultures Reader*, London and New York: Routledge, pp. 216–29.

Colby, Kenneth M., Watt, James B. and Gilbert, John P. (1966) 'A Computer Method for Psychotherapy: Preliminary Communication', *Journal of Nervous and Mental Diseases* 142.2: 148–55.

Connery, Brian (1997) 'IMHO: Authority and Egalitarian Rhetoric in the Virtual Coffeehouse', in David Porter (ed.), *Internet Culture*: 161–80.

Cringeley, Robert X. (1996) *Accidental Empires*, London: Penguin.

Daly, James (1997) 'The Robin Hood of the Rich: Gary Reback May Be the Only Man Bill Gates Fears', *Wired* 5.08: 108–48.

Davies, Simon (1996) *Big Brother: Britain's Web of Surveillance and the New Technological Order*, London: Pan.

de Landa, Manuel (1991) *War in the Age of Intelligent Machines*, New York: Swerve Editions.

DeLoach, Amelia (1996) 'Grrrls Exude Attitude', *CMC Magazine*, www.december.com/cmc/mag/1996/mar/deloach.html, March 1.

Denning, Dorothy (1993) 'To Tap or Not to Tap', *Communications of the ACM*, March: 36–9.

Dertouzos, Michael (1997) *What Will Be: How the New World of Information Will Change Our Lives*, London: Piatkus.

Dery, Mark (ed.) (1994) *Flame Wars: The Discourse of Cyberculture*, Durham, NC: Duke University Press.

Dery, Mark (1996) *Escape Velocity: Cyberculture at the End of the Century*, London: Hodder and Stoughton.

Dibbell, Julian (1994) 'A Rape in Cyberspace', in Mark Dery (ed.), *Flame Wars*, Durham, NC: Duke University Press, pp. 237–61.

di Filippo, JoAnn (2000) 'Pornography on the Web', in David Gauntlett (ed.), *Web.Studies*, London: Arnold, pp. 122–9.

Dr-K (2000) *A Complete H@cker's Handbook: Everything You Need to Know About Hacking in the Age of the Web*, London: Carlton.

Dunne, Steve (2001) 'The Short Life of Kaycee Nicole', *The Guardian*, G2, 28 May: 26.

Dwight, Jeffry, Erwin, Michael, Niles, Robert (1996) *Using CGI*, Indianapolis, IN: Que.

Dyson, Esther (1998) *Release 2.1: A Design for Living in the Digital Age*, London: Penguin.

Ecclestone, Andrew (1999) 'Freedom of Information: an Electronic Window onto Government', in Liberty, *Liberating Cyberspace*: 44–67.

Edwards, Paul N. (1997) *The Closed World*, Cambridge, MA: MIT Press.

Ermann, David, Williams, Mary and Schauf, Michele (1997) *Computers, Ethics and Society*, second edition, Oxford: Oxford University Press.

Escobar, Arturo (1994) 'Welcome to Cyberia: Notes on the Anthropology of Cyberculture', *Current Anthropology* 35.3. Reprinted in David Bell and Barbara Kennedy (eds), *The Cybercultures Reader*, London and New York: Routledge, pp. 56–76.

Featherstone, Mike and Burrows, Roger (1995) *Cyberspace, Cyberbodies, Cyberpunk*, London: Sage.

Foster, Thomas (1993) 'Meat Puppets or Robopaths? Cyberpunk and the Question of Embodiment', *Genders* 18. Reprinted in Jenny Wolmark (ed.), *Cybersexualities*, Edinburgh: Edinburgh University Press, pp. 208–29.

Gates, Bill (1995) *The Road Ahead*, London: Penguin.

Gates, Bill and Hemingway, Collins (1999) *Business @ The Speed of Thought: Using a Digital Nervous System*, London: Penguin.

Gauntlett, David (ed.) (2000) *Web.Studies*, London: Arnold.

Gibson, Owen (2001) 'When the Web Came of Age', *Media Guardian*, 17 September: 42–3.

Gibson, William (1984) *Neuromancer*, London: Victor Gollancz.

Gibson, William (1996) *Idoru*, London: Viking.

Gray, Chris Hables (ed.) (1995) *The Cyborg Handbook*, London and New York: Routledge.

Haddon, Leslie (1999) 'The Development of Interactive Games', in Hugh MacKay and Tim O'Sullivan, *The Media Reader*, London: Sage, pp. 305–27.

Hafner, Katie and Lyon, Matthew (1996) *Where Wizards Stay Up Late: The Origins of the Internet*, New York: Simon and Schuster.

Hall, Jim (2001) *Online Journalism: A Critical Primer*, London: Pluto Press.

Hamilton, Angus (1999) 'The Net Out of Control: A New Moral Panic: Censorship and Sexuality', in Liberty, *Liberating Cyberspace*, London: Pluto Press, pp. 169–86.

Haraway, Donna (1991) 'A Cyborg Manifesto', in *Simians, Cyborgs and Women: The Reinvention of Nature*, London: Free Association Books.

Hausman, Carl (1994) 'Information Age Ethics: Privacy Ground Rules for Navigating in Cyberspace', *Journal of Mass Media Ethics* 9.3: 135–44.

Hayles, Katherine (1996) 'Boundary Disputes: Homeostasis, Reflexivity and the Foundations of Cybernetics', in Robert Markley (ed.) *Virtual Realities and Their Discontents*, Baltimore and London: Johns Hopkins University Press, pp. 12–40.

Heilemann, John (2000) 'The Truth, the Whole Truth and Nothing But the Truth: The Untold Story of the Microsoft Antitrust Case and What it Means for the Future of Bill Gates and His Company', *Wired* 8.11: 260–311.

Heim, Michael (1991) 'The Erotic Ontology of Cyberspace', in Michael Benedikt (ed.), *Cyberspace: First Steps*, Cambridge, MA: MIT Press, pp. 59–80.

Heller, Robert (2001) 'Return of the Silverback', *Business 2.0*, 9 February: 109–14.

Herman, Andrew and Swiss, Thomas (eds) (2000) *The World Wide Web and Contemporary Cultural Theory*, London and New York: Routledge.

Herz, J.C. (1997) *Joystick Nation*, London: Abacus.

Hilden, Julie (2001) 'The Legal Debate Over Protecting Anonymous Speakers Online', www.gigalaw.com/articles/2001/hilden–2001–02–p1.html, 1 February.

Holland, David (1999) *Internet for Students*, Plymouth: Internet Handbooks.

Holmes, D. (1997) *Virtual Politics: Identity and Communication in Cybersociety*, London: Sage.

Jackson, Tim (1997) *Inside Intel*, London: HarperCollins.

Johnston, Rich (2001) 'All Your Base . . .', *The Guardian*, G2, 28 February: 4.

Jones, Steve (ed.) (1997) *Virtual Culture: Identity and Communication in Cybersociety*, London: Sage.

Jonschler, Charles (1999) *Wired Life: Who Are We in the Digital Age?*, London and New York: Bantam.

Kahn, David (1972) *The Codebreakers*, London: Macmillan.

Kandell, Jonathan (2001) 'Yo Quiero Todo Bell', *Wired* 9.01: 126–38.

Khodarkovsky, Michael and Shamkovich, Leonid (1997) *A New Era: How Gary Kasparov Changed the World of Chess*, New York: Ballantine.

Knapp, James A. (1997) 'Essayistic Messages: Internet Newsgroups as an Electronic Public Sphere', in David Porter (ed.), *Internet Culture*: 181–201.

Kroker, Arthur and Marylouise (1996) *Hacking the Future: Stories for the Flesh-Eating 90s*, Montreal: New World Perspectives.

Kroker, Arthur and Marylouise (1997) *Digital Delirium*, New York: St Martin's Press.

Kurzweil, Ray (1999) *The Age of Spiritual Machines*, London: Orion.

Landauer, Thomas (1995) *Trouble with Computers*, Cambridge, MA: MIT Press.

Landow, George (1997) *Hypertext 2.0*, Baltimore: Johns Hopkins University Press.

Lanham, Richard (1993) *The Electronic Word*, Chicago and London: University of Chicago Press.

Leary, Timothy (1991) 'The Cyberpunk: The Individual as Reality Pilot', in L. McCaffery (ed.), *Storming the Reality Studio: A Casebook of Cyberpunk and Postmodern Fiction*, Durham: Duke University Press, pp. 243–59.

Leonard, Andrew (1997) *Bots: The Origin of the Species*, San Francisco, CA: Wired Press.

Levinson, Paul (1997) *Soft Edge*, London and New York: Routledge.

Levy, Steven (2001) *Hackers: Heroes of the Computer Revolution*, second edition, London: Penguin.

Liberty (National Council for Civil Liberties) (1999) *Liberating Cyberspace*, London: Pluto Press.

Lockard, Joseph (1997) 'Progressive Politics, Electronic Individualism and the Myth of Virtual Community', in David Porter (ed.), *Internet Culture*, London and New York: Routledge, pp. 219–31.

Lupton, Deborah (1995) 'The Embodied Computer User', *Body and Society* 1.3–4. Reprinted in David Bell and Barbara Kennedy (eds), *The Cybercultures Reader*, London and New York: Routledge, pp. 477–87.

Lyon, David (1998) 'The World Wide Web of Surveillance: The Internet and Off-World Power Flows', *Communication and Society* 1: 91–105.

McCaffery, Larry (1991) *Storming the Reality Studio: A Casebook of Cyberpunk and Postmodern Fiction*, Durham, NC: Duke University Press.

Mallapragada, Madhavi (2000) 'The Indian Diaspora in the USA and Around the Web', in David Gauntlett (ed.), *Web.Studies*, London: Arnold, pp. 179–85.

Markley, Robert (ed.) (1996) *Virtual Realities and Their Discontents*, Baltimore and London: Johns Hopkins University Press.

Millard, William B. (1997) 'I Flamed Freud: A Case Study in Teletextual Incendiarism', in David Porter (ed.), *Internet Culture*, London and New York: Routledge, pp. 145–60.

Minsky, Marvin (1982) 'Why People Think Computers Can't', *AI Magazine* 3.4: 3–15.

Mitchell, William J. (1992) *The Reconfigured Eye*, Cambridge, MA: MIT Press.

Mitchell, William J. (1995) *City of Bits: Space, Place and the Infobahn*, Cambridge, MA: MIT Press.

Mitra, Ananda (1997) 'Virtual Commonality: Looking for India on the Internet', in Steven Jones (ed.), *Virtual Culture*, London: Sage, pp. 55–79.

Moody, Fred (1995) *I Sing the Body Electric: A Year with Microsoft on the Multimedia Frontier*, London: Hodder and Stoughton.

Moon, Michael and Millison, Doug (2000) *Firebr@nds: Building Brand Loyalty in the Internet Age*, Berkeley, CA: Osborne/McGraw-Hill.

Moravec, Hans (1999) *Robot: Mere Machine to Transcendent Mind*, Oxford: Oxford University Press.

Morris, Stan (2000) 'The Limits of Free Speech on the Internet', www.gigalaw.com/articles/morris–2000–01–p1.html, 1 July.

Moschovitis, Christos, Poole, Hilary, Schuyler, Tami and Senft, Theresa (1999) *History of the Internet: A Chronology, 1843 to the Present*, Santa Barbara, CA: ABC Clio.

Mylott, Thomas R. (1984) *Computer Law for Professionals*, New York: Simon & Schuster.

Nakamura, Lisa (1995) 'Race in/for Cyberspace: Identity Tourism and Racial Passing on the Internet', *Works and Days*, 13.1–2. Reprinted in David Bell and Barbara Kennedy (eds), *The Cybercultures Reader*, London and New York: Routledge, pp. 712–20.

Naughton, John (1999) *A Brief History of the Future: The Origins of the Internet*, London: Weidenfeld and Nicholson.

Negroponte, Nicholas (1995) *Being Digital*, London: Hodder and Stoughton.

Negroponte, Nicholas (1997) 'Digital Era Imposes New Cultural Divide', *New York Times*, available at www.computernewsdaily.com/268_092597_152203_32180.html, 25 September 1997.

Nelkin, Dorothy (1994) 'Information Technology could Threaten Privacy, Freedom and Democracy', in David Ermann *et al* (eds.), *Computers, Ethics and Society*: 20–32.

Nelson, Theodor (1993) *Literary Machines*, Cambridge, MA: Eastgate Systems.

Niederst, Jennifer (1998) *Web Design in a Nutshell*, Cambridge: O'Reilly.

Nielsen, Jakob (2000) *Designing Web Usability: The Practice of Simplicity*, Indianapolis, IN: New Riders

Nixon, Nicola (1992) 'Cyberpunk: Preparing the Ground for Revolution or Keeping the Boys Satisfied?', *Science Fiction Studies* 19. Reprinted in Jenny Wolmark (ed.), *Cybersexualities*, Edinburgh: Edinburgh University Press, pp. 191–207.

Oswald, Michael (1997) 'Virtual Urban Futures', in D. Holmes (ed.), *Virtual Politics*, London: Sage, pp. 37–45.

Pearson, Ruth and Mitter, Swasi (1994) 'Employment and working conditions of low-skilled information-processing workers in less developed countries', *International Labour Review*, 132.1: 49–64.

Plant, Sadie (1996) 'Cyberfeminism', in Rob Shields (ed.), *Cultures of the Internet*, London: Sage, pp. 172–81.

Plant, Sadie (1997) *Zeroes and Ones*, London: Fourth Estate.

Pollock, John (2001) *JavaScript: A Beginner's Guide*, Columbus, OH: McGraw Hill.

Poole, Steven (2001) 'Tooled Up, But Not Turned On', *The Guardian*, 28 June: 2–3.

Porter, David (ed.) (1997) *Internet Culture*, London and New York: Routledge.

Poster, Mark (1997) 'Cyberdemocracy: Internet and the Public Sphere', in David Porter (ed.), *Internet Culture*, London and New York: Routledge, pp. 201–18.

Postman, Neil (1990) 'Informing Ourselves to Death', in David Ermann, Mary Williams and Michele Schauf (eds), *Computers, Ethics and Society*, Oxford: Oxford University Press, pp. 128–36.

Powell, Thomas (2000) *Web Design: The Complete Reference*, Berkeley, CA: Osborne/McGraw Hill.

Powell, Thomas (2001) *HTML: The Complete Reference*, Berkeley, CA: Osborne/McGraw Hill.

Power, Richard (2000) *Tangled Web: Tales of Digital Crime from the Shadows of Cyberspace*, Indianopolis, IN: Que.

Pyle, Forest (1993) 'Making Cyborgs, Making Humans: Of Terminators and Blade Runners', reprinted in David Bell and Barbara Kennedy (eds.), *The Cybercultures Reader*: 124–137.

Rachels, James (1975) 'Why Privacy is Important', in David Ermann *et al* (ed.), *Computers, Ethics and Society*: 69–76.

Reid, Robert (1997) *Architects of the Web*, New York: John Wiley and Sons.

Rheingold, Howard (1991) *Virtual Reality: Exploring the Brave New Technologies of Artificial Experience and Interactive Worlds from Cyberspace to Teledildonics*, London: Secker and Warburg.

Rheingold, Howard (1995) *The Virtual Community: Finding Connection in a Computerized World*, London: Minerva.

Rifkin, Jeremy (2000) *The Age of Access*, London: Penguin.

Rose, Frank (2000) 'Reminder to Steve Case: Confiscate the Long Knives', *Wired* 8.09: 156–75.

Ross, Andrew (1991) *Strange Weather: Culture, Science and Technology in the Age of Limits*, London: Verso.

Rotenberg, Marc (1993) 'Wiretap Laws Must Not Weaken Digital Communications', in David Ermann *et al* (ed.), *Computers, Ethics and Society*: 263–8.

Rushkoff, Douglas (1994) *Cyberia: Life in the Trenches of Cyberspace*, London: Flamingo.

Sandoval, Chela (1995) 'New Sciences: Cyborg Feminism and the Methodology of the Oppressed', in Chris Hables Gray (ed.), *The Cyborg Handbook*, London and New York: Routledge, pp. 407–22.

Sardar, Ziauddin (1996) 'alt.civilizations.faq: Cyberspace as the Darker Side of the West', in *Cyberfutures: Culture and Politics on the Information Highway*, London: Pluto Press, pp. 14–41.

Sardar, Ziauddin and Ravetz, Jerome (eds) (1996) *Cyberfutures: Culture and Politics on the Information Highway*, London: Pluto Press.

Schwartz, Evan I. (1997) *Webonomics: Nine Essential Principles for Growing Your Business on the World Wide Web*, London: Penguin.

Seabrook, John (1997) *Deeper: A Two-Year Odyssey in Cyberspace*, London and Boston: Faber and Faber.

Searle, John (1982) 'The Myth of the Computer', *The New York Review of Books*, 29 April.

Shade, Leslie Regan (1996) 'Free Speech on the Net' in Rob Shields (ed.), *Cultures of the Internet*, London: Sage, pp. 11–28.

Sheff, David (2000) 'Crank It Up', *Wired* 8.08: 186–97.

Sheff, David (2001) 'Betting on Bandwidth', *Wired* 9.02: 145–55.

Sherman, Barrie and Judkins, Phil (1992) *Glimpses of Heaven, Glimpses of Hell: Virtual Reality and Its Implications*, London: Hodder and Stoughton.

Shields, Rob (ed.) (1996) *Cultures of the Internet*, London: Sage, 1996.

Siegal, David (1997) *Creating Killer Websites*, 2nd edn, Indianapolis, IN: Hayden Books.

Silver, David (2000) 'Cyberculture Studies 1990–2000', in David Gauntlett (ed.), *Web.Studies*, London: Arnold, pp. 19–30.

Simon, Herbert (1969) *Sciences of the Artificial*, Cambridge, MA: MIT Press.

Slouka, Mark (1995) *War of the Worlds: The Assault on Reality*, London: Abacus.

Spafford, Eugene (1992) 'Are Computer Hacker Break-ins Illegal?', in David Ermann, Mary Williams and Michele Schauf (eds), *Computers, Ethics and Society*, Oxford: Oxford University Press, pp. 77–88.

Spainhour, Steven and Eckstein, Robert (1999) *Webmaster in a Nutshell*, Cambridge: O'Reilly.

Spinrad, Norman. (1990) *Science Fiction in the Real World*, Carbondale, IL: Southern Illinois University Press.

Springer, Claudia (1996) *Electronic Eros: Bodies and Desire in the Post-industrial Age*, London: Athlone.

Springer, Claudia (1994) 'Sex, Memories and Angry Women', in Mark Dery (ed.), *Flame Wars*, Durham, NC: Duke University Press, pp. 157–77.

Spufford, Francis and Uglow, Jenny (eds) (1996) *Cultural Babbage: Technology, Time and Invention*, London and Boston: Faber and Faber.

Squires, Judith (1996) 'Fabulous Feminist Futures', in J. Dovey (ed.), *Fractal Dreams: New Media in Social Context*, London: Lawrence and Wishart. Reprinted in David Bell and Barbara Kennedy, *The Cybercultures Reader*, London and New York: Routledge, pp. 360–73.

Stallman, Richard (1985) *The Gnu Manifesto*, in David Ermann, Mary Williams and Michele Schauf (eds), *Computers, Ethics and Society*, Oxford: Oxford University Press, pp. 229–39.

Standage, Tom (1998) *The Victorian Internet*, London: Weidenfeld and Nicolson.

Stelarc (1998) 'From Psycho-Body to Cyber-Systems: Images as Post-Human Entities', in David Bell and Barbara Kennedy, *The Cybercultures Reader*, London: Routledge, pp. 560–76.

Sterling, Bruce (1992) *The Hacker Crackdown: Law and Disorder on the Electronic Frontier*, London: Penguin.

Stewart, Fiona and Mann, Chris (2000) *Internet Communication and Qualitative Research: A Handbook for Researching Online*, London: Sage.

Stoll, Clifford (1989) *The Cuckoo's Egg*, New York: Doubleday.

Stoll, Clifford (1995) *Silicon Snake Oil*, Basingstoke: Macmillan.

Stone, Allucquere Rosanne (1991) 'Will the Real Body Please Stand Up? Boundary Stories about Virtual Cultures', in Michael Benedikt (ed.), *Cyberspace: First Steps*, Cambridge, MA: MIT Press, pp. 81–118.

Stork, David (1996) *HAL's Legacy*, Cambridge, MA: MIT Press.

Stratton, Jon (1997) 'Cyberspace and the Globalization of Culture', in David Porter (ed.), *Internet Culture*, London and New York: Routledge, pp. 253–52.

Street, John (1997) 'Remote Control? Politics, Technology and "Electronic Democracy"', *Journal of Communication* 12: 27–42.

Swade, Doron (2000) *The Cogwheel Brain: Charles Babbage and the Quest to Build the First Computer*, London: Little Brown and Company.

Taylor, Paul (1999) *Hackers: Crime in the Digital Sublime*, London and New York: Routledge.

Taylor, Philip M. (2000) 'The World Wide Web Goes to War, Kosovo 1999', in David Gauntlett (ed.), *Web.Studies*, London: Arnold, pp. 194–201.

Tetzlaff, David (2000) 'Yo-Ho-Ho and a Server of Warez', in Andrew Herman and Thomas Swiss (eds), *The World Wide Web and Contemporary Cultural Theory*, London and New York: Routledge, pp. 99–126.

Tomlinson, John (1996) 'Cultural Globalisation: Placing and Displacing the West', *The European Journal of Development Research* 8: 22–35.

Trahant, Mark (1996) 'The Power of Stories: Native Words and Images on the Internet', *Native Americas* 13.1: 15–21.

Tran, Mark (2001) 'Identity Crisis', *The Guardian*, July 5: 10–11.

Tribe, Laurence (1991) 'The Constitution in Cyberspace', *The Humanist* 51.5: 15–21.

Turing, Alan (1950) 'Computing Machinery and Intelligence'. *Mind* 59: 433–60. Reprinted in Alan Ross Anderson (ed.) (1964) *Minds and Machines*, Englewood Cliffs, NJ: Prentice-Hall, pp. 4–30.

Turkle, Sherry (1984) *The Second Self: Computers and the Human Spirit*, New York: Simon and Schuster.

Turkle, Sherry (1995) *Life on the Screen: Identity in the Age of the Internet*, New York: Simon and Schuster.

Wakeford, Nina (1997) 'Cyberqueer', in A. Medhurst and S. Munt (eds) *Lesbian and Gay Studies: A Critical Introduction*, London: Cassell. Reprinted in David Bell and Barbara Kennedy, *The Cybercultures Reader*, London and New York: Routledge, pp. 403–15.

Wakeford, Nina (2000) 'New Media, New Methodologies: Studying the Web', in David Gauntlett (ed.), *Web.Studies*, London: Arnold, pp. 31–41.

Wallace, James and Erikson, Jim (1994) *Hard Drive: Bill Gates and the Making of Microsoft*, New York: John Wiley.

Weinstein, Deena and Weinstein, Michael (1997) 'Net Game Cameo', in Arthur Kroker and Marilouise Kroker (eds.), *Digital Delirium*: 159–64.

Weizenbaum, Joseph (1976) *Computer Power and Human Reason: From Judgement to Calculation*, San Francisco: W.H. Freeman.

Wertheim, Margaret (1999) *The Pearly Gates of Cyberspace*, London: Virago.

Whittaker, Jason (2000) 'Freedom of Information: Scientology on the Net', *The New Humanist* 115.4: 11–13.

Whittaker, Jason (2002) *Web Production for Writers and Journalists*, London and New York: Routledge.

Wilbur, Shawn (1997) 'An Archaeology of Cyberspaces: Virtuality, Community, Identity', in David Porter (ed.), *Internet Culture*, London and New York: Routledge, pp. 5–22.

Williams, Mary (1997) 'Ethical Issues in Computing: Work, Privacy and Justice', in David Ermann, Mary Williams and Michele Schauf (eds), *Computers, Ethics and Society*, Oxford: Oxford University Press, pp. 3–19.

Williams, Raymond (1989) *Television: Technology and Cultural Form*, second edition, London and New York: Routledge.

Willson, Michele (1997) 'Community in the Abstract: A Political and Ethical Dilemma' in David Bell and Barbara Kennedy (eds) *The Cybercultures Reader*, London and New York: Routledge, pp. 644–57.

Wolf, Christopher (2000) 'Racists, Bigots and the Law on the Internet', www.gigalaw.com/articles/wolf–2000–07–p1.html, 1 July.

Wolf, Gary (1995) 'The Curse of Xanadu', *Wired*, 3.06: 137–202.

Wolmark, Jenny (ed.) (1999) *Cybersexualities: A Reader on Feminist Theory, Cyborgs and Cyberspace*, Edinburgh: Edinburgh University Press.

Woodland, Randal (1995) 'Queer Spaces, Modem Boys and Pagan Statues', *Works and Days* 13.1–2. Reprinted in David Bell and Barbara Kennedy (eds), *The Cybercultures Reader*, London and New York: Routledge, pp. 416–31.

Woolley, Benjamin (1999) *The Bride of Science: Romance, Reason and Byron's Daughter*, Basingstoke: Macmillan.

Young, Margaret Levine, Muder, Doug, Kay, Dave, Warfel, Kathy and Barrows, Alison (1999) *The Complete Reference Internet, Millennium Edition*, Berkeley, CA: Osborne/McGraw Hill.

Zickmund, Susan (1997) 'Approaching the Radical Other: The Discursive Culture of Cyberhate', in Steven Jones, *Virtual Culture*, London: Sage, pp. 185–205.

Cultural and media studies

Adorno, Theodor and Horkheimer, Max (1972) *Dialectic of Enlightenment*, trans. J. Cummings, New York: Herder and Herder.

Ang, Ien (1996) *Living Room Wars: Rethinking Media Audiences for a Postmodern World*, London and New York: Routledge.

Appadurai, Arjun (1990) 'Differences in the Global Cultural Economy', in Mike Featherstone (ed.), *Global Culture: Nationalism, Globalization and Modernity*, London: Sage, pp. 291–310.

Barthes, Roland (1973) *Elements of Semiology*, trans. Annette Lavers and Colin Smith, New York: Hill and Wang.

Barthes, Roland (1977) *Image, Music, Text*, trans. Stephen Heath, London: Fontana.

Baudrillard, Jean (1988) *America*, trans. Chris Turner, London: Verso.

Baudrillard, Jean (1993) *The Transparency of Evil: Essays on Extreme Phenomena*, trans. James Benedict, London: Verso.

Baudrillard, Jean (1994) *Simulacra and Simulation*, trans. Sheila Faria Glaser, Ann Arbor: University of Michigan Press.

Berger, Arthur Asa (1998) *Media Analysis Techniques*, second edition, London: Sage.

Bhaba, Homi (1994) *The Location of Culture*, London and New York: Routledge.

Braidotti, Rosi (1994) *Nomadic Subjects: Embodiment and Sexual Difference in Contemporary Feminist Theory*, New York: Columbia University Press.

Bringhurst, Robert (1996) *The Elements of Typographic Style*, Vancouver, Hartley and Marks.

Card, Orson Scott (1990) *Maps in a Mirror: The Short Fiction of Orson Scott Card*, New York: TOR.

Christians, Clifford G., Rotzoll, Kim B. and Fackler, Mark (1991) *Media Ethics: Cases and Moral Reasoning*, third edition, White Plains, NY: Longman.

Clarke, Gary (1981) 'Defending Ski-Jumpers: A Critique of Theories of Youth Subcultures', in Simon Frith and Andrew Goodwin (eds.) (1990), *On Record*, London: Routledge.

Cohen, Stanley (1972) *Folk Devils and Moral Panis: The Creation of the Mods and the Rockers*, Oxford: Martin Robinson.

Collins, Richard and Muroni, Christina (1996) *New Media, New Policies: Media Communication Strategies for the Future*, Cambridge: Polity Press.

Cornish, William R. (1999) *Intellectual Property*, London: Sweet & Maxwell.

Curran, James and Gurevitch, Michael (eds) (1996) *Mass Media and Society*, London: Arnold.

de Certeau, Michel (1984) *The Practice of Everyday Life*, Berkeley, CA: University of California Press.

Deleuze, Gilles and Guattari, Félix (1984) *Anti-Oedipus*, trans. Robert Hurley, Mark Seem and Helen R. Lane, London: Athlone.

Deleuze, Gilles and Guattari, Félix (1988) *A Thousand Plateaux*, trans. Brian Massumi, London: Athlone.

Docherty, Thomas (ed.) (1993) *Postmodernism: A Reader*, London: Harvester Wheatsheaf.

During, Simon (1997) 'Popular Culture on a Global Scale: A Challenge for Cultural Studies?', *Critical Inquiry* 23: 808–21.

Dworkin, Andrea (1981) *Pornography: Men Possessing Women*, London: Women's Press.

Fanon, Franz (1967) *Black Skins, White Masks*, New York: Grove Press.

Fidler, Roger (1997) *Mediamorphosis: Understanding New Media*, London: Sage.

Fiske, John (1987) *Television Culture*, London: Routledge.

Flichy, Patrice (1995) *Dynamics of Modern Communication: The Shaping and Impact of New Communication Technologies*, London: Sage.

Friedan, Betty (1981) *The Second Stage*, New York: Summit Books.

Frost, Chris (2000) *Media Ethics and Self-Regulation* Harlow: Longman.

Gelder, Ken and Sarah Thornton (eds.) (1997) *The Subcultures Reader*, London and New York: Routledge.

Gitlin, Todd (1989) 'Postmodernism defined, at last!', *Utne Reader*, 34: 52–61.

Green, Arnold W. (1946) 'Sociological Analysis of Horney and Fromm', *The American Journal of Sociology*, 51.

Greer, Germaine (1984) *Sex and Destiny: The Politics of Human Fertility*, New York: Harper and Row.

Habermas, Jürgen (1989) *The Structural Transformation of the Public Sphere*, trans. Thomas Burger, Cambridge: Polity Press.

Hebdige, Dick (1979) *Subculture: The Meaning of Style*, London: Methuen.

Herman, Edward and McChesney, Robert (1997) *The Global Media: The New Missionaries of Corporate Capitalism*, London: Cassell.

Humphreys, Laud (1970) *Tearoom Trade: Impersonal Sex in Public Places*, Chicago: Aldine.

Jagger, Alison (ed.) (1994) *Living with Contradictions: Controversies in Feminist Social Ethics*, Boulder: Westview Press.

Jameson, Fredric (1991) *Postmodernism, or, The Cultural Logic of Late Capitalism*, Durham, NC: Duke University Press.

Jeffrey, Ian (1997) *The Photography Book*, London: Phaidon.

Kennedy, Randall (1999) Tanner Lecture in Human Values, cited at www.stanford.edu/dept/news/report/news/may5/rkennedy-55.html, May 5.

Kernan, Alvin (1987) *Printing, Technology, Letters and Samuel Johnson*, Princeton: Princeton University Press.

Lowe, Lisa (1997) *Immigrant Acts*, Durham, NC: Duke University Press.

Lyotard, Jean-François (1984) [1979] *The Postmodern Condition: A Report on Knowledge*, trans. Geoff Bennington and Brian Massumi, Minneapolis: University of Minnesota Press.

McElroy, Wendy (1995) *A Woman's Right to Pornography*, New York: St Martin's Press.

MacKay, Hugh and O'Sullivan, Tim (eds) (1999) *The Media Reader: Continuity and Transformation*, London: Sage.

MacKinnon, Catharine (1993) *Only Words*, Cambridge, MA: Harvard University Press.

McLuhan, Marshall (1962) *The Gutenberg Galaxy*, Toronto: University of Toronto Press.

Morris, Meaghan (1988) 'Things To Do With Shopping Centres', in Susan Sheridan (ed.) *Grafts: Feminist Cultural Criticism*, London: Verso, pp. 193–225.

Oliver, Melvin and Shapiro, Thomas (1997) *Black Wealth, White Wealth: A New Perspective on Racial Equality*, London and New York: Routledge.

Robins, Kevin (1996) *Into the Image: Gender and Politics in the Field of Vision*, London and New York: Routledge.

Rifkin, Jeremy (1995) *The End of Work*, New York: Tarcher/Putman.

Said, Edward (1994) *Culture and Imperialism*, London: Vintage Books.

Sorkin, Michael (ed.) (1992) *Variations on a Theme Park: The New American City and the End of Public Space*, New York: Noonday.

Sreberny-Mohammadi, Annabelle (1996) 'The Global and Local in International Communications', in James Curran and Michael Gurevitch (eds), *Mass Media and Society*, London: Arnold, pp. 177–203.

Stratton, Jon (1992) *The Young Ones: Working-Class Culture*, Perth: Black Swan Press.

Strinati, Dominic and Wagg, Stephen (eds) (1995) *Come On Down? Popular Media Culture in Post-War Britain*, second edition, London and New York: Routledge.

Sudjic, Deyan (1993) *The 100-Mile City*, London: Flamingo.

Tunstall, J. and Palmer, M. (1991) *Media Moguls*, London: Routledge.

Virilio, Paul (1991) *The Lost Dimension*, trans. D. Moshenberg, New York: Semiotext(e).

Weeks, Jeffrey (1977) *Coming Out: Homosexual Politics in Britain from the Nineteenth Century to the Present*, London: Quartet.

Index